The Man Who Lost
His Language

SHEILA HALE

The Man Who Lost His Language

ALLEN LANE
an imprint of
PENGUIN BOOKS

ALLEN LANE
THE PENGUIN PRESS

Published by the Penguin Group
Penguin Books Ltd, 80 Strand, London, WC2R ORL, England
Penguin Putnam Inc., 375 Hudson Street, New York, New York 10014, USA
Penguin Books Australia Ltd, 250 Camberwell Road, Camberwell, Victoria 3124, Australia
Penguin Books Canada Ltd, 10 Alcorn Avenue, Toronto, Ontario, Canada M4V 3B2
Penguin Books India (P) Ltd, 11, Community Centre, Panchsheel Park, New Delhi – 110 017, India
Penguin Books (NZ) Ltd, Cnr Rosedale and Airborne Roads, Albany, Auckland, New Zealand
Penguin Books (South Africa) (Pty) Ltd, 24 Sturdee Avenue, Rosebank 2196, South Africa

Penguin Books Ltd, Registered Offices: 80 Strand, London, WC2R ORL, England

www.penguin.com

First published 2002
1 3 5 7 9 10 8 6 4 2

Copyright © Sheila Hale, 2002

Set in 10/13 pt PostScript Adobe Sabon
Typeset by Rowland Phototypesetting Ltd, Bury St Edmunds, Suffolk
Printed in Great Britain by Clays Ltd, St Ives plc

A CIP catalogue record for this book is available from the British Library

ISBN 0–713–99361–8

For John's children
Sophie, Matthew, Charlotte and John

Contents

Acknowledgements

John and I were immensely fortunate in the friends, family and clinicians who contributed in so many ways to his recovery and enjoyment of life after what might otherwise have been a devastating stroke.

For the physiotherapy that enabled John to walk again, and kept him walking, I would like to thank especially the team led by Carolyn Smith at the Royal Star & Garter Home for Disabled Ex-Servicemen & Women, and Ellie Kinnear, founder and co-ordinator of Integrated Neurological Services. Anna Maria Dreszer, whose loyal and graceful presence in our lives was constant reassurance, supervised his exercises at home.

John's aphasia was treated by two remarkable speech and language therapists, Eirian Jones and Jane Maxim, who stimulated his recovery of reading and some writing, as well as my interest in acquired language disorders. Of the forty volunteers who helped to restore John's language I can mention only Ann Barr, Anthony Besch, Chris Jackson and Susan Raven, all people with many other demands on their time who continued over the years to visit John on a regular basis and to help him find enough words to correspond with absent friends. Camilla Panufnik cared for me as well as John like a second mother during the bleakest as well as the best of times.

In the dark days after the stroke, when I learned that the state would not provide John with the long-term clinical therapy that offered the only hope, a group of friends established a fund that paid for John's rehabilitation and care. Thanks to the generosity of the donors we were able to afford the expert treatments that eventually enabled him to return to a rich and sometimes even adventurous life. I would like to express my gratitude for their financial support to Bill Blackburn, Edie Coulson, Ronald and Betsy Dworkin, Bamber and Christina Gascoigne, Graham C. Greene, Michael Frayn and

Claire Tomalin, Matthew Hale, Teddy Hall, Evie Haynes, Shirley Hughes, Mimi Kilgore, Richard King, Francis and Maureen Nichols, John Julius and Mollie Norwich, Camilla Panufnik, Robin and Catherine Porteous, Bill and Rosemary Righter, Richard and Ruthie Rogers, Garry and Ruth Runciman, Simon Sainsbury, and Anthony and Sally Sampson.

John also received a grant towards his care from the Royal Literary Fund, which provides for authors in need.

When I came to write this book I knew I would be dependent on the guidance of specialist aphasiologists. I could not, however, have anticipated the kindness, patience and encouragement with which all the experts I consulted responded even to my most ignorant questions. Those to whom I am particularly grateful are Dr Niels Birbaumer, Professor Brian Butterworth, Professor Alfonso Caramazza, Professor Chris Code, Dr Emanuel Donchin, Professor Mitchell Glickstein, Jenny Greener, Eirian Jones, Dr Philip R. Kennedy, Dr Alexander Leff, Dr Jane Marshall, Dr Jane Maxim, Dr Jonathan Miller, Dr Arnold Schapiro, Dr Linda Wheeldon, Dr Richard Wise, Dr Jonathan R. Wolpaw and Professor Lewis Wolpert.

I am also indebted to Professor David Howard, who very kindly read the first draft of Chapters 5–15, both for his invaluable comments and corrections and for cheering me on. I doubt if I would have found the spirit to write about a painful personal experience without the warm encouragement of my friend and agent, Anne Engel. I am also more grateful than I know how to say to my publisher, Stuart Proffitt, for responding warmly and constructively to what he knew would be a risky book; to Elizabeth Stratford for the sharp-eyed and sensitive copy-editing that saved me from many an embarrassing slip and to Andrew Barker for his sympathetic design.

The Man Who Lost
His Language

Suppose that you and I are watching a bird in flight. The thought 'bird-in-flight' is in each of our minds and is the means by which each of us interprets his own observations. Neither of us, however, could say whether our lived experiences on that occasion were identical. In fact, neither of us would even try to answer that question, since one's own subjective meaning can never be laid side by side with another's and compared.

Nevertheless, during the flight of the bird you and I have 'grown older together'; our experiences have been simultaneous.

Alfred Schutz, The Phenomenology of the Social World

Just as I can be mistaken concerning myself and grasp only the apparent or ideal significance of my conduct, so can I be mistaken concerning another and know only the envelope of his behaviour. The perception which I have of him is never, in the case of suffering or mourning, for example, the equivalent of the perception which he has of himself, unless I am sufficiently close to him that our feelings constitute together a single 'form' and that our lives cease to flow separately. It is by this rare and difficult consent that I can be truly united with him . . . I communicate with him by the signification of his conduct; but it is a question of attaining its structure, that is of attaining, beyond his words or even his actions, the region where they are prepared.

Maurice Merleau-Ponty, The Structure of Behaviour

I

John

I confess I do not believe in time. I like to fold my magic carpet, after use, in such a way as to superimpose one part of the pattern upon another. Let visitors trip. And the highest enjoyment of timelessness – in a landscape selected at random – is when I stand among rare butterflies and their food plants. This is ecstasy and behind the ecstasy is something else, which is hard to explain. It is like a momentary vacuum into which rushes all that I love. A sense of oneness with sun and stone. A thrill of gratitude to whom it may concern – to the contrapuntal genius of human fate or to tender ghosts humouring a lucky mortal.

Vladimir Nabokov, Speak, Memory:
An Autobiography Revisited

I am studying a photograph of John taken in 1927 or 1928 when he was four or five. It's one I've always liked and kept where I could glance at it from time to time. These days I examine it more closely, searching for clues to the way he is now. I know John at the other end of his life as well as one person can know another. But I want more. I want to know what it is like to be John.

It is high summer in an English garden. John has been persuaded to settle on a rug on the lawn with his two older sisters, Joan and Polly. Polly, the tallest child, is sitting with a large Pekinese sprawled on her lap. Joan, the eldest, has been shelling peas into a colander, which she has set aside for the photograph. The two girls are laughing for the camera. John is not laughing. He is quietly amused, inquisitive, no doubt planning some adventure; possibly already a bit of a ham? He is perched neatly on his heels, wearing shorts and a cotton shirt buttoned up to his neck, hands resting palm to palm between his bare thighs, self-contained, ready to go. He is a very pretty little boy, his thick hair dappled with patches of reflected sunlight. The hair, although you can't see it in the black-and-white photograph, is a colour which John later described to me (not altogether ironically) as a ravishing shade of burnished copper. When it was first cut his mother wrapped a lock of it in tissue paper and preserved it in an envelope, labelled with purple ink in her flamboyant handwriting: 'First cut of my darling John's hair aged 1 year 8 months.' Below this inscription there is another note, in purple ink: 'Another cutting taken on Sept 6, aged 9. Colour hasn't changed. Like two tongues of fire.'

John's father was a country doctor who knew all the music-hall songs and charged his patients what they could afford to pay. Some expressed their gratitude with gifts of family heirlooms – bits of antique porcelain or cut glass; the maple-framed samplers which now hang in our kitchen. He was the kind of doctor who visited the sick at any time of day or night, and he died, possibly of overwork, when John was fifteen.

John's mother was a nurse but she retired when John was born to devote herself to her only son. Her other interests were amateur theatricals, spiritualism and the philosophy of Rudolph Steiner. But it was John who was the centre of his mother's mildly eccentric universe. And her unconditional adoration of the late, unexpected golden boy seems to have been shared by Polly and Joan, already eight and ten when John was born, as well as by all the aunts, uncles and family servants who peopled the stories about his childhood that John was to tell his children at bedtime and after lunch on rainy Saturday afternoons. Some of the stories were surreal, some mock-spooky; many involved elaborate practical jokes. The stories always ended happily with the family comfortably reunited over a delicious tea in the large, safe house in Kent, surrounded by cherry and apple orchards that even a charitable doctor could afford during the depression.

It was in this gentle, bourgeois environment that John developed his compulsion to write. Judging from the prodigious volume of his juvenilia, which his mother returned to him shortly before she died, John, from the age of eight, must have spent many hours of each day writing. He wrote poems, plays, stories, accounts of extraordinary and ordinary days in his life. He wrote a poem about his appendix operation; several stories about his uncle's false nose (the real one having been shot off in the trenches), which was kept in place by an elastic band around his head. He wrote about his favourite puddings (trifle and spotted dick) and about the colours and shapes which were projected on his inner eyelids when he closed them. His letters home from school tended to be either in verse, or to be plays starring 'our lissom, auburn-haired hero, John'. His notes about butterflies and birds, their habits, eggs and calls, are accompanied by rough, expressive sketches, with arrows pointing to those he says he wishes he could draw better.

The copy of T. A. Coward's classic *The Birds of the British Isles and their Eggs* which John won at his school in 1934 as first prize in natural history is, with the photograph in the sunlit garden, one of the talismans I keep on my desk, as though it might act as a passport to the mind of the man I know so well but not well enough. Although T. A. Coward is admired even today by ornithologists for his scientific methods of observation, he could not refrain from anthropomorphic moral judgements, directed particularly against bullies and cowards – two classes of people John has always scorned. The golden eagle, for example, 'in romance is fierce, terrible, and a robber of infants; in reality it is a large, powerful, magnificent bird with a cowardly vulturine character'.

The illustrations in John's 1933 edition are sparse and feeble. You have to peer very hard at the black-and-white photograph of a tree trunk to distinguish the tiny black-and-white tree sparrow 'at nest' on a hole in the bark. But T. A. Coward's descriptive power does the work that colour photographs and television have now made unnecessary. I turn to the section on the peregrine falcon, *Falco peregrinus* Turnstall, 'the largest and most common of our resident falcons . . . commoner, especially around our rocky coasts, than is usually supposed'. The gripping description that covers the following pages is written in a prose that must have influenced John's own mature style:

There is a dash, neatness and finish in the flight of the Peregrine which is purely its own. The wings move rapidly, beating the air for a few moments, and are then held steady in a bow whilst the bird glides forward, sometimes rolling slightly from side to side . . . Near the eyrie the birds have look-outs, some jutting rocks or pinnacles on the cliff face . . . On the cliff-top, near the eyrie, are the shambles, scattered litter of blood-stained feathers and the rejected remnants of many a victim . . . Immediately after giving the fatal blow with the hind claw the destroyer shoots upward, descending later to enjoy its meal. The rush of a swooping Peregrine when heard at close quarters is like the sound of a rocket . . . No nest is made; the two to four richly coloured orange-red or deep brown eggs are placed in a rough hollow scraped on some ledge of a steep crag or cliff.

In the summer of 1937 when John was thirteen he volunteered to take part in a Royal Air Force mission to subvert the mating activities of peregrine falcons on the cliffs of Wales where they were endangering national security by disturbing radar signals. It was John's job to remove the eggs from their ledges and crags. He was lowered by rope down the cliff face, equipped with a soft bag in which he placed, one at a time, the richly coloured eggs so they could be transported to a safe but less intrusive hatching ground.

When John and I met twenty-seven years later, he often talked about his peregrine summer. And two months before our son JJ (John Justin) was born he took me to Wales on a walking tour of the cliffs and made love to me on the one he remembered as the site of his egg-rescuing adventures. Oddly, there is no evidence that he wrote at the time about the experience he was to remember so vividly for the rest of his life. His letters home from school that autumn are mostly about rugby, which he played as scrum half. Everything else is going 'pretty well', but it is rugger that makes the prose light up. Then he is in the school infirmary having hurt his knee in a rugger game.

The bruise developed into osteomyelitis, a bone-wasting infection that is still serious, even now when it can be treated with antibiotics. Doctors have told me that osteomyelitis is so painful that they are sometimes prepared to relieve it with potentially addictive amounts of morphine, which can lead to an extended period in hospital while the patient dries out. John was in a wheelchair for eighteen months.

He nearly lost the leg, at least according to Polly, who believes she may have saved it with her powers as a faith healer. The school doctor gave him nothing stronger than aspirin. Perhaps his father would have been more indulgent; but he was far away, bedridden by what proved to be his last illness. Polly says that their mother, who took a flat near the school, was often hysterical – more, it seems, about John than her husband – but that everyone else, especially John, bore his suffering bravely: gritted teeth, no crying.

Many years later, when I touched the scar, in bed with John for the first time, he told me about how much he had enjoyed reading Darwin's *Voyage of the Beagle* in his wheelchair, and about the fun of watching the leeches suck the pus from his infected knee. He didn't mention pain or frustration, and I didn't think to ask. At forty-one, fifteen years older than me, his auburn hair now streaked with silver as though by a good hairdresser, he seemed to me impossibly glamorous, and impossibly invulnerable.

By 1939 John was up and walking again, well enough to take part in army drills. His attitude to war (which was to be one of his chief interests as a mature historian) was already evident. Marching in the middle of a large company of officer cadets he would occasionally swing the same arm as his leg. The RSM overlooking his body of soldiers was puzzled to see that the symmetry was broken, but could not identify the problem. The young professional schoolmasters had gone off to fight in the war. They were replaced by elderly volunteers who were only too happy to depart from the syllabus and share their particular intellectual passions with John. One introduced him to French and Spanish literature, another to the social theories of Shaw and Ruskin, a third to art history, which was not then a subject formally taught in schools or universities. His battered brown-paper editions of French and Spanish novels, plays, poetry and memoirs, pages all cut, are on the shelves of the library that lines the walls of our tall old house by the river; as is the two-volume edition of the prefaces and complete plays of George Bernard Shaw, which John won as a school essay prize. We once had the Travellers' Edition, Ruskin's own abridged version of *The Stones of Venice*. That has disappeared, perhaps worn out from too many trips to Venice or loaned to some student.

His favourite reading at sixteen was J. A. Crowe and G. B. Cavalcaselle's *History of Painting in Italy*. His three-volume 1908 edition edited by Edward Hutton is still in good condition, possibly because nobody, except John in nostalgic moments, has looked at it since. I have to stretch my imagination to guess what it can have been about these formidably dreary-looking books that appealed so strongly to an adolescent boy. The closely printed pages are heavy with detailed descriptions of works of art John had never seen and closely argued attributions, qualified by footnotes, to artists whose names he could never have previously encountered. The mean little black-and-white photographs of works of art are even less inspiring than the birds in T. A. Coward. But they seem to have had a power for John, as for other art-loving members of his generation, that is lacking in the lavish colour reproductions and educational weekend breaks in 'art cities' that are widely available today.

Sometimes I gaze at John gazing at some work of art in a gallery or church. He can easily spend an hour or more standing absolutely still in front of a single work of art. I see a man in a state of self-transcending ecstasy that is achieved only rarely, if ever, by those of us who grew up later, force-fed with clamorous technicolor images of everything from toothpaste to high art. He is old and lame, but, at such moments, I envy him. I am overwhelmed by the recurring desire to share his ecstatic self-forgetfulness. If I interrupt him with questions about the picture that is absorbing him he points, waves his stick, blows kisses at it; and puts his finger over his mouth as though he were listening to something.

He didn't get to see the originals of the Italian paintings in Crowe and Cavalcaselle until 1946 when he made his first pilgrimage to Florence, travelling across war-torn Europe on his motorbike, with a girl on the back. He abandoned her for ever in the Piazza del Duomo when she failed to share his rapturous enthusiasm for the Baptistery. His first major book, *England and the Italian Renaissance*, a pioneering investigation of the history of the English taste for Italy, is an attempt to explain to himself the impact Italy made on him. Its preface begins with an indirect and rather generalized apology to the girl for his 'priggish' behaviour.

Here is a cutting from the 1941 summer issue of the school magazine. John was eighteen, and it was his last term at school.

On July 12th and 14th, 1941, a small company of performers gave a rendering of the 'comic scenes' from 'Twelfth Night', which will not be quickly or easily forgotten ... The most difficult part, of course, is that of *Feste the Clown*. Here, as J. R. Hale convincingly showed, is something very close to Shakespeare's heart. His wit and nonsense were as spontaneous as his agility – his sly glance at Sir Toby, as he sang about the toss-pots' drunken heads, being particularly pleasing – but above all he revealed the sensitive nature of the character in his reactions to the slightest suggestion of reproach.

At the back of the same issue there are brief notes about the achievements of the final-year boys: 'J. R. Hale. School Prefect; Head of House; Margetson English Essay Prize 40; Gillum English Biography Prize 41; Scholarship to Jesus College, Oxford; Editor of the *Eastbournian*; Chapel Warden; Librarian to Radley Library; Higher Cert.; School Cert.'

John deferred the scholarship to Oxford and went straight from school to train as a radio operator, in preparation for joining the Merchant Navy. The Royal Navy had turned him down on account of his osteomyelitis, which also exempted him from active war service. But he wanted to spend his war at sea, and the Merchant Navy wasn't fussy about the fitness of its men. I don't know if anyone warned him, or his mother, that the Merchant Navy was the most dangerous of the wartime services. Since the crews were mostly working-class career seamen it may not have come out until later that a third of Merchant Navy men died at sea between 1939 and 1945. John's mother in any case loved to show him off in his uniform when he came home on leave.

Here is a photograph of John wearing his dress uniform, standing to attention with his right arm clamping the hat to his side, acting the part, or so I would guess from his expression. His mother was so proud and jealous of him that when he made the mistake of bringing a girlfriend home for tea she chased the girl around the piano with a knife. Her possessiveness may account for the slightly subversive set to John's mouth in the photograph, which I think she must have commissioned.

After the war John wrote *The Waves Between*, a book about his Merchant Navy years, which he had the good sense not to submit to a publisher. The prose is relentlessly ecstatic: 'Over a slow swell we drove on, lifting a shoulder to each smooth fold, meeting it with a sharp shearing hiss that was succeeded by a quiet rippling till we rolled back to meet the next . . .' Discomfort? We read instead about the joy of being alone under the stars on night watch, looking forward to the rum ration due at dawn. Boredom? In his free time he read and taught himself the languages of the ship's destinations (*Teach Yourself Swahili* and *Teach Yourself Portuguese* are on the shelf next to French poetry). Fear? 'Only when a destroyer dashes past flying a black pennant do we follow its movements with care for this means "I am hunting a submarine. Keep clear." Of all the hundreds of charges that explode during the course of a convoy we seldom know whether the result is a U-boat or a good haul of fish.'

Day after day after day the pages of the Oxford pocket diaries he kept for those three years are blank except for the words 'at sea'. It was forbidden to record any other information that might fall into the hands of the Germans. Then suddenly there is the name of a port – Brooklyn, Cape Town, Sydney – followed by a string of female names, operas and ballets. The diary goes on like this, with different girls' names and different operas and ballets, for a few days and then returns to 'at sea'.

Many people had more terrible, or more glamorous, wars; and, when John used to talk to me about his, I'm afraid I listened more in a spirit of conversational give and take than with real interest. It is only now that I want not just to imagine him but to be with him, all those years ago, cooped up, defenceless, tossed around for weeks on end in waters swarming with enemy ships. Then I wonder at his courage and wish I could understand the source of his joyous appetite for life under all circumstances. Whatever it is, it is not passive 'acceptance', that dreary attitude advised by the glib professional 'counsellors' who are forever offering us their services these days. 'Denial', which they suppose to be psychologically unhealthy, may be closer to whatever it was that kept John going then as it does now.

Here is a photograph of John two years after the war, playing the King of Navarre in an Oxford University Dramatic Society production of *Love's Labour's Lost*, splendid in a costume – scarlet and gold, so he told me – previously worn by Laurence Olivier in the film of *Henry V*.

Shortly after I met John many years later he recited the opening lines of the play from the bath in which he was lying:

> Let fame, that all hunt after in their lives,
> Live registered upon our brazen tombs
> And then grace us in the disgrace of death–

John threw himself into acting and directing plays as soon as he went up to Oxford after the war. Our friend Anthony, an Oxford contemporary who later became a professional opera producer, remembers him off-stage – relaxed, elegant, auburn-haired – and on, playing among many roles another king, Haakon, King of Norway, in Ibsen's *The Pretenders*, the messenger in Kenneth Tynan's production of *Samson Agonistes*, and Neptune in a Royal Masque presented to HRH Princess Elizabeth.

John's amateur acting career at Oxford attracted the attention of a film producer who offered him the male lead in *The Blue Lagoon* opposite Jean Simmons. He turned it down. He was still hoping to join the Royal Navy on the chance it would take him in peacetime despite the osteomyelitis. In the end he decided instead to accept the History Fellowship offered by Jesus College, Oxford.

Here is another, in sepia, which I can't date precisely. He is sitting in a meadow, probably in Oxford, wearing an academic gown, surrounded by a group of friends, three apparently from the cast of a play, all of them laughing.

There is an entire album of photographs commemorating the second-hand motorbike, a BSA, on which he travelled in the summer vacations from Oxford – across the United States, or across Europe on his way to the Middle East or Africa. (The children's top favourite of his bedtime recollections of his motorcycle adventures was the one about the moving meat offered to him one night by a hospitable African tribe who considered maggots a delicacy. Would you eat it? He claimed he had.)

There is a photograph of John taken by himself in the mirror of a bar in New Mexico. The photograph is labelled El Bandito Bianco. You can't actually see that it is of John because the face is masked by curved ski goggles over his spectacles, straw cap worn back to front (the elastic of the goggles is clamping the peak in place), with the mouth and chin covered by a large handkerchief. This arrangement, which protected his face from sun, wind and bugs, attracted the attention of a party of American cops who were chasing a real villain and who enchanted John by actually saying, as they arrested him, 'Reach for the sky.'

There are drawers full of Venice: John, me, our son JJ and various friends in various Venetian settings. We lived in Venice for part of each year after he started working in the Venetian archives and brought his university students with him hoping to share with them his intense, exhausting love of every stone, house, church, monument in that city. In his *Who's Who* entry he gives 'Venice' as his only hobby.

1972: in the lagoon reconnoitring for locations for a BBC television documentary about Venice that John was commissioned to write and narrate.

1983: John telling me about his first and last attempt to row a one-man gondola, which he foolishly took into the Grand Canal where it spun out of his control.

And many more: with our baby son JJ riding one of the little lions in the Piazzetta; on balconies and bridges, smoking, glamorous in dark glasses; in a friend's garden where his red cardigan stands out nicely against the wisteria.

1974: John is giving a press conference at the National Gallery, of which he is Chairman of the Trustees. He has just negotiated the purchase of an important picture, Drouais's portrait of Madame de Pompadour.

There are so many from the early 1980s that it's hard to choose. It was a busy time. He was a Trustee of the Victoria and Albert Museum, Chairman of the Theatre Museum, member of the Royal Mint Advisory Commission, member of the Museums and Galleries Commission, Chairman of the Advisory Committee on Government Art Collections, President of the British Association of Friends of Museums, Chairman of the Art History section of the British Academy. In 1982 he organized the Genius of Venice exhibition at the Royal Academy. It was the most stupendous collection of sixteenth-century Venetian painting ever to be shown in Britain.

He wrote and appeared in television programmes, delivered lectures about the meaning of quality in the Renaissance to business conferences all over the world (I remember him complaining to his accountant that he had been well paid for these). Meanwhile there were two lengthy study visits to Princeton.

There is one from that period that I cannot find. He was the university's public orator. Yet another unpaid public service on top of the work for museums and galleries, the lectures to impoverished schools and colleges, the extra hours with students. That's how I see it in my sour moods. But John loves this work. He enjoys researching and composing lapidary eulogies to the men and women upon whom the university will bestow honorary degrees. He adores the dressing up and processing, the presence of royalty, all the trappings that turn English ceremonies into camp theatre. But public speaking doesn't come as easily as he makes it seem. He has learned to turn his slight stutter to histrionic advantage. But after all these years of lecturing he is still nervous before a performance.

Summer 1984: John with me and my mother after he was knighted. The Queen was wearing an olive-green wool dress and looked bad-tempered to me. John said she was charming.

Afterwards we had lunch at the Ritz and then went swimming in the river. John innocent and happy as a swimming dog.

Winter 1984: John and his daughter Charlotte framed by a Picasso sculpture on a freezing day at Princeton. John was working there at the Institute for Advanced Studies on his next big book, *Artists and Warfare in the Renaissance*. I flew back and forth from London. JJ was in his last year at school and I felt I couldn't leave him alone for long. But John wrote to me every day, long letters describing the snow, the new friends he was making, his trips to New York, what my mother had given him to eat for lunch.

Autumn 1991: in the park opposite our house, in his red cashmere cardigan, which now has leather patches on the elbows, an old tweed jacket flung over one shoulder. It is a very good photograph, taken by a professional to go with a magazine article about John's work with museums and galleries, which are, in his opinion, seriously under-financed by the government. He is standing in a patch of sunlight that has pierced a sky loaded with swollen black clouds. The red cardigan stands out nicely against the white Palladian house in the background. You might think from John's commanding expression that he was lord of this manor.

The truth is that he is worried, impatient to get back to his desk. The final chapters of his latest book, *The Civilization of Europe in the Renaissance*, are not writing themselves in his head the way all his other books have done. I know this only because he has been fuelling his concentration with more smoking than ever. Otherwise I would never have guessed how seriously tired he is.

Summer 1997: in his elder son Matthew's garden, wearing the pale-blue short-sleeved cotton shirt that he specially likes because it has many pockets for stowing his comb (he is still vain about his hair, which has turned a brilliant shade of white), his glasses, and the card with his name and address that I insist he carry with him at all times. John is smiling eagerly as though about to take his turn in a lively conversation. This is my favourite of all the recent photographs of John. I keep it on the kitchen sideboard where it will catch my eye as I come down the stairs. Three or four times a day I pick it up and study it, wondering whether, if I didn't know the truth, it would fool me.

His left hand reaches towards the camera, thumb up, his stick resting on the ring and middle fingers, which are crossed between extended index and little fingers. There's a clue. You see this hand posture in Italian art – in Byzantine mosaics in Sicily, in carved pulpits in and around Pisa, on the ceiling of the Sistine Chapel, very often in Mannerist painting and sculpture. I've seen it on mannequins in the windows of high fashion dress shops. It is an elegant gesture, it draws attention to itself and makes still images seem more life-like. In fact, you rarely see it used by real people in real conversation, because the hand does not fall naturally into that position.

When we are in Paris John likes to pay his respects to Raphael's portrait of Baldassare Castiglione in the Louvre. Castiglione was an Italian scholar and diplomat, famous for *The Courtier*, a book of etiquette, which was a best seller in sixteenth-century Europe. Castiglione used the word *sprezzatura* – hard work made to look easy – to describe the behaviour of his ideal Renaissance courtier. The courtier strives to please his Prince, while contributing to the security and welfare of a badly governed Italy with hard-won supremacy in all his attainments. But he never lets the strain show; however hard he labours he never sweats or lets the veins stand out on his arms. John used to tell his students that Castiglione was indirectly responsible for the English Disease: laziness. The first foreign-language translation of *The Courtier* was in English. But, so John said, the ideal of *sprezzatura* was gradually misinterpreted by successive English etiquette books, until it came to mean that the hallmark of gentlemanly behaviour was conspicuous indolence.

Musing over the photograph of John looking as though he were engaged in normal conversation, I can, suddenly and quite clearly, hear his voice talking to me about *The Courtier*. It is one of his favourite books, one of the keys, in his view, to an understanding of the Renaissance ideal of civilization; but, like so much of what he has taught me, I know it only second-hand, through him. Once – I don't remember why, only that we were having lunch in Paris at about the time he was beginning to write *The Civilization of Europe in the Renaissance* – he told me a story from *The Courtier* about an

Italian merchant in Poland who is trying to negotiate terms with some Muscovites on the other side of a frozen river. But it is so cold that their words freeze solid in the air. The two sides can see the words, but they cannot hear or understand them. The Poles, who know how to manage in their extreme climate, light a fire on the river, and gradually the words thaw and the merchants are able to strike a deal. John said it was a popular conceit in the Renaissance to imagine that words – the invisible, ephemeral emanations of breath – were elements that could be transmuted, like water into ice, into substances that were solid, palpable, visible; and then unfrozen by the rays of the sun or the warmth of a fire.

PART I

THE STROKE

There is much about John Hale which calls to mind The Tempest, *of all Shakespeare's plays the one which contains most of the themes essential to the Renaissance. The setting of broad horizons, of travel, of exotic dreams; the characters, the magician and wordsmith Prospero, the mischievous spirit, Ariel, and Caliban, warning us of war and violence; even John's present (it is to be hoped only temporary) deprivation of speech finds resonance in the play.*

War, Culture and Society in Renaissance Venice:
Essays in Honour of John Hale, *ed. D. S. Chambers,
C. H. Clough and M. E. Mallett*

2

The Accident

The moment of a stroke, even a relatively minor one, and its immediate aftermath, are an experience in chaos. Nothing at all makes sense. Nothing except perhaps this overwhelming disorientation will be remembered by the victim. The stroke usually happens suddenly. It is a catastrophe ... The victim cannot process. Her familiar world has been rearranged. The puzzle is in pieces. All at once, and with no time to prepare, she has been picked up and dropped into another realm ...

An explosion quite literally is occurring in her brain, or rather, a series of explosions: the victim's mind, her sense of time and place, her sense of self, all are being shattered if not annihilated. Fortunately, finally, she will pass out. Were her head a pinball game it would register TILT – game over – stop. Silence. And resume again. Only now the victim is in yet another realm ... In this new world, she moves from one space or thought or concept to another without willing or sometimes even knowing it. Indeed, when she moves in this maze-like place, it is as if the world around her and not she were doing all the moving.

Arthur Kopit, preface to Wings

John spent the winter and spring of 1992 revising and finishing *The Civilization of Europe in the Renaissance*. It was his most ambitious book so far and had occupied much of his working and thinking time over the previous four years. The publisher's deadline was set for 30 June. They wanted to take advantage of the coincidence that Europe was scheduled for economic union in 1992, which also marked the fifth centenary of Columbus's discovery of America:

good timing for a book about the age when Europeans were first conscious of a common identity and set out to explore the rest of the world. I delivered the typescript by hand on the afternoon of 30 June.

John looked exhausted. I made him visit the doctor, who turned him over to a nurse, who said his blood pressure was a bit raised 'but nothing to worry about'. I was, nevertheless, uneasy about something I couldn't quite identify. I had read *Civilization* and thought it his best book yet. But who could say whether it would live up to the publisher's high expectations? It had been a tremendous struggle for John, and that was so unusual that it was in itself cause for worry. He had written his previous books from first sentence to last with scarcely a correction, working on them in odd bits of time left over from teaching, lecturing, broadcasting, and his work for museums and galleries. All he needed was a table, a chair, a pad of lined paper, a cheap biro and a pack of cigarettes for the thoughts to flow, the messages in his head to emerge from the clouds of smoke, fully clothed in finely crafted prose, as though delivered by Mercury. Or so it used to seem to me when I lay reading on the sofa in his study while he wrote in the evenings after a day's teaching.

'Th' intertraffique of the minde'.

In 1492 the German poet laureate, ~~and humanist~~ cosmographer and humanist scholar Konrad Celtis delivered at the age of thirty three his inaugural lecture at the recently founded university of Ingolstadt. Speaking as a still young man to a youthful audience, he urged them to learn new things and think new thoughts, for they belonged not just to Germany but to 'the commonwealth of letters.'

By this he meant not the static internationalism of the common texts and syllabuses studied in European universities, but to ~~new and independent~~ novel and personal attitudes to the process of learning and the forms of self-expression. The commonwealth was still a-building. Most of its representatives were Italians; he had met a number of them on his ~~to~~ journey across the Alps. Others, university and school teachers or independent scholars and gifted amateurs were German he had met in his travels across the Empire. There were Frenchmen, similarly ~~impatient with~~ attuned to the 'new learning.' ~~All that~~ ~~they~~ They were just beginning to be linked by the agencies we shall go on to discuss: personal contacts, correspondence, printed books and translations. Their 16th century forbears

When he had finished *Civilization* he talked about a holiday later in the summer in Madrid and Barcelona. It would mean spending eight hours a day on our feet in picture galleries. I suggested we put off the Spanish galleries and accept an invitation he had received to join a cruise in the Adriatic as guest lecturer. But first he wanted to clear his desk. His correspondence, as he called it in his old-fashioned way, had piled up. He kept up friendships by post with people he had not seen since his Oxford years. He wrote regularly to his favourite former students, his old nanny, Niss, his two sisters, Joan and Pauline, his children (even when they were in the same city), and sometimes to me, even when we were in the same house. He answered all letters, including letters from admirers or critics he'd never met or heard of, people who believed that his books contained coded cosmic prophecies or personal messages, people who wrote to him out of sheer loneliness.

He was also busy planning his next two books, the first to be a companion to *Civilization* about art across Renaissance Europe. Then he wanted to write a biography set in the nineteenth or early twentieth century. He said it would make an interesting change to write about one person rather than many, in a period for which there was too much rather than too little documentation.

While John worked purposefully at his desk I tried, and failed, to concentrate on something other than my unfocused anxiety. *Harpers & Queen* sent me to Milan to interview Giorgio Armani. I had thought I would take advantage of the open ticket and enormous fee to spend some time with friends in Venice. But I flew back to London on the same day, with an armful of jackets for John and JJ bought wholesale from the Armani warehouse.

On Tuesday, 28 July we went to a party in London. I drove home because John had had too much to drink. At a red light I glanced at him, and saw on his face the expression of a man crazed by an apocalyptic vision. He laughed it off: 'Is that what you go around saying at parties, "Good evening, you have a crazed apocalyptic look on your face"?' If I had known what that look meant, it is theoretically possible that I might have saved John – at least in the unlikely event that an Accident and Emergency department had seen him immediately, recognized the symptoms and taken action in time.

On Wednesday, 29 July, the day after the party, John worked all morning at his desk, then bicycled five miles down river to the garden centre to visit the Scholar. The Scholar was an old man who sat wrapped, summer and winter, in layers of woollen garments behind the window of the customer inquiry booth. John called him the Scholar because of the way he gazed disapprovingly over his half-moon glasses at customers who wanted advice about the plants for sale, which were in his opinion a waste of money and could just as easily be raised from seeds and cuttings. He made no effort to conceal his contempt for customers who asked for instant solutions to their gardening problems, but if someone asked him a proper horticultural question he would rise wheezing from his seat and look up the precise answer in his pile of reference books.

For John, who loved buying and learning about beautiful plants but had no time for gardening, the Scholar was the main attraction of the garden centre. Over the years John invented a character around him which may have been based on the great, gloomy historian of medieval England – I seem to remember that his name was Bruce Macfarlane – who had taught him in his first undergraduate year at Oxford, and from whom he quickly escaped into the sunnier field of the Italian Renaissance.

I cannot imagine why any commercial enterprise in the 1990s would have employed the Scholar. I don't suppose many customers dared approach this remnant of an era when knowledge mattered more than smooth salesmanship. I certainly didn't. And I was not surprised, several years later, when I revisited the garden centre which had supplied the plants in our long, thin untidy garden and found that the Scholar was gone. In his place behind the customer inquiry window was a cosy middle-aged woman who said, Yes, yes, plants for dry shade are so difficult aren't they dear but I'm sure you'll find something nice if you look around, dear.

John is a great believer in trusting professional expertise. Although nobody knows better than John, the historian, that doctors, bank managers, lawyers and even gardening experts are fallible human beings, capable of carelessness and self-serving dishonesty, he prefers to behave as though English society is composed of men and women who practise their chosen vocations with absolute integrity. Obeying the 'orders' of professionals who know about practicalities, such as money and health, which bore John, saves time for thinking about the many subjects that fascinate him. He used to tell me that when he was first teaching at Oxford, in the years before students were accepted according to their examination results, he had never looked at an applicant's A-levels. He chose his students on the basis of a searching interview, which told him everything he needed to know. He said he was never wrong. And he expected the same confident judgement from people who followed the other professions.

For nearly fifty years he kept the bank account in Oxford that he had opened there as an undergraduate. He was aware that banking had changed since the 1940s, but he continued nevertheless to travel to Oxford in order to ask the bank manager for financial advice or permission to top up an overdraft. I don't know what the person who saw him on these occasions made of this silver-haired relic of a bygone age; I never went with John on his visits to the 'bank manager'. It was only later that I discovered that at a time when banks were paying interest rates of around 9 per cent, he had been advised to invest the lump sum he received on retirement from university teaching in an account that paid 1 per cent interest.

John's elder son, Matthew, a banker in the City, was outraged by his father's cavalier attitude to his own health. He used banker's words like ridiculous, preposterous, foolish, insane. Every now and again John would humour Matthew and me by visiting the local surgery, where a doctor who had never seen him before glanced at him and said he looked reasonably fit for his age. Doctors in his own father's day had given 'orders': before the discovery of penicillin John had been ordered, on pain of losing his leg, to spend eighteen months in a wheelchair. Since his recovery from osteomyelitis he had rarely had occasion to visit a doctor, but when he did he expected to find the sound instincts, the professional expertise and high standards that he had always required of himself.

He chose not to notice that by the time he had passed his sixty-fifth birthday British doctors working in the National Health Service had no time for instinct, no time to inquire about the general health of patients, much less to issue orders to 'geriatric' patients whose age spelled trouble and expense. Rather than monitor his blood pressure, or suggest that he work less or (heaven forbid) give up smoking, they wrote out prescriptions for whatever minor ailment had brought him to their surgeries. This suited John very well: if a doctor said nothing it meant there was nothing to say about his health. And that was the end of that. For a while.

In matters unrelated to his own financial or physical welfare John worked with all the good sense, cunning and determination of a born businessman. As long as the reward was not for his own benefit, he showed a surprising talent for managing and investing institutional money. He founded and ran university departments; as Mrs Thatcher's cuts began to bite, he rescued his own from closure. He managed the finances of the National Gallery, extracted money for education and the arts from tight-fisted civil servants and politicians. He knew how to charm but he also knew which arguments would and wouldn't work with whom; he could calculate to the minute when the time had come to lose his temper. During his chairmanship of the National Gallery he and his director, Michael Levey, bullied successive governments into raising the annual purchase grant from £480,000 in 1974 to £2.9 million in 1981.

Money, as far as John is concerned, should be earned and spent. He had a word for people like Mrs Thatcher (and me in my financially sensible moods) who hoard money for its own sake. I am searching for this word, but can't find it. He used it when, for instance, I resisted the temptation to visit a needy friend abroad because I knew we couldn't at that particular time afford the fare. It was a good word, signifying a joyless, ungenerous short-sightedness about the nature and purpose of the good life. Perhaps it was the name of a person: no one as obvious as Scrooge, of course. But I've lost it, and he can't help me find it now.

If John wanted to top up his university salary he made the extra money from television, journalism, popular books, lecturing about moneymaking in the Renaissance to business conferences in Florida or Hawaii. This kind of work was his hobby, almost as much fun as spending the fees on travel, opera tickets, books, and on the antique furniture, porcelain and old prints, watercolours and flaking oil paintings with which we decorated our house. The house, which we bought in 1970 just as the property market was beginning its upward spiral, was one of his more eccentric purchases. Jerry-built in the early eighteenth century, it had leaned nine inches to one side. The basement was damp, the floorboards creaked, the roof leaked. The location was inconvenient for central London where we both worked. Although the neighbourhood was unfashionable, the price was more than we could afford. John wanted this house and no other because it was beautiful. He could imagine waking up to the sunrise in the wood-panelled bedroom that faced east over treetops. He could see himself writing at the desk he would put in the window of the small room at the top of the house, which overlooked the garden and the setting sun.

We painted his study the colour of a pumpkin, and in it John wrote many of his best books – including *Renaissance Europe, 1480–1520* (1971); *Florence and the Medici: The Pattern of Control* (1977); *Italian Renaissance Painting from Masaccio to Titian* (1977); *War and Society in Renaissance Europe* (1985); *Artists and Warfare in the Renaissance* (1990); and *The Civilization of Europe in the Renaissance* (1993). At his desk in the window, he worked, just as he had planned, writing his own books, editing and contributing to more books, writing scholarly articles, newspaper articles, television scripts, testimonials for students, as well as dozens of long personal letters each day.

John liked the village atmosphere of our neighbourhood. He liked the nodding relationships he developed with people after passing them in the street as the years went by. The small, hopeless shops that had somehow survived competition from the new supermarkets across the river intrigued him. He encouraged the man who sold newspapers at the station to pursue his dream of opening an antique shop. He enjoyed the protective affection he inspired in the two large, comfortable elderly ladies who worked in the dry cleaners: they reminded him of his sisters. Not having as much spare time as he would have liked for chatting, he invented characters for people with whom he had never exchanged a word. The couple up the road who screamed at their cleaning lady and chopped down all the trees in their garden were the Colditzes. The fresh-faced young couple next door, whose wealthy parents had given them their house as a wedding present, were – despite the fact that neither of them ever wore wellington boots – the Greenwellies. For Mr Patel, the shy Indian owner of the paper shop where JJ bought his weekly copies of *Beano* and *The Dandy*, John invented an adventurous life, which began when Mr Patel closed the shop.

On Wednesday, 29 July John returned from the garden centre with his bicycle basket filled with plants for which we had no place left in the garden. We had tea in the garden before going to the theatre with JJ and my mother, who was visiting us from New York. The play was a routine drawing-room comedy which each of the three generations thought the others might be enjoying. None of us wanted to spoil the others' pleasure, which left us with nothing interesting to say in the interval, until John released us. 'Well,' he said cheerfully, 'this is almost like going to the theatre.'

I remember the velvety feel of the summer air on my arms as we escaped after the first act on to the street; and the smell of regale lilies, jasmine and tobacco plants in our garden where we sat for a while drinking white wine, enjoying not being in the stuffy theatre. For supper we had cold chicken and my mother's New York potato salad (flavoured with dill, spring onions and olive oil). I remember that John ate two helpings of everything, and that we sat up late talking. But I can't remember anything John said after, Well, this is almost like going to the theatre.

The accident, as doctors prefer to call it – they don't like the word stroke – occurred the following morning, Thursday, 30 July 1992, shortly before nine. John got up without waking me, which was un-usual. When I reached the kitchen I could see that he had eaten his usual breakfast – muesli, toast with marmalade, coffee. He had also emptied the dishwasher, the one domestic task he enjoyed. But the contents were scattered all over the kitchen: plates, mugs, forks, cups, pots, knives, saucers all jumbled up on the kitchen table and counters.

I heard the crash a few minutes later. It sounded like a heavy picture falling off the wall. I had decided to ignore it – John could deal with it while I finished tidying the kitchen – when the Irish cleaner, who had gone upstairs to spend her usual half-hour saying good morning to John, came running down the stairs screaming: John has fell. She left the house and never returned.

That night our friend and neighbour Camilla who has a key to our house let herself in and noticed that I'd left some beans to soak for our dinner. She said, They'll go off if they're left soaking. She covered them with fresh water, boiled them, and put the leg of lamb that was to go with them in the freezer. It's strange how you remember such things about times of disaster.

He was lying on the floor of his study, next to the desk where he must have planned to spend the morning writing. His eyes were open and his smile allowed me to believe, just for a moment, that this might be the opening scene of one of his more histrionic practical jokes: like the time when he cured me of hiccups by fusing all the lights in a house we'd rented in California and climbing up a drainpipe wearing my long black evening cape. The neighbours, who noticed him peering into a bedroom window hissing, I'm coming to get you, called the police.

But this smile was empty, with none of John's mischief or irony behind it. It was the sweet, witless smile of a baby. He opened his mouth and said, in a weak but otherwise normal voice: *The Walls.*

The receptionist at the doctors' surgery did not recognize our name. She refused to call a doctor to the telephone, because they were all busy with what she called 'patients', in a tone that implied that John, perhaps because he rarely visited the surgery, was somehow not a patient. She suggested I call an ambulance. The emergency operator said that the nearest ambulance was well beyond the other end of London and had several other urgent calls. She couldn't say when an ambulance would reach us. She suggested I call our doctor.

The ambulance arrived forty-five minutes later. The paramedics put an oxygen mask over John's face and carried him downstairs on a stretcher. In the ambulance he smiled at me like an adoring child and stroked my arm with his left hand, saying *The Walls* over and over in a reassuring voice. The paramedics said they were taking us to the nearest hospital. I'd never been to this hospital, but we'd lived in the neighbourhood long enough to know that the locals called it The Feet First. I pleaded with the paramedics to take us just a little further, to another hospital with a better reputation. They were sympathetic but firm. They could not break the rule that required them to take an emergency patient directly to the nearest Accident and Emergency department.

In Accident and Emergency John was immediately attended by a team of doctors and nurses. After about half an hour one of the doctors told me that my husband had suffered a 'cerebral vascular accident' – a stroke. There was nothing to be done except provide him with rest and reassurance. Unfortunately, however, all beds in their hospital were occupied. There was a severe shortage of beds all over London. The doctor really couldn't say whether it would be possible to find a bed for John anywhere.

John beamed his radiant baby's smile at the doctors who were refusing him a bed. Maybe he felt that they, the professional experts, knew best. Or it could be that he was stunned by the euphoria that can follow stroke. Maybe he didn't understand what they were saying, or what it meant. I shall never know exactly what was going on in his head as he lay on that trolley. John remembers nothing about it. But later, when a friend advised me to read the American playwright Arthur Kopit's play *Wings* about a stroke victim he calls Mrs Stilson, I came across what remains for me the most convincing description of the inner world of a mind that has just been shattered:

MRS STILSON (*trying hard to keep smiling*): Yes, all in all in all I'd say while things could be better could be worse, far worse, how? Not quite sure. Just a sense I have. The sort of sense that only great experience can mallees or rake, plake I mean, flake . . . Drake! That's it.

FIRST DOCTOR: Mrs Stilson, who was the first President of the United States?

MRS STILSON: Washington.

Pause.

SECOND DOCTOR (*speaking more slowly than the first doctor did; perhaps she simply didn't hear the question*): Mrs Stilson, who was the first President of the United States?

MRS STILSON: Washington!

SECOND DOCTOR (*to First*): I don't think she hears herself.

FIRST DOCTOR: No, I don't think she hears herself.

The two doctors emerge from the shadows, approach Mrs Stilson. She looks up in terror. This should be the first time that the woman on stage

*has been directly faced or confronted by the hospital staff. Her inner and
outer worlds are beginning to come together.*

FIRST DOCTOR: Mrs Stilson, makey your naming powers?

MRS STILSON: What?

SECOND DOCTOR: Caju spokeme?

MRS STILSON: Can I what?

FIRST DOCTOR: Can do peeperear?

MRS STILSON: I don't believe what's going on!

SECOND DOCTOR: Ahwill.

FIRST DOCTOR: Pollycadjus.

SECOND DOCTOR (*with a nod*): Hm-hm.

Exit doctors.

John lay on the trolley, visited occasionally by doctors, for several
hours. I heard a nurse say, He's getting very dehydrated. Another
nurse took his blood pressure. It's raging, she said to a junior doctor,
who said, He really ought to be on a drip. The tea trolley rattled
relentlessly through the narrow corridor followed by a woman selling sweets and biscuits. A nurse complained that she couldn't resist
chocolate biscuits. Another nurse warned me not to try to give John
water: he wouldn't be able to swallow and might choke.

A hospital porter arrived. He wheeled John's trolley into a concrete building, into a lift that smelled of urine and stale cigarettes,
up to a ward on the fifth floor. It was the closest place to hell I'd ever
been in all my privileged, overprotected, trusting life.

3

Hell

The world will not record their having been there;
Heaven's mercy and its justice turn from them.
Let's not discuss them; look and pass them by.

Dante, The Inferno, *Canto III*

Doctors hate an illness they cannot cure, which is part of
the explanation for the profound and chronic neglect of
stroke patients. (In many provincial hospitals, the out-of-
the-way bed at the back of the ward is often still referred
to as 'the stroke bed'.)
                    Robert McCrum, My Year Off:
                    Rediscovering Life after a Stroke, 1998

From my diary, August and September 1992.

Sunday, 2 August, 4:15 a.m. This is the worst time, when I lie here wondering why John is being punished as though his stroke was a crime. What has he ever done but good? If anybody should be punished it is me, not him. Nearly two hours before I can go to the hospital. I mustn't take another temazepam because I need to be alert all day. There is so much to do and John is so helpless. The other patients scream and scream for help: 'Doctor doctor. Nurse nurse.' But John can't say a single word except for something that sounds like a cross between the wars and the walls. I can tell he understands what I say to him, but if I ask him a simple question – like do you want your book? – he nods yes and then shakes his head for no and then looks completely exasperated. He is very weak and can't move his right arm or leg, and I'm afraid that without words to call for help or explain what he wants he might not survive in that place. If he could talk he would know how to attract the nurses' attention without causing offence. And he would know how to reassure me. I know this is ridiculous, but I need him now more than I ever have. I can just hear him saying, There are good times and bad times. This is a very bad one but we'll find a way to get through it. And then I would say, Oh don't be so bloody *balanced* about everything. This is *serious*. I need you to help me. And then he would find a solution, because that's the way it is in our marriage.

This diary is Christina's idea. Thank God for friends. She says I should keep a record of these terrible days because when it's all over and John is well and life is back to normal I'll forget all about it, the way women are programmed to forget the pain of childbirth. Actually, I'd rather go back to lying curled up in the dark where I can cry. Maybe John will be able to write about it one day.

Monday, 3 August, late afternoon. The ward is very hot. At this time of day the sun glares straight in through the greasy plate glass window and cooks up an almighty stink – the dinner trolley, unwashed bodies, stale urine. The shade rolled up at the top of the window is stuck – nobody can remember when it was possible to pull it down. The window is also permanently sealed – to prevent suicides, according to one of the junior doctors who happened to be passing when I tried to open it earlier today.

I've promised to bring in a fan tomorrow, but Harry, the patient in the bed opposite John, says not to bother because it will only be stolen.

I should be grateful – I *am* grateful – that they found a bed for John after all, and that he is alive, sleeping peacefully in it as I write. I shouldn't be peevish about minor matters, but focusing on problems like the window for which there is, or could be, a practical solution makes me feel a bit less helpless. The doctors in Accident and Emergency said John needed 'rest and reassurance'. So one thing I can do, for example, is stop the dinner trolley lady from waking him up – as she is about to do as I write – with a tray of food presumably intended for a patient who can eat.

J can't swallow yet so they're feeding him from a bottle through a tube in his nose. He also has two needles in his bad – right – arm, one delivering a saline solution to keep him from dehydrating, the other a medication to lower his blood pressure, which, they say, is still dangerously raised. The nurses have explained that the tube and the needles are keeping him alive. But there is never a nurse available when the tube blocks or the bottles are empty. The nurses are obviously tremendously busy and I think not really very well organized. When I run around the other wards looking for someone who knows how to fix John's life-saving equipment I hear the competition, a chorus of bed-bound patients, all pleading, Nurse? Please help me. Nurse!

Tuesday, 4 August. I haven't had time to count, least of all answer, all the cards and letters from John's friends. He's had so many flowers that the ward looks almost festive, like a wedding banquet. I've gummed the postcards on to the wall above his bed, which is now a collage of piazzas, bell towers, landscapes, details from paintings and frescoes.

Now that he is more alert he's very preoccupied by the problem of not wetting his bed. He's not incontinent, at least he doesn't think he is. But because the nurses have no time to take away full urine bottles and bring empty ones he often has no choice but to pee in his bed. They want to catheterize him which may be easier for them but is uncomfortable and humiliating for him. So every night before I leave I have to sneak into the supply room (which is theoretically off bounds for non-staff) and steal three cardboard urine bottles, which he secretes under the bedclothes for use during the night. First thing in the morning I empty them in the visitors' loo.

In the evening, as I'm leaving, Harry, who sits in a chair across the room, and Pete, in the next bed, promise to look after John. They are mates, buddies. They have to be.

Pete is a retired electrical engineer. He had a right-brain stroke, on the other side of his brain from John's. Pete can talk, and because he's been here so long – he's forgotten how long – they've given him a wheelchair that he can manipulate with his good right arm. He is obsessed with time and has several clocks and watches which he is forever asking me to wind and check against mine. He cries most of the day and passes the time wheeling himself to and from the patients' recreation room to try to telephone his wife, which he can't do because the pay telephone has been ripped from the wall.

His family arrives every evening punctually at 5:30. He and his son talk a lot about the hi-fi system Pete installed before his stroke. It's broken. The other bad news is that the hamster has escaped. His wife and daughter, both of whom have office jobs, are dressed almost identically in neat summer dresses and court shoes. The family seems close but remarkably phlegmatic about what has happened to them. I think they may be secretly shocked by the old trousers and T-shirt I've been wearing since John's stroke. I must at least wash my hair.

Today John had 15 visitors. Matthew brought him a book about American cowboys and John entertained us with an imitation of a cowboy's voice. There are no visiting hours, the nurses don't mind who comes or when, but when the parties round his bed get noisy John always indicates that I must ask the other patients if we are disturbing them. They say, no, it's nice seeing people around.

Wednesday, 5 August. While watering the plants, which get very dehydrated in the heat, I discovered three thermometers stuck in the soil of a hydrangea, and a syringe in the gardenia. Matthew has brought John a radio but John doesn't like listening to it. Music in particular seems to cause him pain. So I gave the radio to Harry, who says it will only be stolen. Harry is a retired gardener. He can't walk following a thrombosis in his right leg but seems otherwise fairly OK. He's been in hospital for a year because the social services haven't got round to adapting his cottage for his wheelchair. His wife Joanna is 91, a few years older than Harry. She is already in the ward every morning when I arrive at about 8. They sit together all day holding hands and looking quite content – gazing at the comings and goings on the ward with detached interest, like Darby and Joan on holiday in a Spanish café.

The sister gave John a bed bath today, his first. It was a joy to watch her work. I've been trying to keep him clean by myself and so I know how difficult it is to move a paralysed body without doing harm. The sister said his right arm should be stretched out at all times on a pillow. But there are no spare pillows. The sister says if I bring some from home they will be stolen. So I stole a blanket from the supply room and use that rolled up instead.

Pete's son came in this afternoon with news. The hamster has eaten the wires at the back of the hi-fi set. That's why it won't work. John warned me not to laugh by waggling his eyebrows and shaking his head.

Thursday, 6 August. John has been here for a week. I've made friends with three of the nurses. Maria trained in Jamaica, Eileen in Ireland. David is still training at a college nearby. Maria and Eileen both say that they were brought up to believe that nursing in England was the best in the world, that it would be an honour to work in an English hospital. The reality is so disappointing that they're thinking of leaving the profession. They don't mind working hard but they hate the attitudes that seem to put patients' welfare at the bottom of the list of priorities. David went into nursing because he likes caring for people, especially old people. He is not good at book learning, but is now required to go part-time to a college to learn about medical technology, which he hates.

I've not seen a sign of the consultant who is supposed to be in charge of John. The consultant's name is Dr X. I know this because there's a filthy card above John's bed printed with the words 'In the Care of Dr X', just visible through the grime. The nurses say they don't know where I could find Dr X. But this morning an exhausted junior doctor pointed me in the direction of his office. Eventually I found a door with his name on it. The woman who answered my knock looked not so much outraged as astonished. Dr X, she said very slowly, Does Not Speak To The Relatives Of Patients. I guessed that there was no point in explaining that the patient in question couldn't speak to anyone.

Saturday, 8 August. Yesterday we were taken by ambulance to another hospital for John's CT scan. This hospital doesn't have a scanner. The CT scan will give the doctors more information about John's stroke. Since no nurse could be spared to accompany us Christina kindly agreed to come along. This was a great help because I couldn't have managed John by myself. He is unable to move and still attached to the life-saving bottles of food and water.

In the ambulance I could tell that J was enjoying the outing. It was the first time he'd been out of the ward for 10 days. He chatted with

Christina and gazed out at the familiar west London streets as excited and interested as a child. He had managed to forget all about the reality of our situation – until he put up his hand to straighten his hair and it brushed the tube in his nose, and I could see the dejection and embarrassment in his eyes. Why do I have to share his feelings as though they were my own? Everyone tells me that my desire to take his place, to do the suffering for him, is bad for both of us.

The paramedics put John's stretcher on a trolley in the centre of a round room which was the hub of six straight corridors. There was nobody in sight and not a sound. After an hour and a half Christina said, This is hospital time. Hospital time is different from real time. But John's drip bottles were nearly empty. I ran up and down the corridors and eventually bumped into a Chinese nurse. She said there was no appointment booked for Hale that day. She then followed me to John's trolley, peered down at him and said, What seems to be the matter? I said, My husband has been lying on this trolley for two hours. His bottles are empty and if he stays here much longer his life will be in danger. The nurse, directing her question at John, repeated: What seems to be the matter? John gave her his radiant smile and said, The walls, the walls. I explained our problem once again, and once again she asked John, What seems to be the matter?

They went back and forth like that for a while. Then Christina went off to find a pay telephone and try to persuade someone at our hospital to send a nurse with fresh bottles or an ambulance to collect us. The nurse arrived by taxi 20 minutes later, just as a doctor was wheeling John off to have the CT scan for which the appointment had not been booked.

Sunday, 9 August, late at night. I don't dare go to sleep for fear of the small hours. At 2 this afternoon when John was sleeping and I was reading in the reception area a man came up and said, I gather you wanted to see me. He had a fixed social smile on his face and was rocking back and forth on his feet as though judging how to swing a golf club. This was Dr X! Dr X said that a first reading of the CT scan had proved what 'everybody here' had known from the beginning. John's case was hopeless. Dr X was not prepared to accept him in the hospital's rehabilitation programme. It would be a waste of limited resources. He suggested I put John in a home. After all, he said, You're still relatively young. You don't want to spend the rest of your life tied to an infarct. I've looked up this word. It means a region of dead tissue caused by a blocked artery.

I found myself telling him what a remarkable man John is, how he risked his life in the Merchant Navy during the war, how much of his time and talent he has devoted to public service. Which is why we have no money for private treatment. Surely he deserves something in return? Dr X said, There are no privileged patients here. Everybody is treated exactly the same. I knew I was irritating him but I couldn't stop myself. What if we could somehow raise some money? Would that buy him treatment? Dr X said, I've seen patients carried out of here on stretchers and flown to America. It doesn't work. Nothing does. Your husband is not going to walk out of this hospital. Take my advice. Put him in a home.

Tuesday, 11 August. I don't trust Dr X. To be honest, I hate him. Maybe he's right, he is a doctor after all. All I know now is that I must get John out of here. I spent yesterday and this morning on the telephone. The Stroke Association will supply a list of stroke rehabilitation units but will make no recommendations or provide any personal advice or help. The Wolfson Centre at Atkinson Morley's Hospital, which is supposed to be one of the best stroke rehab places in England, categorically refuses to take any NHS stroke patient over the age of 65, however deserving, however active their lives before the stroke. They will, however, be happy to accept John in their private branch, which is more than anyone who is not insured or very rich could afford for more than a few weeks. Queen Mary's Roehampton isn't sure what their policy is about geriatric stroke patients. They may be closing their stroke unit altogether.

Anthony, who knows how things work in this country, says I must play the old-boy network. Does John have any connections in the medical profession?

Wednesday, 12 August. This morning I telephoned a famous neurologist at Queen Square who treated a cabinet minister whose wife is an acquaintance of ours. It's a pretty feeble link but the neurologist did come to the phone and sounded, briefly, impressed either by the connection or by John's title. Who did you say your husband is? Distinguished historian and former Chairman of the National Gallery didn't quite make the grade. He agreed to examine John for a fee if I had him delivered to Queen Square by private ambulance.

Next I'm going to try a certain Dr Y, whose name has been mentioned by several people as being an eminent neurologist who is also interested in Italian history, particularly Machiavelli and Vico. Perhaps he knows John's work?

I told John that I might have found someone who could help. He responded, in falsetto, with an imitation of me (emphatic American accent) talking on the telephone.

In the afternoon a nurse took the tube out of J's nose. He ought to have been able to swallow a few days ago but the nurse had to wait until the speech therapist was free to be there in case J had any swallowing difficulties. I watched him take his first sip of water and mouthful of food in nearly two weeks. Some disgusting-looking pudding, but the look of bliss on his face! He'll have to be on soft food for a few days. I'll bring him some nice things like hummus and ice cream.

The speech therapist is a pretty Scottish lass wearing a floaty summer dress and sandals with very high heels. I told her that John can read and can understand absolutely everything said to him and she said, I wouldn't be so sure. She put four objects on John's bed tray: a razor, a clock, a pencil and some keys. Then she spoke each word very clearly and asked him to point to the correct object. It was obvious he hadn't a clue what she wanted him to do or how he could do it. Then she wrote the words on separate labels and asked John to match them to the objects. Once again, John was stumped. I panicked. If John can't match the simplest of words to the most ordinary of everyday objects does it mean he has less language than a trained ape?

The speech therapist said that although John appears to understand us he is in fact only guessing from clues given by our gestures and tone of voice. As for his reading, he is turning the pages out of what she calls habitual behaviour. I had to admit that he does not persist with the books I bring him. All his adult life he has comforted himself in times of trouble by reading detective stories and thrillers. Now he starts a book eagerly but soon abandons it. On the other hand he really does seem to understand his academic journals and offprints. I can tell this because he marks them in what seem like appropriate places and answers questions about them by pointing to relevant passages. And he's been reading the newspapers I bring him. They are full of photographs of Serbian death camps and beautiful Muslim women arriving in England on boats. I feel guilty that I am not more bothered by the terrible things happening in other parts of the world.

The speech therapist admitted that she had heard a theory that reading for pleasure and reading for information might be two dissociated functions. Perhaps John's ability to read for information has been partially spared, although it seems unlikely given his performance with the keys and the razor.

Friday, 14 August. When I came into the ward yesterday morning John was sitting in his chair bent over double and moaning, clutching his paralysed leg. I've never seen him show such pain. I found a nurse who said she couldn't give him a strong enough painkiller because addictive drugs are kept in a locked cupboard on another floor of the hospital. It would take about 15 or 20 minutes to fetch the pills. Two nurses must be present when the cupboard is opened. Dr X would be doing a ward round in the morning – this morning. Maybe I could catch him then.

I came in at 6. Dr X arrived at 8. Ignored me, as usual. I shadowed him for an hour or so until he reached J's bed. I asked what might be causing John's pain. Oh, you never know with infarcts, said Dr X. They fall downstairs. But how could he fall downstairs when he can't even get out of bed? Dr X beamed his social smile at me and began to shout: I gave you a whole hour of my time on Sunday and that's as much as you're going to get. I told you that your husband isn't going to receive special treatment. If you go on making fusses he'll suffer for it. His voice was very loud. The ward sister appeared, tapped him on the shoulder and said he was wanted on the telephone. Shortly afterwards two nurses arrived with the painkiller. Later this afternoon the sister summoned me into her office. She wanted to know if I had been 'bothered' by Dr X's 'tone'. He was very busy, as I could see, but of course John's leg would be examined by one of the junior doctors. She said she thought it might be phantom pain, as experienced by amputees. I said I wasn't bothered. And that I was extremely grateful to know that someone would be available to look at John's leg. Geriatric stroke victims are the lowest of the low. We are at the mercy of Dr X and can do nothing but bow our heads to his authority and figure out an escape.

Sunday, 16 August. Amused myself last night when I couldn't sleep by imagining what a television crew from a more civilized country would make of Dr X's hospital. How different would it look from makeshift hospitals in third-world war zones that we see on our television? I can just hear the reporter's smug, sing-song voice ticking off horrors that could never happen here: the stench, the filth, the shortage of trained nurses and doctors, the breakdown of organization, the patients begging for help, dying from neglect.

Everything I read about stroke and everyone I talk to who knows about it say that it is crucial that the affected limbs be exercised, passively if necessary. If not the muscles may be permanently cramped and never able to recover. Fortunately, I remembered that a neighbour, a woman with whom I'm on chatting terms only, once told me she used to be a physiotherapist. I knocked on her door and to my surprise she actually agreed to come with me to the hospital. She showed me how to bend and straighten and stretch his right arm and leg. Then she got him into his chair and told him to try to push himself up, not only with his left hand but also with his paralysed one which she held in place on the right arm of the chair. John stood up! It was so unexpected that the three of us started laughing while Harry and Pete applauded. Then five nurses led by the sister came running in. The sister shoved John back into his chair saying that physiotherapy was not allowed on the ward because the hospital was not insured for it.

But there is good news! Dr Y has agreed to visit John at the hospital on Tuesday. He was in the States when I first telephoned, but his secretary, who has a kind voice, said she was sure he would ring back on his return, and he has. He says he's read some of J's books, heard him lecture and even met him – although he doesn't suppose John will remember him – at a conference at the Warburg Institute. I've told John that he had jolly well better remember him, which actually it seems he does.

Monday, 17 August. On Saturday, while I was giving John his supper – his favourite, crab with mayonnaise – he suddenly, with no warning, shat himself. I couldn't find a nurse anywhere, and when I got back from searching he was shaking and very pale. I started trying to clean him up but this is not easy. He's lost a lot of weight but he's still a big man. My admiration for nurses has gone up yet another notch as a result of trying myself to do one of their routine tasks. After about 45 minutes a nurse arrived and took over from me. John used to say that the one thing he most dreaded about old age was humiliation. Seeing him like this was worse than seeing him in pain.

Then Richard arrived to visit John and take me out to dinner. When we left the hospital Richard said, He's going to be fine. He's still got the old fire in his eyes. I started to cry and found I couldn't stop, which was actually a relief because I'd thought I was beyond tears. Richard took me home, went out to get a Chinese takeaway and a bottle of champagne. Then we lay together on John's and my bed, he in his good City suit and me in my excrement-smeared trousers, and for the rest of the night Richard talked to me about his business, his children, their sailing holidays, his wife's bee-keeping. Towards morning I said, Why do I have to feel this pain? Why do I suffer so much for John? Richard told me Ovid's story about two people called Baucis and Philemon who were so happily married that the gods made them grow old together as entwined trees. I don't know whether the gods intended to reward or punish them.

Tuesday, 18 August, late at night. In the morning everybody was busy making preparations for Dr Y's arrival. John was given his second bed bath in nearly 3 weeks, the floor of the ward was washed (first time since we've been here). At 3:30 Dr X appeared in the reception area within sight of the lifts, and engaged in businesslike conversation with the sister and a junior doctor. Dr Y emerged from the lift at 4:00, exactly on time. He is 60-ish, small and wiry with a sallow complexion. Dr X stopped rocking back and forth on his feet and welcomed the king to his provincial but well-ordered domain. His body language said: for all our difference in status we speak a common language, the language of medical science which gives us the power to decide who will and will not be saved.

Dr Y spent a long time examining J's CT scan and then came to see John. He spoke to John with what seemed like real respect. He examined the paralysed leg, pricked it here and there asking J how much he could feel, asked him to push against his hand as hard as he could. Meanwhile he was chatting away about the Machiavelli conference where they'd last met. When he'd finished examining John he said, This must all seem like a ghoulish nightmare, but you will get your speech back. Now I'm going to have a talk with your wife and then with Dr X. Don't worry, you are in good hands.

When we were alone Dr Y repeated that we needn't worry about J's speech. He would recover because all highly intelligent, naturally verbal people do, especially if they are polylingual. I shouldn't waste money on professional speech therapy. He recommends instead a method devised by a retired businesswoman called Valerie Eaton Griffith who devised a system of games and puzzles for the actress Patricia Neal after her stroke. They are all things that can be done by volunteers. Then he said that there was however something he hadn't said in front of John. John has very little reaction in his right leg. The chances are he will never walk again.

Wednesday, 19 August. I telephoned Dr Y from home this morning and asked if he could help me find another hospital for John, perhaps the hospital in central London where he is a consultant neurologist. He said, My hospital is a dump. You're better off close to home.

He added that Dr X had assured him that John was doing very well, considering the severity of his stroke, and was receiving the care that a man of his distinction deserved.

When I came into the hospital at about 10 Dr X made an appearance and told me that he's changed his mind about accepting John in the hospital's rehabilitation programme. Nevertheless, I'm working on a letter to Dr Y that will somehow manage to convey how desperate our situation is without seeming to cast aspersion on a fellow doctor. The medical profession is inclined to close ranks. Camilla, who is very good at being both tactful and tough, has read one draft and rejected it as being implicitly too critical. It's not easy to get the tone exactly right.

Thursday, 20 August. Morning. Camilla approved third try at letter to Dr Y. JJ will deliver three copies on his motorbike – to Dr Y's home, private practice and hospital.

Saturday, 22 August. 5:30 a.m. The telephone rang last night at about 11 while Camilla and I were having supper in my kitchen after the hospital. The voice said, Buona sera, signora. I admire your shrapnel technique. It was Dr Y, who had received all three copies of the letter. He said – breaking into his not very good Italian every now and again – that a former student of his, a certain Dr Z, was in charge of geriatric medicine at a hospital in north London. Dr Z had sometimes taken in distinguished patients like John who had no private insurance or whose policies had run out. Dr Y had spoken to Dr Z about John and there might be a bed for him. But it would not be easy to transfer John to a different health authority. According to the Patients' Charter, every patient is supposed to be allowed to have the hospital of his or her choice. In practice it is rarely possible. He then wished me good luck and signed off with, Remember your Machiavelli!

Camilla and I opened another bottle of wine and danced around the kitchen.

Monday, 24 August. Sometimes The Walls sounds more like The Wars, or more often like a cross between the two: *the*, or *da*, *woahs*. When the speech therapist floated in today, bringing, as before, a welcome note of glamour to our bedraggled company, I told her that as a historian John was in fact interested both in war and in walls (fortifications). She said nobody knows whether these recurrent utterances, as they are called, represent real words, perhaps something the patient was thinking about just before the accident, or whether they are just a sound that is easy to make. Sometimes people who have lost their expressive language are left with embarrassing words like shit. Sometimes they keep repeating the same meaningless sentence over and over, such as Let's go to the gate.

Then she drew a circle, a square and a triangle and asked John to copy them. John did this so easily that she gave him some letters to copy. No problem. No problem either with copying words or even whole sentences. He doesn't seem to mind writing with his left hand, but what he can't do is write so much as a single word out of his own head.

Then she gave him some sums to add and subtract which he did without difficulty. She said When were you born John, and he wrote 1923. She said, Something very complicated is going on here. Before leaving she told us that his recovery of speech might begin with swear words, which are apparently lodged in a primitive part of the brain, or with automatic language such as counting or saying the days of the week.

When she had gone I lay on the bed next to John and whispered four-letter words into his ear. This made him laugh. When I counted up to ten over and over and recited the days of the week, he patted my hair and said *Da woahs, da woahs*. I dozed off until I heard Pete's wife say, She's fallen asleep wearing only one shoe.

Thursday, 27 August. It's three days since I delivered my letters requesting the transfer. I suppose it's too early to expect a reply. I've also tried to telephone the health authority, the hospital administration office and Dr X. The telephones are engaged or don't answer.

Friday, 28 August. Meeting with Dr Z at his hospital. He is about fortyish, with a public-school accent and an absent-minded manner. He asked if John has any movement at all in his right leg and when I said just an occasional twitch of the big toe he said Good, we'll have him up and walking in a few weeks. Do you have stairs in your house? Good, I'll get the physios to give him stair practice. I was afraid he might not accept John if I confessed that Drs X and Y were certain that he would never walk. So I just nodded when he told me J will need gym shoes and a track suit, and that between sessions with the physios he will walk on the ward with the nurses. Are you prepared to take risks? said Dr Z. Because there are going to be some bumps and lumps.

Dr Z says he isn't a stroke specialist. What interests him most is a certain valve associated with incontinence in the elderly, which is why it suits him to run a geriatric ward. He will put John on 75 mgs of soluble aspirin twice a week. This is less than the conventional dose. If that worries me I can read his article about it in the New England Journal of Medicine.

He showed me round the hospital, which looks very nice. He believes that Victorian hospitals, properly refurbished, work better than modern buildings. He says there is a stigma attached to them as relics of the Dickensian age. The corridors are freshly painted, prints by contemporary artists on the walls, the wards clean and full of light. But what if I can't get John here in time? Dr Z can hold the bed until 14 September, but not a day longer.

Saturday, 29 August. There is nothing we can do about the transfer until after the bank holiday.

Tuesday, 1 September. Still no reply to my letters and nobody in any of the offices who has seen them.

Thursday, 3 September. When I came into the hospital this morning, later than usual after my usual round of trying to reach some official about John's transfer, I found Dr X standing by John's bed. I asked him if he had received my letter. He said he would address his remarks to John, who is his patient. I said I would like an answer to my letter, please and soon. And then we had the following dialogue:

DR X: In my opinion a transfer would not be in your husband's best interests.
ME: I'm very sorry but I'm afraid I must try to give him the chance of having some rehabilitation.
DR X: But I've told you that he has been accepted in our rehabilitation programme.
ME: Yes but he hasn't actually been given any physiotherapy at all.
DR X: Yes he has.

ME: No he hasn't.

DR X: What makes you so sure?

ME: Because John, Pete and Harry all say that he hasn't.

DR X: What makes you think you can trust those infarcts?

ME: I'm sorry, but I must find the best possible care for John.

DR X: He will get the best possible care in this hospital. He might have died here. Do you know why he hasn't? Because everybody here loves him.

I've just rung Camilla in tears. Only a week to go and no sign of release papers.

Monday, 7 September. At 8:45 this morning, Camilla, who had just washed her hair, picked me up in her Daimler wearing her best Dior suit and a splendid hat over her wet hair, mumbling I hate bureaucracy. She drove me to the hospital, parked in the Officials Only space in front of the admin building, sailed majestically up to the receptionist and said, I understand Sir John Hale is being held in this hospital against the wishes of his family. I'm sure there has been some mistake but would be tremendously grateful if you would inform the manager that we expect arrangements to be made immediately for his transfer to the hospital of his family's choice.

My diary for 1992 ends there. John was taken by ambulance to Dr Z's geriatric ward on 14 September.

The Wolfson Centre at Atkinson Morley's Hospital abandoned its age limit in 1995.

In the autumn of 2000 and again in the spring of 2001 – nearly nine years after our escape – an inspection by the Department of Health gave the hospital its lowest rating for internal cleanliness and tidiness for common areas and wards, furniture and visitors' lavatories. In the spring of 2002, nearly ten years after John's stroke, a routine assessment by the Commission for Health Improvement found the hospital's Accident and Emergency department to be a 'potentially unsafe environment'. The inspectors reported that it was overcrowded, and had excessive waiting-times, high nursing vacancies and a lack of leadership. Pete died there, shortly after John left. Harry was eventually released, still in a wheelchair.

4

The Geriatric Ward

*God help old people on their own with no-one to fight
their corner – and believe me fight is the appropriate word.*

A *female carer quoted in M. Kelson* et al., Speaking Out
About Stroke Services: The Views of People Affected by
Stroke, *a survey to inform the implementation of the
National Service Framework for Older People*

Dr Z's geriatric ward is long and narrow, lit by rows of windows on
both long sides, like the carriage of a train. The patients' cubicles
are on either side of the wide corridor, which has a scrubbed wooden
floor. Each cubicle is equipped with a bed, a locker, a curtain, which
can be drawn against the corridor for privacy, and a window that
can be opened. There is light, air and space, as stipulated by Florence
Nightingale in her successful campaigns to reform the design of
British hospitals in the nineteenth century. It seemed to us an
altogether better place than the airless ward in the 1960s block from
which we had escaped.

John's window overlooked the dusty tops of old chestnut and
sycamore trees growing in the Victorian hospital's cemetery, which
now serves the neighbourhood as a park. As the days grew shorter
and the leaves fell we could see the evening traffic flowing downhill
towards the West End. Sometimes I would look up the entertain-
ments listings in the paper and pretend to choose which operas and
plays we would see when John was strong enough.

Most of the other patients were women, some old enough to be
John's mother. Mary, whose hundredth birthday we celebrated soon
after John arrived, was partially blind but otherwise relatively
healthy and sharp-witted. But she had outlived all her relatives and
friends, and the nurses said they could find no local authority with

a record of her existence. The nurses, who had grown fond of Mary, knew very well that 'long-term care in the community' was likely to be a euphemism for a lonely death in an under-heated house or squalid old people's home. The Alzheimer's patients, who wandered half-dressed around the ward mumbling and shouting, were not supposed to be there either, because their condition, being untreatable at that time, was considered by the health authorities to be a waste of hospital space. None was dismissed in the time John and I were there. The nurses wore their own clothes, mostly the jeans or long hippie-style skirts favoured by the idealistic young and poor, because Dr Z thought the patients would feel more at home that way. They worked closely with the physiotherapists and helped the patients with their exercises in the ward.

Viewed from the safe haven of Dr Z's geriatric ward, Dr X's terrifying regime began to look like an exceptional piece of bad luck, not worth dwelling on. The conditions I had witnessed there could not be typical. If they were, surely we would have heard about them from some latter-day Dickens or Orwell? Some of our friends who had seen Dr X's hospital for themselves urged me to do something about it – write an article, complain to the authorities. I went so far as to contact the medical correspondent of a national newspaper. He refused to believe me. I asked a wise and famous old journalist if he thought people knew what went on in some British hospitals. He said, yes, he thought people knew. I put my diary in a drawer. I had mastered the trick, essential to anyone who faces a dark future they cannot control, of living and thinking from one day to the next.

And for John and me, fresh as we were from Dr X's underworld, each day seemed to bring new miracles. Within an hour of his arrival in the geriatric ward John was provided with a wheelchair that he could move about by manipulating the left wheel with his good hand. A speech therapist brought him a green felt-tipped pen and a large pad, and asked to see what he could write. Starting in the centre of the page he wrote the letter f, followed by the letters – descending in a diagonal towards the right bottom corner of the page – o, r, k. The speech therapist said this meant that his writing was better preserved than Dr X's report had suggested.

Supported by a physiotherapist and a nurse John took his first steps the next day. A few more days and he was walking up and down a quarter of the length of the ward with his special nurse, Rosie, hanging on to the belt of his trousers: he had got so thin they had outgrown him; I must buy him new ones. I discovered the fascination of watching skilled physiotherapists coax movement from muscles which have been disconnected from their control centres in the brain. I was more excited by John's first steps at the age of sixty-nine than by our baby son's at one year. The physios told me that he would have walked anyway before long, but it was important that he should not develop bad habits that would lead only to further complications.

So we were lucky. I never discovered why Dr Z admitted John. He may have been backing a hunch, or impressed by John's record of public service; or he may have been doing Dr Y a return favour. Whatever his reason, he gave John the opportunity to do what he likes best: work hard, learn about something new, overcome obstacles, start each day without knowing how it will end. On fine days John would make me wheel him straight from the morning physiotherapy session to the cemetery next to the hospital. We would eat our sandwiches under the trees; and then John would want to attempt a few more steps on the uneven ground between the Victorian headstones.

Leaning heavily on my shoulder, John took a few more steps each day than the day before. We hadn't spent time together outside a hospital ward for nearly two months, and John was enchanted by our afternoons in the cemetery. He tilted his face up towards the misty autumn sunlight. He inspected the worn inscriptions on the old headstones, laughed at the children who popped out from behind them playing games of hide and seek. He smiled at the young mothers and old tramps who sat on the benches. It all seemed so normal that I sometimes beguiled myself into imagining that we were coming to the end of the most harrowing of the stories about his youthful adventures that John used to tell the children.

Supper in the geriatric ward was served at 5 p.m. I thought it a good sign when John began to reject the food, which was bland and mushy for the sake of the mostly toothless patients. Eager to satisfy his revived appetite, Ruthie sent hampers of food from her restaurant. Or Cynthia would bring him unusual pasta dishes from an Italian delicatessen in Soho; or Rosemary would arrive with smoked salmon and good bread wrapped in a huge damask napkin. The friends started arriving in the evening at about 6:30, with their news, love problems, gossip. Garry entertained John with indiscreet, elegant accounts of the royal commission he was chairing. One evening I found John with the curator of prints and drawings at the British Museum, which had kindly kept John on as a Trustee, the two of them bent over facsimiles of two prints by Pietro da Cortona, discussing which one the Museum should buy. John was saying *Da woahs da woahs, woahs da woahs*, the curator replying, Yes, Sir John, I entirely agree that the area around the bridge is damaged but the quality of the rest is superb.

The speech therapist for whom John had written *fork* on our arrival seemed very interested in his case. She questioned me closely about his life and interests. Searching for lost language, she said, 'is a great voyage of exploration.' Unfortunately, she had already accepted a job in another hospital. At our final meeting she said she couldn't be sure but she thought John's semantic system was intact: he could access meaning but not language. Her assistant, a timid girl fresh out of college, continued to see John. She tried to get him to say P, which she said is one of the easiest sounds to re-teach because it involves only the lips and breath, and, unlike sounds made at the back of the mouth, the patient can see how it's done from a drawing or watching another person. John tried and tried to say P. He puffed out his cheeks until I feared his face would burst. But it always came out as *woahs*. And each time he looked at his audience expecting congratulations, as though he had actually succeeded in enunciating P.

The assistant speech therapist also made him sort pictures of objects into their respective categories: animals or vehicles, tools or foods; fruits or vegetables was a favourite. He found this exercise difficult at first but soon mastered it. For the next few months, whenever he was given a reading task with a different purpose that happened to contain the words for fruits or vegetables he would dutifully underline them in different colours according to category. By now John was as quick as any normal person at pointing to objects when we named them or showed him written labels. When I asked the assistant speech therapist if these advances were signs that he would soon recover the rest of his language she looked, I thought, embarrassed, and said nothing.

I got hold of a copy of Valerie Eaton Griffith's book, *A Stroke in the Family*, as suggested by Dr Y. Valerie Eaton Griffith was an energetic and kindly woman who lived in the village of Great Missenden in the 1950s. After her retirement from Elizabeth Arden she was looking for a challenging project at just the time when the actress Patricia Neal was hit by a series of strokes. When Patricia Neal's husband, Roald Dahl, appealed to Valerie Eaton Griffith for help, she knew she had found her second career. She organized other people in the village with spare time – none of them had any qualifications for dealing with stroke patients – and evolved methods of teaching which were, as she confessed, 'truly hit or miss'. The writer Alan Moorehead, whose language was worse affected than Patricia Neal's, soon joined in the daily lessons, which continued for four years. In *A Stroke in the Family* and her two later puzzle books, Valerie Eaton Griffith details the games, puzzles and exercises with which she and her helpers stimulated the minds of her two distinguished pupils, and, subsequently, many other stroke patients.

I lent the books to our friends. As Valerie Eaton Griffith had found, so I discovered to my surprise that even the busiest of them really wanted to help. Some were former students of John and happy to return the favour. Like many people who have been well taught they enjoyed teaching, and *A Stroke in the Family* was an inspiring source of ways they could go about teaching John to write and talk. Before long we had fifteen volunteer teachers who came to the hospital on a regular basis.

Everyone thought it important to appeal to John's highly developed aesthetic sense. They brought him art books and exhibition catalogues and contributed to his collection of postcards. Susan made charming drawings of different categories of objects with the words for each written in her beautiful handwriting on separate tags. Ann devised simple crossword puzzles, which he could not do. Betsy worked with him, unsuccessfully, on exercises from junior English grammar books. Jonathan recommended seeing if John could make words out of Scrabble tiles.

We were fascinated by the uncanny paradoxes of John's mysterious condition. After his success with *fork* he did not write another real word. But if you gave him a pencil and pad he would grasp the pencil in his left hand – he scarcely seemed to notice that his right hand was paralysed – and write earnestly, purposefully, evidently certain of his message, in strings of letters, each string obeying the rules of English orthography, each separated from the next by a space and grouped into punctuated sentences. If I asked him to write something for me while I was away he would cheat by fleshing out his text with a few phrases copied from a newspaper or book. He filled entire notebooks like this: *An da rodor wesh rof; rand brinste trab. Refugees from the former Yugoslavia. Blook cridder was droosed. A bracelet of bright haire about the bone. Ah! And the and.*

But if you gave him Scrabble tiles, with the letters of a word jumbled up, he could sort them into that word, or, given the chance, a joke. Ruth, one of our more seductive friends, put down OESR and asked for the name of a flower. John arranged the letters to spell EROS. He could play Boggle quite well. And if you wrote a long, complicated sentence, cut it up into individual words and mixed them up, he could recreate the sentence without much difficulty.

I heard that some people who are unable to speak words can sing them. Accompanied by Bill on the piano in the hospital recreation room we tried, and failed, to lure John's language from its hiding place. I heard that some people lose one language but retain others. We tried working with him in the foreign languages he knew – Italian, French and German. Although he seemed to understand them they failed to prompt words of his own.

John could read well enough to help with the proof-reading of *The Civilization of Europe in the Renaissance*. David Chambers, a professional historian who had been one of John's early students at Oxford, agreed to see the book through the press, but only on condition that John should approve each stage of the editing. This was generous, because John could certainly not work with his former precision and speed. His concentration wavered. He spotted some errors and infelicities but missed most. What he could unfailingly do was to tell David where to locate any references he needed to check. He did this by pointing to the location of a library on a map of London, or by drawing detailed plans of his library at home. There was a crisis. The deadline for the edited book was approaching, but John had not delivered the bibliography with the manuscript. It consisted of hundreds of titles and would have been impossible to recreate. John drew a floor plan of his study (which he hadn't seen for two months), showing the position of his two desks, three chairs, filing cabinet. He marked one of the desks with a cross. But the desk was piled high with unfinished business. I couldn't find the bibliography. John must have been mistaken. David came to the house, searched patiently through the papers, and found the bibliography exactly where John had indicated. He has never been mistaken, then or now, about the location of anything.

One evening in October all the friends happened to leave early. I was alone with John, facing him across the bedside locker on which I had laid out the supper that I'd cooked at home and warmed up in the hospital's microwave. Supper, in our previous life, had been our favourite occasion of the day, the time when we exchanged the thoughts we'd been saving up all day like Christmas presents. I watched John preparing to enjoy his food and my company, and listened to his voice – *da woahs, da woahs, da woahs?* – asking me to talk to him, tell him about my day. Suddenly I was tired, too tired to carry the burden of a one-sided conversation. I thought about all the unmarried women I knew who said they preferred the company of their pet animals to having a man around: animals, they say, understand more than you think; they whine and purr and bark when you tell them your problems; some dogs even howl in tune to music. I was too weak to resist a quick, forbidden glance into the future. And what I saw there was a succession of meals, sitting across a table from a husband who was no more, or less, companionable than an affectionate dog.

That was not the first moment of hopelessness, although it may have been the first John noticed. The worst times were when I got home late at night with the smell of hospital and traffic fumes in my unwashed hair and clothes, knowing that I could allow myself only a few hours of sleep before grabbing a few more hours of trying to keep sane by catching up with my own work before driving back to the hospital. My mother, who could never remember the five-hour time difference between London and New York, got into the habit of telephoning after midnight London time. She was angry because I was too tired to talk to her properly and because she was too old to help. She lost her temper.

Of all the family the one who seemed most in control was John, whose unfailing courtesy and apparent good humour was impressive, but also slightly worrying. A doctor I met at dinner with friends explained that John was enjoying a condition described by the French nineteenth-century neurologist Jean Martin Charcot as *la belle indifférence*, the sublime indifference that can accompany mental imbalance. He was mistaken. Although I was too distracted by self-pity to notice it, John had woken from the euphoric trance that can indeed follow severe stroke. He hid his despair from me until one afternoon when I came into the ward earlier than usual, hoping to surprise him, and saw him before he saw me. His stillness and the angle of his neck told me what he would have never revealed in my presence. He was sitting in his chair, newspaper neatly folded on the table in front of him. His head was bowed, his face covered with his left hand. There was an atmosphere around him of extreme concentration that I recognized from his writing days. He was thinking very hard, trying to think his way out of his dilemma, and he needed no words to tell me that the only solution he could find was suicide. When I put my arms around him, I felt the tears on his face. He was crying for the first time since I'd known him.

He pushed me away. He opened his mouth and pulled at his tongue and lips. He grabbed a pencil and scribbled violently in the air then threw it on the floor. He did a wordless imitation of himself trying to enunciate words. He mimed himself as an idiot, head lolling, index finger in his mouth, eyes rolling. He began to talk in his wordless voice. I listened and realized that I understood what he was saying. With a phonetic range more restricted than a baby's he spoke to me by modulating his voice: its pitch, rhythms, timbre, timing, intensities as eloquent as ever.

I reminded him that he had always believed suicide to be the most disgusting and unjustifiable of acts, as immoral as murder. Nobody, he used to say, owned their own life; it belonged to all the people affected by that life. I told him, which was true, that I needed him now more than I ever had. He concluded the conversation with a bang of his fist on the rickety bedside locker and a resounding *WOAHS*. It meant: OK then. You win. Let's have a go and see what happens.

From then on we have continued to talk about whatever is on our minds, almost as we did before his stroke. Often it is just chat about the feel of the moment we are sharing: the taste of a glass of wine, the pain of a toothache, the fragrance and colours of plants in our garden. Sometimes I ask him what it feels like to have no words. And he answers me in his long, richly nuanced sentences, his voice rising, falling, emphasizing, pausing for thought, qualifying, as naturally as though he were explaining to an eager student some particularly interesting but complicated moment in the history of the European Renaissance. I don't always understand exactly what he is saying, but I think I may have a better idea of what it is like to be John just from the sound of his voice when he exclaims at the sight of our bright red azalea, always the first splash of vivid colour after the long, dreary English winter, and from the way he pretends to warm his hand in front of it on chilly spring days.

5

The Royal Star & Garter

Lack of organisation of stroke services in the National Health Service means that more people die from stroke than should; more are left with greater disablement than need be; and money is wasted on a huge scale.

S. *Pollack, ed.,* More Positive Steps

In the middle of October Dr Z said it was time for me to think about taking John home. He could now walk the length of the ward supporting himself on a high stick; he could climb a few steps gripping a railing with his left hand. Although Dr Z considered that John would benefit from another five or six months of therapy, he had not succeeded in finding a National Health Service rehabilitation unit that would accept a patient over sixty-five. I contacted several private hospitals that specialize in stroke rehabilitation. We could have just afforded the six months by selling or taking out an annuity on our house.

John came home for a trial overnight visit. I filled the house with flowers and cooked the things he liked to eat. But it was clear to us both that I had neither the physical strength nor the experience to look after this large, fragile man who could not speak or write or walk more than a few yards. Seeing John at home forced me to accept how much our lives had been changed by his stroke. An occupational therapist from social services arrived by appointment. She said that John would not be permitted to live in our house until the lavatory seat was raised by one and a half inches and a grip installed on the wall next to the bathtub. She wanted to know if I would require counselling. I said I would rather have a wheelchair and some practical help. She looked around our shabby but comfortable book-lined house and said that help for carers was means-tested.

So I was no longer a journalist or travel writer or even John's wife. I was John's 'carer', a full-time job for which nothing in my life so far had prepared me. I asked her if stroke physiotherapy was available in the community. She said there was a geriatric rehabilitation day centre but it was oversubscribed. There was a waiting list and she doubted if John would qualify anyway because he would probably not make enough further progress to justify a place.

Towards evening John began to shiver. He didn't have a fever, and he didn't seem to be having an epileptic fit, something that I had been warned can happen after a stroke. But I panicked. I wrapped him in a blanket and telephoned the hospital to say I was bringing him back. But I knew we had only a few more weeks in Dr Z's safe haven.

A group of family and friends clubbed together and offered to contribute to a fund that would cover the cost of private physio-therapy as well as some help with looking after John at home. I hesitated for twenty-four hours, and accepted without consulting John, who would probably have refused. Then I heard from old friends, who live in Richmond, about the Royal Star & Garter, a home and rehabilitation unit for disabled ex-servicemen and -women, which is partly financed by charitable contributions and can therefore adjust its fees according to ability to pay. The fund, which could not have stretched to other private rehabilitation units I'd investigated, would cover the cost of a course of residential rehabilitation at the Star & Garter.

We weren't sure whether John's war service in the Merchant Navy would qualify him as an ex-serviceman; and if so whether we would, half a century later, be able to find documentary proof. John drew a map of England and marked Liverpool and Plymouth as the ports from which his ships had sailed. On this evidence alone the Star & Garter agreed to admit him. On 4 November, the day Bill Clinton was elected President of the United States, JJ and I collected John from the geriatric ward and drove him to Richmond.

The Royal Star & Garter for Disabled Soldiers, Seamen and Airmen occupies a large foursquare redbrick building overlooking the Thames from the brow of Richmond Hill. This impressive monu-ment was purpose-built, on the site of a grand Edwardian hotel from which it takes its name, for the care and rehabilitation of servicemen and -women disabled in the First World War. Some of the treatments for brain damage pioneered at that time are still used for the rehabilitation of victims of stroke, which is now the biggest cause of disability in the developed world and the third biggest killer after heart disease and cancer. Although I didn't immediately recognize their common illness, the majority of the inmates of the Star & Garter had, like John, been wounded by 'cerebral vascular accidents'.

The entrance hall was designed to welcome war heroes. The floor is polished marble, the high coffered ceiling is supported by marble columns with ram's-head capitals. On either side of the hall are little sitting-out alcoves and straight ahead a deep, broad terrace from which you can enjoy the famous view of the curving Thames, as painted by Turner and Reynolds. John's cubicle on the fourth floor had the river view. He shared it with Commander Brooke, a retired naval officer. The nursing staff had thought that with their common naval backgrounds the two of them might get on, and so they did. Commander Brooke, who was much less disabled than John, looked after him tenderly, sometimes even shaving him and tying his ties. Although we soon became quite intimate Commander Brooke always called me Lady Hale, and I called him Commander Brooke.

John was once again wheelchair bound, this time by the physiotherapists, who said that if he walked at this early stage he would develop bad habits that would be difficult to break later. But he did at least have the freedom of the entire building, every part of which is accessible to wheelchairs. On weekdays John would wheel himself to the well-equipped gyms where the Bobath-trained physios instructed him, muscle by muscle, in the normal pattern of walking and tried to revive his right arm, which was still limp apart from a slight twitch in his right shoulder. He could also wheel himself to the bar; or to the dining-room, which served straightforward, wholesome food; or, in his spare time, to the library or one of many sitting-rooms or terraces. On some evenings there were concerts in the large hall next to the dining-room. But most of his free time was spent with the friends who continued to visit in ever greater numbers as more and more heard about his stroke and offered to take part in the effort to revive his speech.

The most striking first impression of the other inmates was the differences between them. They all had disabilities markedly different from John's, and, as far as I could see, from each other's. Many were in wheelchairs, some walked on one stick, or two sticks. Some sat all day in their chairs dribbling or crying. Some were bedridden while others appeared to be physically normal, even healthy, but could not read or write or speak. One refused to acknowledge that his paralysed left arm was paralysed. A few were incontinent, doubly or singly. Some had been blinded by their strokes, some had lost the right or left visual field, while some of those whose vision was unimpaired could not recognize the closest members of their families. Some could hear but could not understand what was said to them. Some had lost their balance; others their sense of direction and couldn't find their way round the building.

In the months that John was in the Star & Garter I spent a part of every day in the company of men and women who had suffered strokes. I listened to their stories in the bar and over meals, at first as a matter of common courtesy, increasingly because I was eager to know what it was like for other victims, other families and friends. I spent my spare time quizzing friendly doctors, reading in science libraries, trying to master the medical jargon that would answer my questions about stroke. What causes it? Can it be prevented? Why and how does it affect the minds and bodies of its victims in so many different ways? Is it, or is it not, curable? As the shock of John's stroke gave way to a better understanding of what had happened to him, I slowly came to register that what had happened to us was far from the unique personal tragedy it had seemed in the early days of our new life.

Even now when I see a group of stroke patients gathered together in one place I find it hard to believe that they have all been undone by the same illness. And yet the stories they tell about the onset of their strokes have this much in common: the time, date and place are recorded as though on a certificate of birth, marriage or death. And the details of their ordinary, everyday lives, as they remember them just before the life-changing accident, have that quality of ominously heightened normality that you sense at the beginning of horror stories.

Here, for example, is Dr Johnson, in a letter to Mrs Thrale of 19 June 1783 written shortly after his stroke: 'On Monday, the 16th, I sat for my picture and walked a considerable way without inconvenience. In the afternoon and evening I felt myself light and easy, and began to plan schemes of life. Thus I went to bed . . .' And this is the opening sentence of *Stroke: A Diary of Recovery* – a masterpiece in the sparse genre of personal accounts by stroke survivors – written by Douglas Ritchie, a broadcaster for the BBC, five years after his stroke: 'On 7th May 1955, a Saturday, my 17-year-old daughter Anne and I went by train from London to Dorking. We were met by my father at 2:30 p.m. He invited me to drive the car'; and Guy Wint, a journalist, on the minutes just before his stroke, in *The Third Killer*, published in 1965: 'The day was bright and sunny. It was about noon on the 28th September, 1960. The engine of my train, as it puffed into the station, seemed to be wearing a festoon of white smoke, and looked very gay.' A. H. Raskin, a former deputy editor of the *New York Times*, described the onset of his stroke in the 19 September 1992 edition of that paper: 'On September 29, a Saturday, Marge and I went to the funeral of a union leader at St. Patrick's Cathedral. We walked home and had lunch . . .'; as did Robert McCrum, a publisher and novelist, in the opening pages of *My Year Off: Rediscovering Life After a Stroke*: 'the truth is that no one will ever know exactly what happened inside my head on the night of 28/29 July 1995. . . . It was just another bright summer Saturday morning. . . . Downstairs, the grandfather clock was chiming the hour: eight o'clock.' Arthur Kopit's play *Wings*, which is, as far as I know, the only successful fictional account of the experience of stroke, opens with a woman who is about to have a stroke sitting comfortably in an armchair, absorbed in a book. A clock ticks a trifle louder than normal, then skips a beat.

And yet the majority of strokes do not in fact come out of the blue. They are not Old Testament curses or, as was believed in the Middle Ages, 'strokes of God'. They are not really 'accidents' either: many can be predicted, and some prevented or delayed. The number one villain in the aetiology of stroke is not God or chance but high blood pressure, which wears down the walls of the arteries. High blood pressure is easily measured and easily controlled by medication. The risk of stroke caused by hypertension could be halved by proper treatment of high blood pressure. Other predisposing conditions that should be watched carefully are: diabetes, atrial fibrillation and high blood cholesterol.

It is now known that simvastatin, a type of statin usually prescribed only to people with high cholesterol levels, also benefits those who may have low cholesterol but suffer from heart problems or diabetes. Simvastatin, furthermore, seems to cause no serious side effects. A seven-year Heart Protection Study involving 20,000 volunteers aged between forty and eighty concluded that simvastatin reduces heart attacks and strokes by a third in those at risk. In an interview published in the *New Scientist*, Rory Collins, director of the study said: 'Doctors need to be aware of just how definite these results are . . . They are the results you dream of . . . The default has changed, so doctors should now ask if there's a good reason not to give the drug.'

Smokers with uncorrected hypertension are twenty times more likely to have a stroke than people who neither smoke nor have high blood pressure. Smoking is harder on the arteries in combination with drinking than either habit is alone. Other avoidable behavioural risks are lack of physical exercise and obesity. A diet rich in fruit, vegetables and oily fish helps to reduce oxidation damage to arteries and cerebral vessels; and there is evidence that vitamin E has a similar beneficial effect. (It may be that simply eating less is preventative. During the Second World War – when smoking was fashionable, stress unavoidable and food in short supply – there was a marked fall in deaths from arterial disease in Norway, Sweden, England and Wales.)

Although aspirin has been known since the 1980s to reduce the risk of blood clotting the most effective dose is still controversial. Dr Z prescribed 75 mgs twice a week; others prefer 150 mgs a day. Aspirin plus dipyridamole may be more protective than aspirin alone. But there are newer drugs on the horizon that may be even more effective. In 2001 a large Australian-based study called PRO-GRESS, involving 172 hospitals world-wide, found that stroke patients with clots who were given perindopril or perindopril plus Indapamide (a diuretic) had a more than 25 per cent reduced chance of another stroke; for patients who had suffered cerebral haemor-rhage, the risk was cut by nearly 50 per cent. A surprise outcome of the trial was that the drugs benefited patients with normal as well as high blood pressure, from which the Australian scientists concluded that blood-pressure-lowering drugs should be given to everyone who has had a stroke. Another study is now exploring the effectiveness of new 'super aspirin', clopidogrel, also known as Plavix.

There are also drugs that can increase the chances of stroke, and doctors alert to stroke prevention should be aware of them. Phenylpropanolamine (PPA), which is contained in cold remedies such as Benylin Day and Night, Sinutab, Contac 12-hour cold cap-sules and Mucron, has been linked by studies in the United States to haemorrhagic strokes in people between the ages of eighteen and forty-nine.

Any general practitioner can get a rough idea of the rate of blood flow through the arteries by a simple digital examination or by listening with a stethoscope. Suspected occlusion of the internal carotid artery – the cause of most strokes – can be confirmed by ultrasound. If the blockage is more than 30 per cent surgery may be called for. The operation, carotid endarterectomy, is risky but on average reduces the chance of a first or subsequent stroke by six- to ten-fold. Another warning sign is damage to the capillaries at the back of the eye. (A blocked capillary impaired the sight of John's left eye fifteen years before his stroke.) Now a study at the University of Wisconsin has discovered that of a sample of 10,000 patients nearly all of the 110 who suffered strokes had damaged blood vessels in their eyes.

And yet doctors who might react quickly to symptoms of cancer or heart disease frequently fail to carry out procedures that might detect early warnings of stroke. In Britain even the monitoring of blood pressure has only recently been introduced as standard prac-tice, and is still often neglected by busy general practitioners.

One woman in five and one man in four between the ages of forty-five and eighty-five has a stroke: after the age of fifty-five the incidence doubles with each successive decade. There are a million new strokes each year in the United States and in the European Union. About a fifth of the victims die in the first four weeks, half of the survivors are permanently disabled. The prediction is that as the population ages the incidence will increase by 30 per cent in the first quarter of this century. But these tragic 'accidents', some of which need never have happened at all, are not only the consequence of inevitable ageing. Stroke is not – as most of us like to think until a stroke affects our lives – something that happens only to people older than ourselves. Twenty per cent of British stroke victims are under sixty-five, 10 per cent are under fifty-five. Robert McCrum was forty-two. Donal O'Kelly, a barrister, had his stroke in court one morning when he was forty-three. The hospital casualty doctors assumed from his funny clothes and Irish name that he was drunk. Donal O'Kelly recovered well, against all predictions, and founded a charity, Different Strokes, which offers encouraging and much-needed practical advice about prevention, treatments, and rehabilitation to young stroke victims – some of whom, because stroke is so closely associated by doctors with old age, have wound up in geriatric wards.

To be fair to the medical profession, the symptoms that may herald a stroke are often reported by patients after the event, and are so various that they could be anything from harmless to indications of many other illnesses. A stroke may be preceded by unusual headache, irritability, anxiety, tiredness, depression, loss of concentration, an increased need for alcohol, an inexplicable dissatisfaction with a contented life or absorbing career. But strokes have followed a period of acute eyesight or unaccountable sense of well-being. Some, at least in retrospect, seem to have been triggered by an unusually happy or successful event.

Guy Wint, in an attempt to find a temperamental predisposition for stroke, made a random list of famous sufferers. On his list are four British prime ministers: the Duke of Newcastle, the Duke of Liverpool, Lord Melbourne, Sir Winston Churchill; four British monarchs: Edward III, James II, Queen Anne, George I; also the Duke of Marlborough, Sir Walter Scott, Dr Johnson, Handel, Jawaharlal Nehru, Woodrow Wilson, Walt Whitman, Palmiro Togliatti, Louis Pasteur, Madame de Staël, Lenin, Stalin, and, possibly, Attila the Hun.

Wint surprised himself by concluding that the average stroke victim was not 'of the satanic type, lantern jawed, moving among the furniture of the world with a lamp which he is busy shining on unknown places. Rather he is gregarious, comfortable, enjoys the society of his fellow-men, is not a solitary, and is not given to extreme concentration.' He added that some of the people on his list might also have put themselves under more strain than their physiques could tolerate: the word stress was used less often in the 1960s than it is now.

My own arbitrary list includes the playwrights Robert Bolt and Dario Fo; the composer J. S. Bach; the poet Charles Baudelaire; the actors Patricia Neal, Alec McCowen and Sharon Stone; the media guru Marshall McLuhan; the writer Alan Moorehead; the film directors Michelangelo Antonioni and Ken Russell; the American president Dwight Eisenhower; the Great Train Robber Ronnie Biggs; Princess Margaret . . . I could go on. But star-gazing tells you nothing about stroke, except that it is extremely common. People who achieve a lot tend to challenge themselves and work hard, but they don't all have strokes. Although the hormones released by a stressful situation can certainly trigger a stroke that is already on its way, the long-term effects of stress are difficult to measure and vary greatly from individual to individual.

About 15 per cent of strokes are preceded by a Transient Ischaemic Attack (TIA), a temporary disruption of brain function which can cause weakness, difficulty with speaking, loss of sensation or orientation, followed by complete recovery after twenty-four hours at the most. The crazed expression I saw on John's face two days before his stroke may well have been a TIA. He made a joke of it. But a doctor – had I been bold enough to consult one of the over-burdened strangers in our local practice – might have been less amused to be consulted about a funny look on my husband's face. TIAs are in any case commonly dismissed or misdiagnosed by general practitioners in Britain. According to one survey, less than 3 per cent of doctors consider themselves specialists in stroke medicine, only a fifth have defined minimum standards, only a third have access to guidelines or protocols on TIAs, and a mere 20 per cent have access to a TIA clinic. And the chances of seeing a neurologist about a TIA, or indeed about any other neurological problem, are slim. There are fewer than 400 consultant neurologists in the UK, a ratio of one consultant for every 150,000 people. (In the Netherlands, just to take one contrasting European example, it is one per 25,000.)

The World Health Organization definition of stroke is 'disturbance of cerebral function, with symptoms lasting twenty-four hours or longer or leading to death, with no apparent cause other than vascular origin'; 10–15 per cent are cerebral haemorrhages; 85–90 per cent are infarctions, blockages caused by clots, which can be pumped up to the brain from large arteries elsewhere in the body (embolism) but are more frequently generated in the carotid or cerebral arteries (thrombosis). The stroke itself is painless. The brain, which can alert us to the slightest disturbance in other parts of the body, cannot send out distress signals on its own behalf. It is for that sinister reason that stroke victims do not always recognize or report the event.

The kilogram of pale, soft tissue consisting of the one hundred billion brain cells whose activity controls everything each of us is, thinks and does is the greediest and most fragile of our organs, depending for its life on the uninterrupted supply of oxygen and glucose provided by the fresh blood that circulates through its vascular system. Capable of making a billion neuronal connections per millimetre, each one travelling at a rate that can reach 220 miles an hour, the brain burns oxygen and glucose at ten times the rate of other body tissues at rest and cannot live without them for more than a few minutes. When the supply system is blocked by a clot or flooded with stale blood, some neurones will die within minutes; others, as the flow of fresh blood slows to a trickle and dries up, in the course of the next hours. Excessive glutamate, a neurotransmitter used by one cell to excite another in the normal brain, is released into surrounding areas, over-exciting and killing more nerve cells, while others further afield may be stunned or damaged by swelling or the knock-on effect of the trauma.

The smallest strokes affect only a few cells with results that are barely noticeable. The cumulative effects of recurrent small strokes, which are most common in older people, can result in dementia. Big strokes, like John's, block the cerebral vascular system – which does

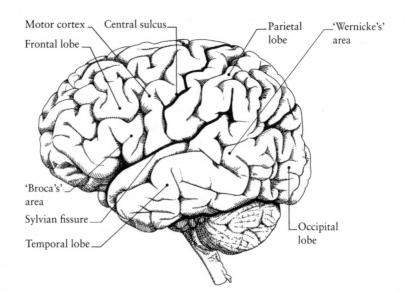

Motor cortex Central sulcus Parietal lobe 'Wernicke's' area

Frontal lobe

'Broca's' area

Sylvian fissure

Temporal lobe

Occipital lobe

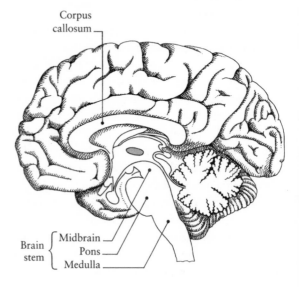

Corpus callosum

Brain stem { Midbrain
Pons
Medulla

not respect the brain's topographical boundaries – ravaging whole populations of neurones, cutting off their lines of communication. The effect on the victim depends in the first instance on the location, extent and depth of the infarction – the area of dead tissue left in the wake of the stroke.

The brain consists of two hemispheres, near-identical mirror images of one another but controlling different functions. The wrinkled surface layers of brain cells – the cerebral cortex or so-called grey matter (cortex comes from the Latin for bark) – are divided in each hemisphere by deep ravines or 'sulci' into four lobes: frontal, temporal, parietal and occipital. The motor cortex – a strip at the back of each frontal lobe – of the right hemisphere controls movement of the left side of the body, and vice versa. The cerebral structures that support language are usually in the temporal, parietal and frontal lobes of the left hemisphere, but there are exceptions. Vision is received in the occipital lobes at the back of the brain but interpreted in many other areas. Personality and higher cortical functions – such as decision making, planning, problem solving – involve many areas, across both hemispheres, but are particularly dependent on the prefrontal cortex.

The classic stroke, the one most often seen by doctors, is a thrombosis somewhere along the course of one of the middle cerebral arteries, rising into the brain from the internal carotid arteries on both sides of the neck which branch into tributaries carrying nourishment to large areas of the cerebral hemispheres. John's was that kind of stroke: an occlusion of the left carotid artery causing extensive destruction in the vascular territory of the left hemisphere, paralysis of the right side and loss of speech.

The stroke continues to inflict damage for days after the 'accident' as toxins released by the attack cause more cells to 'commit suicide'. Since John's stroke in 1992 drugs have been developed that could have prevented much or all of this ongoing destruction. One is injection of magnesium sulphate within the first twelve hours post stroke. Magnesium sulphate is safe, inexpensive, and easy to administer. It has been used in the United States for some years and has been in trial in Britain since 1998. Abciximab, which inhibits the formation of platelets in the blood, seems to be effective even when given up to 24 hours after the onset. Another drug, being developed in Australia, is a compound called AM-36, which seems to protect nerve cells if administered within the first six hours post stroke. AM-36, however, will not be available until 2010.

In April 2001 Dr Michael Chopp of the Henry Ford Health Sciences Center in Detroit announced the results of a research project that may benefit stroke victims sooner. Rats injected with infused bone marrow stromal cells one to seven days after induced strokes showed 'significantly improved neurological function'. Dr Chopp described the cells as 'smart cells that selectively migrate to the site of the injury and become little factories producing an array of helpful molecules to repair the tissue'. In August 2001, in the first operation of its kind on a human patient, bone marrow cells were removed by a surgeon in Düsseldorf from a forty-six-year-old man's pelvis and injected into arteries in his heart. The cells migrated to areas damaged by a heart attack and turned into healthy muscles which began to beat. The use of bone marrow stem cells for the treatment of stroke may be just around the corner. One great advantage of the treatment is that it need not be given immediately after the stroke, when the patient is in a dangerously weakened condition; another is that the cells are taken from the patient's own body, which means there is no risk of rejection, and no ethical problem, as there is with the use of foetal cells.

The most exciting development in the treatment of thrombolytic stroke is the use of clot-busting drugs, such as recombinant tissue plasminogen activator (rt-PA), which can prevent most or all of the damage. They must, however, be administered within three hours of the 'accident' and are only suitable for strokes caused by clots. In the United States, where rt-PA has been available since the mid-1990s, a doctor tells me he has seen patients with strokes as severe as John's walk out of the hospital on the same day.

Clot-busting drugs are given in Britain for heart attacks. And some British doctors administer rt-PA to stroke patients who arrive at well-equipped hospitals within the three-hour time limit. It is not, however, yet suitable for widespread use in Britain – where more than three-quarters of consultants are 'uncertain' about the effects of thrombolytic therapies. Patients must first be scanned in order to determine that the cause of stroke is not haemorrhage, in which case an rt-PA would be fatal. Unfortunately, just under half of British consultants can get a computerized tomography (CT) scan on the same or next day; and the time it takes to get a magnetic resonance imaging (MRI) scan, which is more expensive and produces a more detailed picture, is even longer: only a little over half of consultants' main hospitals are equipped with MRI scanners, and only 10 per cent of consultants scan with MRI on the same or next day. Most stroke patients, like John, are scanned, if at all, many days after the 'accident' – too late for the administration of clot busters or, for that matter, for operations that might save the lives of patients with bleeding strokes. The unreliable ambulance service, furthermore, as well as the reluctance of British patients to report symptoms and of their doctors to act quickly all mean that the median time from 'accident' to hospital is four hours – too late for rt-PA.

Once a stroke has taken its toll it is still not too late to prolong life and improve chances of recovery, even from the most severe strokes, and prevent subsequent strokes. There is evidence that the damaged arteries that cause most strokes may, given a chance, heal. A diet rich in fruits, vegetables, nuts and seeds – and a low intake of animal fats – is important for recovery, as for prevention – as is, of course, abstaining from smoking. Nevertheless, anyone who has had one stroke is at risk of another and should have regular monitoring of blood pressure and take appropriate protective drugs. And yet, although the majority of doctors consider aspirin to be useful in secondary prevention, fewer than half of patients outside hospital who would benefit from it actually take aspirin. I had a hard time persuading our doctor to prescribe dipyridamole for John.

Stroke patients nursed from day one in specialized units (which provide integrated care involving doctors and nurses trained in stroke, as well as physiotherapists and occupational therapists) have a 30 per cent greater chance of survival, and of recovering independence, after the first year than those treated in general wards. Given physiotherapy, two-thirds of survivors will walk independently within the first year; without it they may suffer from irreversible muscular cramp, degeneration of the muscles, and other painful and sometimes fatal complications.

There is strong evidence that early and ongoing physical and cognitive rehabilitation can make the difference between a helpless, hopelessly restricted and shortened life, and at least some degree of independence. There is in any case no other treatment for the physical and mental consequences of stroke. Nevertheless, a survey by the Stroke Association in 1999 showed that only 50 per cent of stroke patients in Britain have access to organized stroke services. The result is 4,500 to 7,000 avoidable deaths and institutional placements per year with deaths accounting for about half.

The cost of stroke to society is enormous: £2.3 billion a year in Britain. Stroke takes up about 20 per cent of acute hospital beds and 25 per cent of long-term beds. Survey after survey shows that holistic rehabilitation, although initially expensive, results in long-term savings in the costs of hospital and community care. Why then are doctors, especially in Britain, so reluctant to prescribe therapy? Why would Dr X not even allow John to try to stand up? Why do doctors fail to monitor blood pressure? Why do Accident and Emergency departments, which may be on their toes to do something about incoming heart patients, fail to apply the same standards to stroke?

Some middle-aged general practitioners blame the neglect on the medical schools, which, they say, taught them only the bare basics about stroke and encouraged a prejudice against 'geriatric' patients. Some doctors admit they are bored by stroke because recovery is so difficult to predict and takes so long. Some say they are required by their paymasters – health authorities, government, insurance companies – to limit expenditure to drugs and operations proven effective by control trials. One told me that in his opinion physiotherapy and speech therapy were 'about as useful as peanut butter' and should not be confused with a caring attitude. One confessed that he didn't like to think about stroke because it is the illness he most fears for himself.

In the seven years I've spent trying to understand what was in Dr X's mind when he ignored and ridiculed the 'infarcts' in his care, I've met only a handful of doctors who are interested in stroke. One is Dr Richard Wise, a British consultant neurologist with the Medical Research Council, who specializes in scanning the brains of recovering stroke patients, and who helped me with some of the research for this book. Dr Wise believes that neurologists tend to avoid stroke patients because 'Strokes are dirty, messy, all over the place. There's a lot of confusion. You could spend two hours a day for days examining the cortex of a stroke patient and be none the wiser.' Another is an American neurologist practising in Atlanta, Georgia, who amazed me by saying that he is fascinated by stroke, precisely because its effects are so heterogeneous and unpredictable; and, he added, because stroke patients, given proper rehabilitation, 'usually do better than you think'.

That, however, was many years after the Star & Garter told me they would be discharging John in April, because, they said, he had 'plateaued': there was nothing more they could do for him. The occupational therapist gave us a wheelchair and advised me that I would need help but would not get it from the social services unless I used cunning. Lie! she said cheerfully. Pretend you have a bad back.

I panicked. I'd got used to living alone. John's overwhelming joy at his release from institutional life did little to still my fears about how I would cope with him back at home – needy, dependent, living with me again day by day in the house we had once shared but which had become, for me, a private retreat, the place where every evening I escaped from the realities of my husband's diminished condition.

6

Vermeer

[The speech therapist] picked up a book with some child's drawings.

'What is that?' she said, showing me a drawing of a grandfather clock.

It took me two minutes to say again: 'Tarch-tarch-tarch.'

'A clock,' she said, enunciating clearly and slowly.

I shook my head. 'Tarch-tarch,' I said. I could not bear it in that small room, with the speech therapist's face not a yard from mine, and her treating me like a small child. Currents or switches, or clutches, things like that, that was the right way to treat me. A concealed door – that is, concealed from me, a speech therapist ought to know where it was – this was what I wanted.

Douglas Ritchie, Stroke: A Diary of Recovery

When John came home from the Star & Garter at Easter time, the garden, which I had neglected for eight months, was alive with blue-bells and blossom. He walked up and down it pointing with his stick at the shrubs, mourning the dead ones, leaning forward to inspect the fresh leaves of those that had survived the winter. He climbed up the stairs to his study and sat at the desk in the window overlooking the garden as he had when writing his books. He pulled up a chair to the bookshelves that hold English and foreign-language editions of his published work, and sat there for hours gazing at them.

John was alive, with me at home. His vision, hearing, balance, sense of taste and smell had been spared. *He* had been spared. He was himself. We slept curled around each other, as before. When we talked I sometimes forgot he couldn't talk. When we made love, as naturally as ever, I forgot that his right hand didn't work.

When he was discharged from the Star & Garter he could walk about fifty yards. He could wash and dress himself (apart from tying his tie and shoelaces and buttoning his left shirt-cuff); prepare and eat food that didn't need cutting; lever himself on his good leg, and, with some help, in and out of the bath. The physios who told me that he had 'plateaued' left it to me to work out whether that meant that he might, or might not, make further progress. But for the time being he could at least manage the ordinary business of daily life. He was handicapped, but not disabled.

His repertory of sounds had expanded to include – as well as the staple *das* and *woahses – ach, ah, ga, gwoahs*; and, very occasionally, when we resorted to Twenty Questions and still failed to catch the subject he was proposing, *Oh my God*. He made us laugh with his imitations of foreign accents and environmental noises – cars, planes, birds, the telephone ringing. He was beginning to develop a very crude sign language. Laying his head sideways on the palm of his hand meant after or before a night's sleep, that is to say yesterday or tomorrow, followed by the number of days counted on his fingers. Weeks were seven fingers.

He identified friends either by mimicking their voices or by locating their houses on a map or, if they lived near us, drawing the route from our house to theirs. If he wanted me to buy something for him he would indicate the shop where it could be found with a detailed street plan, a floor plan of the shop and a drawing of the item as it might appear in its packaging: socks, for example, in their boxes with little hooks for hanging on display stands. When I asked him why he didn't just draw a sock – or shirt or tube of toothpaste or whatever – he was bewildered by the question.

The house was full of friends – there were now forty volunteers coming in turn to work on the language games that we still hoped would stimulate John's recovery. Often they stayed for a meal. When the talk around him was in full flow he sometimes indicated that he had lost the gist, and asked for a repeat, making forward and backward gestures until we'd returned to the exact point in the conversation where we'd lost him. Although he could read newspapers, letters, and articles in his academic journals, he was unable to get through whole books and had lost his appetite for fiction. Music of any kind continued to cause him extreme pain, although he couldn't explain where he felt it.

Anie, a Polish friend of Camilla, came in every morning to work with John on the maintenance exercises recommended by the Star & Garter physios or to take him out in his wheelchair for walks along the river. Then we had a stroke of luck. The general practitioner who had agreed to take John on as a patient sent round a physiotherapist to assess him. I prepared myself for the usual gloomy lecture on acceptance and what the health and social services were not prepared to do for John. Instead, she noticed that his walking was impeded by a dragging right foot. She prescribed a splint, which was made for him at Queen Mary's, Roehampton, an excellent hospital which was being dismantled by the government at that time but still had the remains of one of the great orthotics departments in the country. The splint was made of lightweight plastic, with a hinged heel to allow movement if and when the muscles that were failing to lift the foot recovered. It meant buying two pairs of the same shoes at a time: one in John's usual size 9 for the left foot, one for the right foot in size 10 to accommodate the foot plate of the splint. But the splint itself was paid for by the NHS. And it did not escape my attention, or John's, that both the physiotherapist and the specialist who made the splint seemed to think that further recovery was not out of the question.

The splint, which John could strap on and off himself, was his key to liberty. He started going out for long walks on his own, from which he would return with some purchase – a book or a bag of peanuts – tucked into his shirt, presumably by a friendly shopkeeper, and tell me where he had been with drawings of street plans, bridges, pubs. One day he came back with a small plant in his shirt and making bus noises: he had been to the garden centre on the bus. I put away the wheelchair. Soon he was able to walk around the house without the splint or his stick. We started going out to parties, operas, exhibitions, plays. Then one day, while rummaging through his desk drawers looking for some scrap paper, I found a list of recent books about European Renaissance art copied out with his left hand – presumably from the academic journals and booksellers catalogues he still received and read. The list was written with his left hand in the neat, round childlike letters that had replaced his former cramped, semi-legible right-handed writing. John was planning his next book.

One evening when I had opened a bottle of wine and was chatting away at John about my day, he raised his left hand like a policeman stopping a car. He made a circle of his thumb and index finger, put it to his eye and then thrust it forward as far as his arm could stretch, making a noise like wind by breathing through his lips. He did this again and again, pausing only to describe little bird-like question marks with his voice. A telescope? Wind? I should have caught his meaning sooner. John had always been the planner in our marriage. He was asking me about the future. It was time to get back to work.

I found a speech and language therapist. She wore a starched white coat, like a doctor's. She tried, and failed, to make him repeat words or syllables after her. When he couldn't do that, she tried, and failed, to teach him Amerind, a simple gestural language which he hated. For 'yes' and 'no', which he was supposed to indicate with thumbs up or down, he preferred a radiant smile or an exaggerated expression of distaste. For 'woman', which he was supposed to indicate with a curvy gesture, he insisted on a lascivious grin and flashing eyebrows. As homework she gave him exercises of simple sentences with a word missing, such as: The baby was ——, I watched a —— match, We were —— in the pool; John had to select the correct word from a list at the bottom of the page: crying, football, swimming.

I've kept all these worksheets in chronological order. Although he filled most of the blanks effortlessly and correctly, he could not do the ones that required him to find words with opposite meanings, or the words that completed the titles of familiar Christmas carols. For opposites he guessed, for example, at 'clever' as the opposite of 'first'; the Christmas carols became 'Good Royal Wenceslas', 'Oh Little Angel of Bethlehem', and so on.

Jill, one of our literary friends, decided that John was irritated by such banalities. Her versions are scrawled on a pad in her large confident handwriting. On one the words GOOD and BAD are on one side and on the other MUSIC MURDER LOVE ART WAR CIVILIZATION HOLIDAYS PIERO DELLA FRANCESCA. John has drawn lines connecting each of these words, appropriately, either to GOOD or BAD, and she has written on the top of the page '100 per cent!' On the next HARD and SOFT are connected, again 100 per cent correctly, to STEELY TOUGH LIGHT MISTY ADAMANTINE FLUFFY GRANITE FEATHERY. On another sheet she has written 'Lay your sleeping head my ——' followed by HATE DOG CAT LOVE; 'The quality of mercy is not ——' FUN SIEVED STRAINED BAD. On each of these pages Jill has written '100 per cent – no problem at all'.

Next, as I sort the pile chronologically, comes the last of the speech therapist's opposites tests. After the word 'Opposites' at the top of the page John has written: '= antagms', which is followed by a note in my handwriting: '? = antonyms'. From then on he was able to chose opposites with no difficulty. Had the idea of what opposite means been restored by his recollection of another, less usual, word for it?

I thought this was progress, but the speech therapist said he was unresponsive to therapy, possibly because he was over-tired by playing games with his friends. She tested his comprehension by asking him to read little childlike stories followed by questions like: Who was waiting at the bus stop? When did the bus arrive? Where was it going? What did Mary buy at the shop? John, who was supposed to point to or copy out the answers from the relevant sentences in the stories, was stumped. He didn't seem to understand what she wanted him to do. When she repeated 'Who was waiting at the bus stop, John?' John shrugged and looked mystified.

He couldn't do it. And the harder we tried to explain the idea of it the more he was baffled and exasperated. The speech therapist said this failure to understand the stories proved that his comprehension was getting worse. And yet, given the choice of words, he quickly and correctly filled in the blanks of sentences like: A fin is to a fish as a —— is to a plane; A spider has —— legs. So he must, I reasoned, be able to comprehend what he read. At the same time our friend Nina was amusing John with a game from the *Reader's Digest*, where she had once worked on the editorial staff. It tested readers' knowledge of rare or pedantic words, such as persiflage, thyrsus, drupe, fuliginous. There was a choice of five definitions for each word. John got on average 97 per cent correct, which according to the *Reader's Digest* put his vocabulary in the top percentile of its readers.

The speech therapist remained unimpressed. She dismissed my suggestion that John might be merely bored by the childlike stories. And about that she was right. He may indeed have been bored, but boredom, as I was to discover much later from a more experienced language therapist, was not the reason for his inability to answer questions beginning with the words who, what, where, when and why.

Finally, the speech therapist invited me to a meeting in her office without John. I remember the crisp folds of her immaculately laundered white coat and the box of paper handkerchiefs that she nudged across her desk in my direction as she said: I can do nothing more for John. You have to accept that you will never again have a conversation with your husband.

Fuelled by energizing fury I flew to New York where I was introduced, by the wife of an acquaintance who had had a stroke similar to John's, to Dr Arnold Shapiro, director of the Communication Disorders Center at Mount Sinai Hospital. He confirmed what I was beginning to suspect: 'Nobody can say who will recover language after a stroke, or how much or when – or, to be honest, how it happens. Anybody who uses the word "sure" about it doesn't know what they're talking about.'

He did think that John's lack of frustration was a bad sign. 'From what you say your husband is a very loved man, but it might help him more if his friends were less ready to interpret his non-verbal language.' He suggested we continue with as much intensive language work – he called it 'total immersion in language' – as John could take, adding to what the friends were doing Standard Aptitude Tests (SATs), which are used to assess students applying to American universities. Examples can be bought at any paper shop in the United States. One advantage, he said, was that SATs tested intelligence and educational level from the most basic to the most sophisticated: so John would be able to find his own level; another was that the answers were all multiple choice, which would allow John to work with language without having to find his own words.

John's scores on the SATs would have qualified him as scholarship material for Harvard. He excelled on spatial relations, but also on vocabulary (including words with opposite meanings). On tests of grammar and morphology, he could invariably spot errors or infelicities that might have escaped the attention of a more careless or less linguistically able person. Here are two examples of multiple choice questions from a test designed to 'measure skills that are important to writing well'.

If there is an error, select the <u>one underlined part</u> that must be changed to make the sentence correct. If there is no error, select E:

Some researchers A *have theorized* that B *there may be* a connection between hormones C *with* the body's D *ability to* heal damaged organs. E *No error.*

Select the answer that produces the most effective sentence, one that is clear and exact. Choose answer A if you think the original sentence needs no revision:

(A) *Josh was relieved to find his lost keys walking along the street in front of his apartment building.*

(B) *Much to his relief, Josh found his lost keys walking along the street in front of his apartment building.*

(C) *Walking along the street in front of the apartment building, Josh's keys were found by him, much to his relief.*

(D) *Josh, relieved to find his lost keys, while walking along the street in front of his apartment building.*

(E) *Walking along the street in front of his apartment building, Josh found his lost keys, much to his relief.*

Dr Schapiro's final piece of advice had been: 'Dump the lady in the white coat and find yourself a speech therapist who understands the problems. It might not work, but you never know.'

I don't think that John and I were convinced that more professionally guided work would necessarily be rewarded. What was important was to do *something*, not so much to keep hope alive as to ward off the dreariness and despair that would otherwise follow our idyllic celebration of John's homecoming. The question was: where could I turn for advice? The English Stroke Association, under a scheme originally organized by Valerie Eaton Griffith, organizes local volunteers to play stimulating language games with stroke victims. But we already had plenty of friends doing that. John pointed at me, picked up the telephone and spoke to the dial tone in a nervous falsetto that was all too recognizable as my own voice: *Woahs? Ach ga woahs da woahs* . . . I was, after all, a journalist. I should start networking.

Since I didn't know quite what sort of person or expertise I was looking for I floundered for a while. I read what came my way about John's condition, which, as I discovered from the leaflets sent out by the English Stroke Association and Action for Dysphasic Adults (now called Speakability), was called aphasia or dysphasia. But their descriptions of aphasia didn't seem to tally with John's case. They didn't say when or whether he would recover, or, very precisely, what I could do about it. Then, after several false leads and dead ends, I turned to Laura, who had succeeded John as Professor of Italian at University College London. Laura's husband Giulio was a professor of linguistics, a subject about which I knew absolutely nothing but thought vaguely might be relevant to John's loss of language. Laura and Giulio set me on a trail which led eventually to Jane, a speech and language therapist who specializes in aphasia and lectures about it at the National Hospital's College of Speech Sciences.

Jane agreed to treat John for no charge as a research project investigating the use of volunteers for aphasia therapy. She proposed a collaboration between our forty friends – who, as she said, inevitably knew John and his interests in a way that no stranger, however qualified, could match – and her College, which would try to teach the friends something about aphasia and how it could be addressed.

Jane soon identified some of John's particular problems, which seemed, as she had warned us they would, bizarre in the extreme. I was not surprised when she found that John, given a long, random list of real and non-words, could cross out the non-words without hesitation, or that he could do this whether the words were printed in upper or lower case. But then she showed him rows of single letters and asked him to point to the letters as she named them. He got only about 40 per cent, and had the same difficulty if prompted by the sounds of the letters or by words that began with them. So he could recognize words made of letters but not the letters that made up words. She then discovered that John could not tell whether two words did or did not sound alike. Not only could he not say whether dog and fog sounded more alike than dog and dig, he had no idea at all of what it meant for words to sound alike. The concept of rhyming had been wiped clear out of his brain.

But I was more excited than dismayed by Jane's revelations. She had opened a door into John's mind and was locating which bits of the machine were working and which were out of order. It seemed the logical first step to fixing the damaged parts. She showed us diagrams of the way language is supposed by some psychologists to be assembled, from the message one wishes to convey to its representation in speech or writing. These models, which looked like the instructions for wiring a machine, bored most of our friends. A few agreed to work with John on the letter, rhyming and word-finding exercises devised by Jane. But most preferred to be guided by Valerie Eaton Griffith, or their own instincts and methods. The race was on to see who would be the first to conjure forth a word from John.

It came on a rainy afternoon in July, almost a year after the stroke. John and I were sitting by the fire in Camilla's drawing-room. John was looking through his collection of postcards of Old Master and modern paintings, amassed over many years of travel. He paused at a picture of a young woman seated behind a table where she is tuning a stringed instrument. Her face and eyes are turned away from the instrument towards the window on her right, which lights the yellow sleeve of her dress, her forehead, hands, and the pearl ear-ring dangling from her left ear. Her self-absorbed smile could mean that she is listening for the correct pitch of a note, or, perhaps, for the footsteps of a partner who will make music with her on the viola that rests on the floor in the shadow of the table. A map of Europe hangs on the wall behind the girl.

John stabbed his index finger over and over at the postcard, accompanying the gesture with the emphatic grunting noises that he made when something moved or excited him. He raised his left hand and drew a sign in the air that looked like the letter V. I found a pencil and paper. He wrote V e r. I yelled for Camilla who, Martha-like, was preparing supper in the kitchen. She arrived just in time to witness the completion of the miracle: m e e r: Vermeer!

In the next days and weeks, the picture side of postcards prompted more artists' names. He wasn't allowed to cheat by turning the postcards over, and he had no need to. The names he wrote were not always perfectly spelled, but it was clear that he knew them, and the obscure names came to him as easily as the most famous. They started as, for example, H. Boimlpnb, Georg Faedrick Kerstong, Niklauc Nanuel, Gandeneo Farrori and Wichilengolo. Although I thought this was good enough, John recognized that they were not right and painstakingly corrected each one, over and over, letter by letter, until he got it right: H. Bosch, H. Memling, Georg Friedrich Kersting, Niklaus Manuel, Gaudenzio Ferrari, Michel-angelo. But he could not even make a guess at words like table, chair, cup, cat, or even Sheila.

How could this be possible? As I began to read more about aphasia I came to understand that language, the awesome intellectual skill we acquire without the slightest effort by the age of three and grow up taking entirely for granted, is one of the great remaining scientific mysteries. It is also more vulnerable than most of us suppose.

PART II

APHASIA

The workings of language are as far from our awareness as the rationale of egg-laying is from the fly's.

Steven Pinker, The Language Instinct

You cannot say anything without saying something. *But the notion of saying something can be treacherous . . . a sequence can be coded in any way we like, and all that is linguistically necessary is that we should be able to identify it as a structured set of signs, and experience it as a single line of language, as it might be called.*

Jonathan Rée, I See a Voice

7

The Varieties of Aphasia

To be dumb and yet to have clearly formulated in one's own mind what one wishes to say, is one of the most grotesque predicaments which can be conceived.

Guy Wint, The Third Killer

Before John's stroke and for some time after neither of us had more than a very vague idea of what the word aphasia describes or entails. Few people who are not directly affected by aphasia recognize or understand the condition, which is why aphasics are sometimes taken for drunk, or committed to psychiatric care, or ignored by busy doctors who don't always record the condition in their patients' case notes. Neither of us had ever knowingly met an aphasic. If we had we would probably have dismissed that person as stupid or mad – as carelessly as Dr X had written off the 'infarcts' in his care. If anyone had suggested to John that it is possible for a person with a normal mind, a working set of vocal organs – or at least a pen and paper – to lose the power of verbal expression from one minute to the next, as though it were a bunch of keys, he would have flashed his eyebrows up and down in the way he still does to indicate amused scepticism.

And yet chronic aphasia is quite a common condition, affecting approximately the same proportion of the population as multiple sclerosis or Parkinson's disease: up to 200,000 in Britain and one million in the United States. And despite its name – from the ancient Greek *aphatos*, meaning without speech – people who suffer from aphasia are not necessarily speechless. Aphasia can destroy, or impoverish to a greater or lesser extent, any or all or some components of verbal language – speech, writing, auditory comprehension, reading. It may, or may not, be accompanied by paralysis or weakness of the limbs, usually of the right arm and leg. It can, but doesn't always, involve loss of control over the vocal muscles (a condition known as apraxia).

Aphasia is not like the stroke that paralysed Jean-Dominique Bauby, the author of *The Diving Bell and the Butterfly*, nor is it like the motor neurone disease that afflicts Stephen Hawking. Although both are physically incapable of speaking or writing, they have produced great books: Bauby by signalling with the blink of one eye the letter or word he wished to use, Hawking by using a computer program with word prediction and a built-in voice. Despite their inability to move more than a few muscles both retained access to their language: their problem was not loss of language but loss of control over their vocal organs and writing hands.

Unlike developmental dyslexia, which shows up in childhood, or Alzheimer's disease, which gradually destroys all cognitive functions, the onset of aphasia is typically sudden. The normal language system that you have taken for granted since it was given to you as your birthright by around the age of three, and which you regard as an inalienable part of the human condition, is disabled from one minute to the next as though by an invisible bullet.

Unless complicated by other neurological disorders, aphasia does not usually affect personality or diminish cognitive functions that are not directly related to language. John, in the early stages of his aphasia – when he could not match a razor or watch with the words razor or watch – could play chess, add and subtract (but not multiply or divide), recognize people he hadn't seen for years, write down all the historic dates he ever knew or how much you ought to pay for a house or car or what time someone was coming to tea. Although he had difficulty signalling 'yes' or 'no' he could indicate by facial expression and tone of voice whether or not he agreed with a friend's theories about any subject that had ever interested him; he could read or draw maps, plan a day or a journey, find his way around town. His memory, short-term and long-term, for facts and for episodes of his life, was and is better than mine, for everything except the days immediately before and after his stroke.

The study of aphasia suggests that meaning, concepts and facts are stored differently in the brain from the dictionary of words and grammatical rules that are used to represent them. Shown a drawing of a pyramid and different species of trees (a standard test for semantic memory known as 'Pyramids and Palm Trees'), John, although unable to write or speak any of the relevant words, unerringly chose the palm tree as the one most closely associated with the pyramids.

About a third of aphasics lose, at least for a time, all meaningful speech. Some of those who are able to articulate some words speak hesitantly, with a minimum of grammatical words (articles, prepositions, and so on), as though dictating a telegram. Others babble fluently and grammatically, but using many non-words. Like Lewis Carroll's poem about the Jabberwock, their output makes a sort of sense. The Czech linguist Roman Jakobson suggested that these complementary patterns of non-fluent and fluent aphasia represent pathological extremes of the two poles of normal styles of language. Think of Ernest Hemingway's prose as opposed to William Faulkner's. Most of us tend to one or the other.

The following interviews, conducted by Howard Gardner and reported in his book *The Shattered Mind*, illustrate these two aphasic styles. The first is a thirty-nine-year-old former Coast Guard radio operator, DF, after a stroke:

HG: Were you in the Coast Guard?

DF: No, er, yes . . . ship . . . Massachu . . . setts . . . Coastguard . . . years. (*Raises his hands twice indicating the number nineteen.*)

HG: Oh, you were in the Coast Guard for nineteen years.

DF: Oh . . . boy . . . right . . . right.

HG: Why are you in the hospital, Mr F—?

DF (*pointing to his paralysed right arm*): Arm no good (*then to his mouth*), speech . . . can't say . . . talk, you see.

HG: What happened to make you lose your speech?

DF: Head fall, Jesus Christ, me no good, str, stro . . . oh Jesus . . . stroke.

This, by contrast, is a seventy-two-year-old retired butcher, PG:

HG: What brings you to hospital?

PG: Boy, I'm sweating, I'm awful nervous, you know, once in a while I get caught up, I can't mention the tarripoi, a month ago, quite a little, I've done a lot well, I impose a lot, while, on the other hand, you know what I mean, I have to run around, look it over, trebbin and all that sort of stuff.

(HG *breaks in*)

HG: Thank you Mr G—. I want to ask you a few . . .

PG: Oh sure, go ahead, any old thing you want. If I could I would. Oh, I'm taking word the wrong way to say, all of the barbers here whenever they stop you it's going around and around, if you know what I mean, that is tying and tying for repucer, repuceration, well we were trying the best that we could while another time it was the over there the same thing . . .

Aphasics like John with more severely impaired speech may repeat the same sound or word over and over. Nobody can say whether John's *da woahs* derives from a real word; or if it is just the sounds he happens to be able to articulate, or if so why it is those sounds and not others. Some aphasics know that they are speaking in non-words but can't help it. Those who recognize their problem stand a better chance of recovery than aphasics like John who are unaware of what they are saying, or rather not saying, and who cannot repeat their utterances at will.

This was the case with Mr G, an Australian aphasic who, unlike John, produced his automatism within an otherwise relatively fluent framework. Mr G, who was videotaped in conversation with his therapist in the 1980s, was passionately interested in Bristol cars. The following is a transcript from the video:

CLINICIAN: Um, um. Yes, tell me, how old is the oldest car?

MR G: Ah, the oldest car is a week about, oh . . . nineteen thirty-three or something.

CLINICIAN: Nineteen thirty-three.

MR G: No reams assessor! Anyway it's reams assessor right back. And its reams as . . . sessor, and it's reams assessor, reams a, reams a, reams assessor and that . . . and so on, you see.

CLINICIAN: Um, um. Are there many of them in Australia? I know they're a British car.

MR G: Oh yeah, oh well they're very reams assessor. Not many people could buy them anyway. Reams assessor, reams assessor . . .

CLINICIAN: Are they pretty expensive?

MR G: Oh yes.

CLINICIAN: Good. Okay. All right, moving on Mr G . . . ah . . . tell me. What is a car? Can you give me a definition?

MR G (*astonished to be asked such a simple question*): Oh, by all means, a car is a car. It's a reams assessor and reams assessor. It's a reams assessor or reams assessor and reams assessor and nothing's reams assessor at all.

CLINICIAN: Um, um. Is it a method of transport?

MR G: Reams assessor. Oh, reams assessor and reams assessor and not [*nontranscribable gibberish*] reams assessor. Pick [*nontranscribable jargon*] things. But here it's a reams assessor.

CLINICIAN: Is a car something to carry you in?

MR G (*chuckling at the simplicity of the question*): Oh yes, it's a reams assessor.

Professor David Howard tells me that such substitutions for content words are known as predilection forms. He had a patient who resorted, when in need of content words, to saying *gaygums* or *vackles*. Most specialists have diagnosed John's unvaried meaningless output as an extreme form of the aphasia that affected Howard Gardner's patient, the retired butcher, PG. Some, however, class it with telegraphic, ungrammatical speech demonstrated by the former Coast Guard radio operator DF.

The great British neurologist John Hughlings Jackson, who was the first to make an extensive study of what he called recurrent utterances, believed that they represented the last proposition, or part of it, that the patient had uttered or been about to utter before aphasia struck. His most famous example is that of a lexicographer who had a stroke just after he had finished preparing a dictionary and was left with the automatism *list complete*. There are many such anecdotes, including the one about an attractive young woman whose cerebral haemorrhage reduced her to repeating *not tonight, I'm tired*; and about the man who, after sustaining brain damage in a street fight, could only repeat *I want protection*.

Other common speech automatisms – such as *I can't, I can't talk, I want to, I'm a stone, sister, sister* – might represent a response to the calamity. Just as John sometimes says *Oh my God*, which would be a very natural response to the aftermath of brain damage, some French aphasics repeat *Sacré nom de Dieu* (Charles Baudelaire could say only *cré nom nom*). Others – *it's a pity, paper and pencil* – may echo something the patient has heard from a nurse or speech therapist.

Three common utterances visited on patients who in their previous lives were never heard to swear are *fuck fuck fuck, fuck off, fucking, fucking, fucking hell, cor blimey*. The usual anecdotal example is the vicar who can produce nothing but such expletives. This class of speech automatism probably has nothing to do with anything the aphasic was thinking, said or heard, before or after brain damage, or with any language the patient would have used before the injury. One theory about it invokes the regression hypothesis, according to which the most primitive language is the last to be destroyed by brain damage. Dr Wise says that automatic speech – it can take the form of counting, reciting or singing (usually old familiar songs) as well as swearing – is generated in the right brain, but needs left structures for articulation. Another interpretation is that the neurochemical activity that accompanies stroke may suppress limbic mechanisms that control inhibition.

But many non-lexical utterances probably never had any meaning at all. Mr G's *reams assessors* may once have referred to reams and assessors, or they may have sounded like those words. John may have been thinking about wars or fortifications while sitting at his desk on the morning of his stroke, or it may have seemed to him, after the stroke, that he was the victim of war or enclosed by walls. I wish I knew the origin of the familiar all-purpose *da woahs*. But I have to accept that whether or not it ever represented a fragment of John's thoughts it is now as meaningless as the bark of a dog.

But there are also aphasics whose speech is apparently normal, but whose language is impaired in other ways: they may have difficulty with reading and/or writing and/or understanding the speech of others and/or repeating what they have just heard. There are aphasics who can read but not write; aphasics who can write but not read, not even what they have themselves just written; and aphasics who can write only if they don't look at what they are writing. Dr Barbara Lacelle, an American psychologist who became aphasic after a car accident, describes the effort to complete her Ph.D.: 'I could *talk* about the material that I *heard* in lectures or conversations. I could write, as in exams, content that I had *read* about. But I could not talk fluently or spontaneously about what I had read, and I could not write about what I had heard.'

Some aphasics who can't speak can sing the words of familiar songs. Proper names are difficult for some aphasics – as, indeed, they are for some normal people. Guy Wint was at first unable to recall the names of the friends who visited him in hospital. But he could remember their telephone numbers, and so would report to his wife that Sloane 2381 had been to see him, or the flowers had been brought by Mayfair 9643. Some have difficulty with other classes of nouns, colours for example. There are aphasics who can demonstrate that they experience colours normally; they can match different hues or put the correct colour on a black-and-white photograph of, say, a banana or grass. But they have problems naming or understanding the names of colours, and will frequently, for example, identify 'blue' as 'green'. In extreme cases, all nouns may become problematic, while verbs and grammatical words remain intact.

Most aphasics produce paraphasias or paragraphias, spoken or written words that are in some way associated with the target, such as *mug* for cup, *pen* for pencil, *breakfast* for lunch, *black* for white, *yes* for no. John, for a month or so after his stroke, could not even choose the appropriate gestures for *yes* or *no*. Although the tone of his grunts made it clear which he meant, he would often nod or give the thumbs up for no, or shake his head with thumbs down for yes. Some confuse semantically related words only when they are reading aloud or writing to dictation. Some aphasics are disproportionately impaired for long, unusual words, others for the shortest and most familiar words, such as *and, the, was, in*. A recovered Swiss aphasic described in his memoirs having had more difficulty pronouncing the French for *if* and *since* than *Nebuchadnezzar* and *Popocatepetl*. Some have more trouble with verbs than with nouns and vice versa. Some can speak nouns but not verbs, but when reading aloud it is the other way round. There are aphasics who can say or read aloud certain words, such as *park, walk, play*, as nouns but not the same words in their verb form, or vice versa. A case has been reported of a man who can say the plural noun *cuts* but cannot say, read aloud or even repeat the final -s of the third person singular of the verb 'to cut'.

Dr Nancy Kerr, a rehabilitation psychologist at Arizona State University, who became aphasic after a left-brain stroke, was able to write digits but unable to repeat the words for them when she heard them. Like some aphasics who produce garbled, ungrammatical sentences, she felt that grammatical rules were intact in her brain; the problem was that she 'had no idea what a sentence was or what it was intended to communicate'.

Because aphasia is almost always selective some specialists call it dysphasia – with impaired speech. The strictest purists prefer 'acquired language disorder', which avoids the misleading association with speech alone and makes the point that it strikes mature, normal language systems. Nevertheless, aphasia, the name it was given in 1864 shortly after it was first recognized as an independent neurological disorder, has stuck, contributing to the general mystification of non-specialists, including those aphasics whose doctors or therapists don't quite know how to explain it and presume their patients wouldn't understand if they tried.

Ninety per cent of aphasias are caused by stroke (about a third of people disabled by stroke have aphasia). Other causes are cysts, infections, inflammations such as encephalitis or meningitis, car accidents, gunshot wounds, or taking Ecstasy. Although the majority of aphasics are elderly (the average age of stroke is sixty-eight, John's age when he had his stroke), the incidence of young aphasia is rising due to improved survival rates after road accidents and drug abuse.

It is not yet known how the brain makes it possible for me to write these words and sentences, for you to read them, and for us to talk or write – should we decide to meet or correspond – about anything we choose. What can be said with certainty is that the conversion of my semantic concepts into language and thence into your thoughts, and vice versa, requires a particular swathe of our brains; and if all or part of that territory is destroyed, all or part of the conversion of thought into language and language into thought will be impeded.

In about 95 per cent of adults the brain systems dedicated to words and syntax are mainly located in the left cerebral hemisphere along the banks and within the fold of the deep lateral cleft known as the Sylvian fissure, which runs from around the level of the temple towards the back of the head, separating the temporal from the parietal lobe. Dr Wise describes this as 'A very neat arrangement: the language areas are surrounded by the regions that receive visual and auditory input and bodily sensations.' But it is not known why the arrangement is usually, but not always, primarily located in the left rather than the right hemisphere, which is anatomically all but identical.

It may be that the evolution of verbal language was preceded by the ability to think and plan sequentially which is one of the essential features of language. What is certain is that at some point quite early in evolution, for no reason that has ever been satisfactorily explained, sequential communication migrated to the left hemisphere while the vocal tone, emphases and emotional gesturing that can change or underscore meaning went to the right. (Think of all the different meanings you can give a simple phrase like *Thank you very much indeed*.) Left-brain dominance for communicating in meaningful sequences is present in a large number of vertebrate species. Some songbirds – including male canaries – are silenced by lesions in the left side of their brains. Rats and dolphins use the left brain for detecting auditory signals. Monkeys interpret other monkeys' vocalized communications in a part of their frontal lobes thought to be analogous to the area of the human brain necessary for comprehending syntax. If this area is damaged, monkeys show an impaired ability to communicate.

Although human babies are born with two separate but equal brains, not yet connected, by the age of five or so their left brains have begun to specialize in words and syntax, and by late adolescence most people rely heavily, but not exclusively, on the left hemisphere for speaking and writing. If your left hemisphere were to be put temporarily to sleep by the injection of a mild barbiturate into the left carotid artery, the chances are that you would experience something of what it is like to be aphasic.

There are, however, exceptions to left-brain dominance for language. About half of left-handed people process verbal language in the right hemisphere or are bilateral for language. There is some evidence that women, including right-handed women, have a greater tendency than men to use both hemispheres. The hemispheres of female brains tend to be more symmetrical than men's; the fibres that connect the two hemispheres are thicker, which may facilitate neuronal traffic between the two; and women seem to make better recoveries from aphasia. I am right-handed but bilateral for language. I discovered this when I volunteered as a normal control in a project directed by Dr Wise, who uses positron emission tomography (PET) imaging to chart the cerebral activity of aphasic subjects. I was the only bilateral of the nine controls. According to Dr Wise, my brain 'looked distinctly different from the other normals'. Although such clear variations from the norm are rare, recent evidence is beginning to suggest that hemispheric specialization for verbal language may vary in subtle ways from one individual to another.

The most baffling, but also the most interesting single thing about aphasia is its variety and what that suggests about the intricate machinery that operates normal language. All higher cognitive functions are the product of assemblies of neuronal circuits sending out signals from control centres in diverse brain areas. Vision, the most researched brain function, is now better understood than language, and the often bizarre consequences of selective visual deficits have engaged the popular imagination thanks to readable books like Oliver Sacks's *The Man Who Mistook His Wife for a Hat*, and V. S. Ramachandran and Sandra Blakeslee's *Phantoms in the Brain*. Language, which comes second in the most-studied league table, has been slower to give up its secrets to science, and there are some specialists who suspect that language, like consciousness itself, may be beyond the reach of human understanding.

It seems that all languages can be impaired by damage to the language centres, even those that rely on right-hemisphere specialities like tone or the analysis of visual input. Any system of communication that consists of discrete arbitrary symbols ordered according to abstract rules is vulnerable: tone languages like Chinese, deaf and dumb sign languages, even musical notation. Performing musicians and composers may lose the ability to read or write music but still be able to play and sing from memory. An Italian-based team of researchers recently reported the case of an aphasic professional organist who could read the names of musical notes in the key of G but not in the key of F, although she could recognize both keys when she heard them and could play in both on the piano at sight. Brian Butterworth, Professor of Cognitive Neuropsychology at University College London and the National Hospital for Nervous Diseases, Queen Square, has worked with an aphasic musician who could read words but not music.

In bilingual or polylingual people different languages may be affected in different ways. There are bilingual German Jews, who have refused to speak German since childhood, only to find either that they have mercifully lost it altogether or that they are unable to communicate *except* in German. Or different languages spoken by the same person may be impoverished to different degrees, in different ways, and show different patterns of recovery. Professor Butterworth once knew a patient, bilingual in English and Japanese, who was dyslexic only in English.

Professor Butterworth, who is particularly interested in numeracy, believes that the capacity to manipulate numbers is, like verbal syntax, innate, and that the inbuilt neuronal circuits that enable numeracy and grammar to develop in the human brain are closely connected and may overlap. Nevertheless, although some aphasics are innumerate, some are not; and some, like John, are able to add, subtract and do simple algebra, but not to multiply – possibly because multiplication is usually memorized verbally in the times tables recited by schoolchildren.

The breakdown of language seems to be as complex as language itself. It has been calculated that there are 16,383 varieties of acquired dyslexia alone, and dyslexia may be only one component of an individual case of aphasia. Nevertheless, the human intellect is driven by its very nature to make sense of complexity and confusion, to explain by putting things into categories, a predisposition which may well have preceded language and which has certainly been reinforced by it. Normal people cannot make sense of the world without classifying it into cups and mugs, knives and forks, pots and pans. When John was unable to sort the contents of our dishwasher on the morning of 30 July 1992, he was losing a crucial requirement of language. Once he had regained it he could not remember what it had been like not to be able to distinguish a Flemish painting from an Italian one, or to put oranges, lemons, pears and apples in one pile and spinach, peas and lettuce in another.

8

Silent in Sadness

Nous parlons avec l'hémisphère gauche.

Paul Broca, 1864

It only remains for us to state the view that the speech area is a continuous cortical region within which the associations and transmissions underlying the speech functions are taking place; they are of a complexity beyond comprehension.

Sigmund Freud, On Aphasia

Although loss of language is likely to be as old as language itself, the first documented mention we have of aphasia does not appear until about 2800 BC in an Egyptian papyrus discovered in Luxor in 1862. The author, a surgeon, recommends softening the head of a speechless patient with grease and pouring milk into both ears. A copy, dated some 500 years later than the original, and now in the New York Academy of Medicine, translates the by then archaic Egyptian word for speechless: 'As for "he is speechless", it means that he is silent in sadness, without speaking . . .'

In subsequent millennia, the main varieties of aphasia recognized today were reported. Around 400 BC Hippocrates described loss of speech as aphonia. In AD 30 Valerius Maximus identified selective problems with reading. The word aphasia seems to have been applied for the first time to language problems by Sextus Empiricus, not in its present sense but to describe 'a condition of mind, according to which we say that we neither affirm nor deny anything'. He may have been referring to a common symptom of the early stages of aphasia when some patients cannot indicate *yes* or *no* either with words or gesture.

Some modern scholars believe that the Egyptian surgeon, who

describes the convoluted surface of the human cortex, understood something about the relationship of cognitive function and particular areas of the brain. But the question of which part of the body generates thought and language remained the subject of intense debate for millennia to come. Hippocrates and, later, Galen, both experienced physicians, identified the brain as the organ of intellect. But Aristotle was only the most influential of those ancient thinkers who preferred what has been called the 'cardiac hypothesis': he saw the heart, which is warm and active, as the engine of thought, and gave the brain the role of cooling the blood.

Although Graeco-Roman physicians observed that loss of speech and language was associated with paralysis of the right side of the body, they did not relate the phenomenon to any particular area of the brain. Throughout the Renaissance acquired speechlessness was attributed either to paralysis of the tongue or to verbal amnesia, and often confused with other disorders such as deafness, mutism, stuttering or Hottentotism (being able to understand but not to articulate intelligently). From the middle of the seventeenth century some observant physicians noted that disordered language did not necessarily involve damage to the vocal organs or loss of memory. But they continued to prescribe treatments – bleeding, stinging enemas, blistering with the application of dried Spanish flies – which were scarcely an improvement on those recommended by the Egyptian surgeon. The scientific methods developed for the study of the planets and the human body were for the first time applied to the mind, but with strange results. René Descartes, with the approval of the Catholic Church, gave the mind its principal seat in the brain, but put its source somewhere or other outside the body, where it was received by the pineal gland.

Cartesian dualism was not really challenged until the end of the eighteenth century, by which time the central role of the brain was better understood. The revolutionary concept that the mind is not an ethereal gift of God, but a material consequence of the brain, was first popularized – despite the displeasure of the Church – by Franz Joseph Gall, the brilliant Austrian-born physician and inventor of phrenology. The ingenious propositions elaborated by the phrenologists were that faculties are located in the brain, that well-developed faculties represent large areas of cortex, and that the degree of development can be detected by the shape of the skull. The first was correct. The second is also, somewhat surprisingly, true. It was, however, the third – totally misleading – proposition, that the skull is a guide to the mind, that caught the imagination of the public. That bubble lasted well into the twentieth century – John remembers being taken to a phrenologist by his mother in the 1930s. It collapsed for the lack of supporting scientific evidence, and the ceramic phrenological skulls you can still find in antique shops are now mainly desirable as amusing relics of a famous scam. But phrenology was not entirely ridiculous. Although cognition cannot be charted by examination of the skull, the principle of cognitive modularity, which the phrenologists introduced, continues to exercise neuropsychologists to this day.

Gall placed language in the frontal lobes, a view that was accepted, on the basis of his own clinical studies, by the French physician Jean-Baptiste Bouillaud, who, in 1825, delivered a paper to a scientific meeting in France in which he argued for the frontal lobes as the source of language. Although wide of the mark, it was the first scientifically respectable suggestion that language can be destroyed independently of other brain functions. It was also in 1825 that another French physician, Professor Jacques Lordat, Dean of the Faculty of Medicine at Montpellier, suddenly found, after a fever lasting two weeks, that he was unable to speak. Later he wrote about the experience, describing many of the principal features of what was not yet called aphasia. When he tried to say *raisin* it came out as *sairin*; *musulman* came out as *sumulman*. When he wanted a book he found himself asking for a handkerchief. And, just as alarming for a man 'accustomed to so many years of literary studies', he was unable to read: 'In losing the memory for the meaning of spoken words, I had also lost the meanings of their visible signs.' It is one of the most detailed accounts of John's illness before it had either a name or an accepted scientific explanation. Yet Bouillaud's repeated insistence on the frontal lobes as the source of language had been firmly rejected by the Académie de Médecine.

It has been suggested that the pioneering French interest in cerebral anatomy may have been stimulated during the French Revolution by the copious supply of freshly severed heads available for dissection. It was in any case in post-Revolutionary France that the connection was at last made between language impairment and damage to the left hemisphere of the brain. The discovery was first made in the 1830s by Marc Dax, an obscure provincial physician. Because the two halves of the brain appear to be symmetrical, the idea of hemispheric specialization was at that time so far in advance of orthodox thinking that Dax did not broadcast his findings beyond his immediate circle of colleagues and friends. And so it was left to another man to demonstrate that speech is generated in a specific area of the left hemisphere.

In 1861 Paul Broca, a French surgeon and anthropologist, performed a post-mortem examination on the brain of a recently deceased fifty-seven-year-old man by the name of Leborgne. Around the hospital where he had been a patient for many years Monsieur Leborgne was known as Tan because *tan* was the only utterance he made – apart from *Sacré nom de Dieu* when he was very angry or upset. Tan was able to use his tongue and lips normally; his intelligence and comprehension of spoken language were also considered normal by those who knew him in the hospital. Broca's autopsy revealed a fluid-filled cavity about the size of a small hen's egg at the back of the third convolution of the frontal lobe of Tan's left cerebral hemisphere – the area that has been known as 'Broca's' ever since. Three years later Broca had collected twenty similar cases, some with even more circumscribed lesions and including one in which a lesion in the homologous area of the right hemisphere had *not* impaired speech. He was now ready to deliver to the scientific community the famous pronouncement – 'We speak with the left hemisphere' – which launched modern neuropsychology and established the doctrine of left-hemisphere dominance which remained unchallenged until the middle of the twentieth century.

Broca, wishing to distinguish 'loss of the faculty of articulated language' from verbal amnesia, or failure to connect ideas with words, chose the word aphemia (from the ancient Greek for without voice) for the condition he had located. But in 1864 another member of the French medical establishment, believing – so the story goes – that aphemia meant 'infamous', introduced his own word, aphasia.

In 1874, thirteen years after Broca had planted his flag on the left frontal lobe of Tan's brain, Carl Wernicke, a twenty-six-year-old German physician and psychiatrist, published a short monograph describing two patients with a different variety of what was by then called aphasia. The speech of Wernicke's subjects was copious but full of neologisms and circumlocutions, which made it difficult or impossible to follow. And unlike Broca's subjects they had trouble understanding the speech of others. Wernicke located the disorder, which still carries his name, in the posterior two-thirds of the superior temporal lobe, across the Sylvian fissure from Broca's and further towards the back of the brain.

Wernicke, on the basis of his findings and Broca's, devised a model of language production that postulated that aphasia could be caused by interruption of the pathways between areas as well as by local damage. His model, as elaborated by Ludwig Lichtheim in 1885, proposed seven varieties of aphasia, including Broca's (some comprehension but impaired volitional speech, writing, repetition, reading aloud, writing to dictation) and Wernicke's (fluent but disturbed speech, impaired comprehension of speech and writing; difficulties with repetition, writing to dictation and reading aloud).

The other five syndromes were hypothetical; and they were not in fact tested against real patients until the 1960s. *Conduction aphasia*, as it is now called, would leave speech and writing as well as auditory comprehension and silent reading intact, but cause problems with repetition, reading aloud and writing to dictation. *Transcortical motor aphasia* would spare understanding of speech and writing, repetition, writing to dictation and reading aloud but impair volitional speech and writing. A condition that is today known as *apraxia* would affect the organs of speech but leave comprehension of reading and writing intact. *Transcortical sensory aphasia* would be characterized by preserved speech, writing, repetition, reading aloud and writing to dictation; but comprehension both of speech and writing would be lost. Lichtheim called a seventh aphasic type 'isolated speech-deafness'. Today it is known as *pure word-deafness* because, while volitional speech, writing and reading are all intact, the patients, despite unimpaired hearing, cannot understand what they hear, repeat it or write it to dictation.

For several decades after Broca's discovery neuropathology was dominated by what Freud in his monograph *On Aphasia* called 'the idea of "localisation", that is, of the restriction of nervous functions to anatomically definable areas'. Freud rejected the Wernicke–Lichtheim model in favour of a more dynamic and holistic view of what he called the 'speech apparatus', which he described as 'a continuous cortical area in the left hemisphere extending between the terminations of the acoustic and optic nerves and the origins of the motor tracts for the muscles serving articulation and arm movements'. Language, according to Freud, was a process not of neurological locations and connections but of associations, the result of crossing points where images met words.

Freud's paper on aphasia, his last as a neurologist, is by now something of a period piece, interesting mainly for what it contributed to the development of his subsequent ideas about the unconscious. The 'speech apparatus' gave birth to the 'psychic apparatus', which inherited some of the same characteristics. The concepts of 'projection' and 'representation' also make their first appearance in *On Aphasia*, as does the Freudian slip, which is similar to aphasic paraphasia, the choice of a wrong word in some way related to the target.

His theory of aphasia, however, was not original. Its core ideas are an acknowledged tribute to the British neurologist John Hughlings Jackson. As early as the 1860s Hughlings Jackson had divided the aphasias into two classes: one 'speechless or nearly so', the other with 'plenty of words but mistakes in words'. He agreed, furthermore, that language was generated in the left hemisphere. But he and Wernicke–Lichtheim drew from the neurological evidence very different conclusions, which, although modified in detail over the years, continue to divide aphasiologists to this day.

Jackson's own ideas were strongly influenced by those of the philosopher and psychologist Herbert Spencer. It was Spencer who introduced the powerful notion of a hierarchical nervous system, developed level by level over successive stages of evolution, from the earliest and most primitive to the most recent and complex.

Hughlings Jackson, following Spencer's lead, envisaged language as represented in the brain by a hierarchy of anatomical structures developed in our species in the course of evolution, and in the individual during the acquisition of language in childhood. According to Hughlings Jackson's aphasiology, automatic and serial language – the swearing, counting, reciting the days of the week which are often preserved in otherwise mute aphasias – is at the most primitive level, and is represented in the right as well as the left brain. At the top of the scale is propositional speech: 'To speak is not to utter words, it is to propositionise . . . Single words are meaningless and so is any unrelated succession of words. The unit of speech is proposition . . . Loss of speech is therefore the loss of power to propositionise.' In the normal brain the most recently acquired cortical regions, those which generate complex functions like proposition, repress the lower, more bestial levels. When they are damaged they lose control over their primitive ancestors, thus releasing the symptomatic language, or non-language, of aphasia. Freud formulated this principle of 'functional retrogression' as follows: 'under all circumstances an arrangement of associations which, having been acquired later, belongs to a higher level of functioning, will be lost, while an earlier and simpler one will be preserved'.

It is a seductively plausible theory, perhaps all the more so to those of us who are conditioned, whether we know it or not, by Freud and Darwin. And it persisted in some quarters of aphasiology well into the second half of the twentieth century. As recently as 1940 the 'regression hypothesis' was invoked by Roman Jakobson, who asserted that 'the dissolution of the linguistic sound system in aphasics provides an exact mirror-image of the phonological development in child language'.

According to the regression hypothesis, auditory comprehension, which is the first component of language to develop in infancy and by which language is learned, is less vulnerable to aphasia than speaking, reading and writing; and a first language is less likely to be disturbed by brain damage than languages acquired later in life. But the regression hypothesis, tested against the realities of aphasic language, falls apart. Many aphasics, including those who cannot say real words, make sounds that no baby could make. Others cannot manage the earliest baby-sounds. John cannot say *goo*. He can read German, French, Italian as easily as before his stroke; and he can manage as well as before with Dutch, Spanish and Portuguese.

Hughlings Jackson's rejection of 'locationism' was, and is, less easily dismissed. He proposed an extensive and dynamic model of cortical activity according to which all parts of the brain participate in all aspects of cognitive function. He argued that aphasic language could not be caused by damaged areas, precisely because those areas were destroyed and therefore no longer operational. Aphasia, which must therefore be the product of concerted activity in the remaining brain, was seen as the consequence of a general lowering of intellectual function and therefore a problem of thought as well as language.

Hughlings Jackson's ideas were enthusiastically adopted by a number of influential neurologists. Sir Henry Head, his colleague at the National Hospital for Nervous Diseases in Queen Square, denounced the 'diagram makers' and their simplistic models of neurological activity represented by boxes, for the language centres, and arrows, for the neural pathways connecting the boxes. The French neurologist Pierre Marie caused a stir by insisting that Broca's 'third frontal convolution did not play any special role in the function of language'. True aphasia, according to Marie, was caused by damage to the posterior brain. Tan's difficulty, therefore, was one of articulation, not of language loss. (Marie's theory was put to the test in 1979, when Tan's brain, which had been preserved in alcohol and was at that time kept in the cellars of the Paris Medical School, was removed from its bottle and examined with a CT scan. The results of the scan confirmed Broca's original finding.)

In a paper published in 1938 the respectable American neurophysiologist Karl S. Lashley took the anti-locationist position to its furthest extremes. Lashley contended that loss of intellectual function after brain damage was the result not of the location but of the amount of lost brain tissue. But his ideas were based on experiments with rats and pigeons which have never been repeated and were eventually abandoned.

While neurologists debated the biological sources of aphasia, psychologists brought other perspectives to the problem of how acquired language disorder can best be explained and treated. The inspired concept of Gestalt, introduced in 1890 by the German psychologist Christian von Ehrenfels, was widely adopted on the Continent. Gestalt psychology envisages mental activity as better analysed in terms of interactions than discrete elements. Just as a melody or painting or story is determined less by its component parts than by their relationship, so the patterns of cognition are more than the sum of their parts.

A modified version of Gestalt psychology was applied to aphasia and imported into America in the 1930s by Kurt Goldstein, a brilliant German-born neurologist and psychologist. Goldstein – who had been a student of Carl Wernicke, a founding father of the reductionist attempt to explain all aphasic symptoms by their location – was an arch opponent of localizationism. According to his 'organismic psychology', brain damage unbalanced the cerebral equilibrium, causing behavioural changes as well as loss of function. The excessively rigid reliance on routine that characterizes some aphasics' behaviour is explained as a way of avoiding situations that might provoke a 'catastrophic reaction' – an emotional breakdown caused by challenges with which the aphasic cannot cope. Brain-damaged patients, according to Goldstein and his followers, are fundamentally different from normal people in that they lose the power to appreciate the abstract principles that lie behind the salient details of a pattern or situation. He called this loss of mental flexibility a 'concrete attitude', as opposed to the 'abstract attitude' which enables the normal person to adjust to new situations in the light of new information.

By the time Goldstein reached the United States such imprecise generalizations from the continental *fin de siècle* had been challenged by an opposing school of psychology, behaviourism, founded on the eve of the First World War by John B. Watson, Professor of Psychology at Johns Hopkins University. Watson and his disciples rejected all theories about psychological data that could not be directly observed and measured. The private, invisible realm of mental states was beyond the reach of science and therefore to be explained solely by observable behaviour: the significance of having a pain is that you complain, groan, take a pill or consult a doctor about it. Words like feeling, mind, consciousness, innateness, reason, were taboo. Although the circumlocutions necessitated by the banning of such words make behaviourist prose hard going, the behaviourists did find in the philosopher Gilbert Ryle's book *The Concept of Mind* (1940) an elegant and powerful – if ultimately unconvincing – exegesis.

Two fundamental assumptions of behaviourism were that all living organisms, from an amoeba to a human being, are essentially the same, differing only in the complexity of their responses; and that all behaviour, animal or human, normal or pathological, can be explained only by the environmental conditioning that has caused it and can be measured only by behavioural responses to stimuli. The rules that govern human behaviour could therefore be derived from experiments with laboratory animals: rats could be conditioned to press bars, dogs to salivate when they heard certain musical tones. Language was nothing more than one directly observable characteristic of human behaviour. Thought, as Watson put it, was merely 'talking with concealed musculature'.

In the years after the Second World War behaviourism became the dominant school of psychology in Britain and the United States, where its implications exerted a powerful influence on social scientists and philosophers; and on linguistics, including two of the greatest American linguists, Leonard Bloomfield and B. F. Skinner, whose empiricist methodology necessarily eschewed the knotty problem of the relationship of words and sentences to the meaning the speaker intends to convey.

Behaviourism, like Hughlings Jackson's principle of functional regression and Goldstein's organismic psychology, invited the intuitively appealing but baleful interpretation that aphasic language reflects impaired intelligence. (Hughlings Jackson went so far as to compare aphasics to dogs.) But aphasics are not dogs, rats, pigeons or wild children who have never been exposed to language. They rarely lose all aspects of language, and can sometimes use what little they have to bootstrap with remarkable and surprising results.

Six weeks after his stroke I found next to John's bed in Dr Z's geriatric ward an enormous textbook. The title of the book – *Cognitive Neuropsychology* – meant nothing to me; nor did the names of the authors, Rosaleen A. McCarthy and Elizabeth K. Warrington. But when I asked John who had brought this book he pointed to the names of the authors. I said this was unlikely because we didn't know them and I was pretty sure they didn't know John. He pointed once again at the book. I rephrased the question: Where did the book come from? He pointed yet again at the book. Well then: When did it get here? He opened it and drew his finger under chapter headings. He closed it and jabbed his finger at the spine. He laughed in a patronizing way: evidently my obtuse quizzing amused him. I resorted to Twenty Questions. Was it a man? Was it a woman? Was it a friend? Was it meant for someone else? My voice was shrill, my hands were clammy, my heart was racing. I was experiencing what Goldstein (of whom I had not yet heard) might have called a 'catastrophic reaction' – except that it was I, not the aphasic patient, who couldn't cope with what was happening.

It was for me an essential article of faith that John could think as clearly as ever and understand what people said to him. Any evidence to the contrary was intolerable, and I often wondered what I would have done if Alzheimer's rather than aphasia had afflicted him. For more than half my life I had taken John's superior intellect and imagination for granted. John was my encyclopaedia, problem solver, the window through which I enjoyed life. Everybody – apart from Dr X and the speech therapist in the white coat – was impressed by the way he could, without uttering a single intelligible word, follow, and take part in, even the most rapid and demanding conversations. I think I was more proud of him now than I had ever been of his great achievements and the honours they had brought him; and I continued to rely on his judgement about all matters, not least the quality of my own thinking.

I could accept his loss of speech because the fire in his eyes, the lively modulation of his voice and the way he shaped it with his left hand told me that John was still John. I could accept that he didn't seem to recognize the words for razors and pencils and keys and the like, because he was so quick to respond to complex ideas. But I could *not* bear his inability to deal with these simple, reasonable questions: Who brought the book? Where did it come from? When did it arrive?

John remained calm, waiting for the storm to blow over in that maddening way he always has when I lose my temper. My questioning became more sarcastic: I suppose you're telling me, John, that this book brought itself? It sprouted legs and walked in? He hung his head, and I could see that he was not so much upset as sad. So I gave up the quiz and offered to take the book away and read it for him. He grasped the volume in his left hand, hugged it to his chest, and spoke a real word: 'No!' He was going to read this book himself, and discover from it what was wrong with his head.

Each afternoon when I came to visit him I could tell from the slips of paper between the pages that he had got further into *Cognitive Neuropsychology*. Then one day it disappeared, as mysteriously as it had arrived. In its place was a drawing of a brain, with parts of the left side shaded. The words 'Wernicke's' and 'Broca's' were written to one side of the drawing in a tiny, unfamiliar handwriting, with arrows pointing to the shaded areas.

It was several weeks before I discovered during a chance encounter with Dr Z that it was he who had loaned John the book. He had done so because John seemed eager to know more about his condition. They had had a long discussion about it in my absence, and Dr Z was satisfied that John had understood it well enough to point to certain passages that might be relevant. John had wanted to know exactly where the source of his problem was located, so Dr Z had made a sketch of what he believed, from John's symptoms, to be roughly the picture a scan would show. I asked Dr Z how John, who couldn't match the printed word *razor* to a razor, could possibly have worked his way through the technical prose of a textbook on a subject about which he knew nothing. Dr Z shrugged: 'Gestalt?'

When I told John that Dr Z had revealed himself as the bearer of the book John performed a mime of their conversation. He transformed himself into Dr Z – the same forward tilt of head and shoulders, the same steady gaze, the identical light tenor voice – explaining; and then back into himself listening attentively – left hand, palm open and facing forward, touching his ear, beckoning – sometimes understanding (triumphant smile), sometimes not (corners of mouth down, shaking of head).

Later, when I boasted to our friends about John's feat, the friends agreed with me that it might be explained by his profession: historians have to be able to sift through vast amounts of unfamiliar written material. But I abolished, from my story and from my mind, his failure to answer my questions about who had given him the book. It was a non-event. It hadn't happened. And in fact it didn't happen again for a while because I instinctively avoided asking him questions that began with words like *who, what, when* and *where*; and when I did, John saw the danger signals and bluffed his replies.

Some months later, when the speech and language therapist in the white coat advised me that John's comprehension was failing – because he could not tell her who, in the little stories she gave him to read, was waiting at the bus stop, or where, or when – I dismissed her as incompetent. It turned out that we were both right. He did understand the stories. What he didn't understand were the questions.

9

Aphasia Today

. . . in the next few years, we will have to engage in 'post-phrenological thinking', formulating a new view of brain organisation for language to replace the nineteenth-century perspective that has held sway for most of the twentieth century.
E. Bates and F. Dick, 'Beyond phrenology: brain and language in the next millennium'

Since Paul Broca's momentous discovery that we speak using the left hemispheres of our brains, philosophers as well as psychologists and neurologists have been grappling with the apparent paradox that the human mind, whether it likes it or not, is the product of the human brain. Like Thomas Huxley, who wondered 'that anything so remarkable as a state of consciousness comes about as a result of irritating nervous tissue', many people even today find it difficult to accept the intuitively improbable idea that our most private feelings, original perceptions, special skills, hard-won achievements – our individuality, consciousness, our very souls and our ability to explain ourselves in language – are entirely determined by the electrical-chemical activity of a soft, wrinkled, grey-and-white lump of matter that you could comfortably hold in one hand.

Before John's stroke the mind–body problem was for me an abstract issue, somehow unrelated to the anatomy and physiology of the unlovely organ that apparently makes all of us what we are. It was only after a part of his brain was blasted that I was driven to try to understand something about what had happened to it and therefore to him. An obsessive curiosity drove me into science libraries and laboratories. It gave me the courage to knock on the doors of world-class neuroscientists, who referred me to other neuroscientists or sent me back to the libraries with lists of references to more books and articles.

My research was at first haphazard, but I soon learned that neuropsychology, the science dedicated to explaining human behaviour in terms of its sources in the brain, has not yet explained or located the so-called 'ghost in the machine'. As the neurologist and opera producer Dr Jonathan Miller warned me, 'Compared to the human brain the universe is a clockwork toy. One square millimetre of brain is *unbelievably* complex.' Nevertheless, there has been progress. Neuropsychology is now a burgeoning, many-headed discipline. And the study of aphasia remains one of the headquarters for neuropsychological research.

In the early 1960s, a century after Broca's dramatic announcement of the role of the third frontal convolution, the challenges posed by his immediate successors, Wernicke and Lichtheim, were taken up by a group of neuropsychologists based in Boston and led by Harold Goodglass of the Boston Veterans Administration Medical Center and Norman Geschwind of Harvard Medical School. Wernicke and Lichtheim had predicted hypothetical types of aphasia, which, however, could not be described in detail because they had not at that time been observed.

In a series of important articles about the behavioural consequences of brain damage, Geschwind and his colleagues turned back the tide in favour of attempts to classify aphasic symptoms by their anatomical sources. One of these papers described the case of a forty-one-year-old policeman who, following the removal of a tumour in his left frontal lobe, had, as might have been expected, a weakness of his right hand. Luckily his language seemed to have been spared: he had no problems with speaking or comprehension. His left hand was not affected, but when he tried to write or type with it he surprised himself by making spelling mistakes; he wrote *yonti* for yesterday, for example. When common objects were placed in his left hand while he was blindfolded he could demonstrate their use but could not say what they were: he made hammering movements with a hammer but defined it verbally as a comb; he mimed cutting with a pair of scissors but said he would use it to light a cigarette. When the blindfold and the objects were removed he remembered and correctly identified them. When asked to carry out simple instructions – draw a circle, mimic shaving, wave goodbye – he could do them with his weak right hand but not with his physically unaffected left hand. Geschwind's hypothesis was that the policeman's language centres in the left hemisphere were cut off from the right hemisphere where his left hand was controlled. He predicted damage to the corpus callosum, the bundle of fibres that connects the two hemispheres. And when the policeman died, the hypothesis was supported by an autopsy.

Another more severe disconnection syndrome was demonstrated by the case of a twenty-one-year-old woman who had been found unconscious in her kitchen where she had been poisoned by carbon monoxide from an unlit gas jet of her water heater. The woman never again spoke spontaneously except for a few stock phrases. Sometimes she would sing along with the radio, and finish the songs when the radio was switched off. Although completely unable to understand the meaning of what was said to her, she repeated it in a normal voice. This condition, known as echolalia, had been observed before. It was given a neuroanatomical explanation for the first time when she died ten years later and an autopsy revealed that the whole of her language cortex – Wernicke's, Broca's and the pathways between them – had been spared but was surrounded by areas of destruction which had isolated it from the rest of the brain.

The Boston neo-classical model confirmed the Wernicke–Lichtheim syndromes and added three new ones:

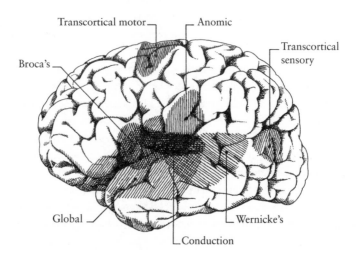

the isolation syndrome, a combination of the classical transcortical sensory and transcortical motor aphasias; global aphasia, the severest type, affecting all components of language and caused by extensive damage throughout the language cortex; and anomia, also known as verbal amnesia, which Geschwind attributed to lesions in parts of the inferior parietal lobe which are unique to the human brain and which he believed were the regions from which all other aspects of language originally developed.

Anomia, difficulty in finding individual words, is one of the most common aphasic symptoms and the one for which normal people are most likely to have a fellow feeling. When we are tired or speaking a foreign language, or as we grow older, most of us occasionally experience the frustration of reaching for a word that we know perfectly well, would recognize instantly if we saw or heard it, can define and place correctly in a sentence, but can't quite catch. Word-finding difficulties are a feature of all aphasias and of many dementias (and it is now known that they can be caused by lesions anywhere in the language zone). Other aphasic symptoms sometimes resolve to what Geschwind identified as pure anomia, in which word finding is the only or the primary deficit. In some cases only nouns are affected, in others verbs also, but sentence structure and closed-class grammatical words (articles, prepositions, conjunctions, and so on) are in place. The result is 'empty' speech, with much reliance on words like *thing . . . whatsit . . . you know . . . I mean . . . like . . . whatever* – rather like the fashionable speech mannerisms of some young people today.

Decades before the Boston neo-classicists revived the Wernicke–Lichtheim system of localizing and classifying aphasic types, the Russian neuropsychiatrist Alexander Luria had formulated a similar set of classifications, but by way of a different, less reductionist theoretical route. Luria's conception of language drew on the ideas of I. P. Pavlov about the dynamic nature of organic function; on his experience as a clinician treating brain-damaged patients during the Second World War; and on structural linguistics, which he had studied in the 1930s. He proposed a synthesis of the holistic and localizing doctrines whereby constricted cortical areas undoubtedly contributed to language, but were only parts of a complex network of fields of sub-components which process all cognitive functions. The notion of neurological locations was replaced in Luria's aphasiology by the concept of neural networks, which, following brain damage, could be 'reconstituted' by training the aphasic patient to employ different physiological processes that would achieve normal or near-normal results by abnormal methods. Luria's philosophy of disordered language spread rapidly throughout Eastern Europe but did not reach the West until 1965 with the English translation of his book *The Higher Cortical Functions in Man*. Although researchers and clinicians in America and Britain have been unable to locate some of the symptoms he describes within the syndromes he postulates, his theories are admired even today for their coherence and precocious sophistication.

Luria was not the first aphasiologist to apply to the study of aphasia principles that are believed to underlie normal language. But he and a fellow Russian, Lev Semyonovich Vygotsky, and the Czech linguist, Roman Jakobson, were twentieth-century pioneers of a systematic application of the idea that the structure of normal language might have a bearing on patterns of disordered language. Jakobson, in 1940, was the first linguist to appreciate that the observation of aphasic deficits might enlighten linguistic theory.

Abstract linguistics, the discipline concerned not with individual languages but with the principles underlying all language, has been described as the most humane of the sciences and the most scientific of the humanities. More than a century ago the subject was characterized by the avant-garde Swiss linguist Ferdinand de Saussure as operating on the borderland between thought and sound. It is in this very borderland – so easy to take for granted but so difficult to map and describe – that aphasics lose their way. But it was not until the early 1970s that there was a widespread exchange of ideas between academic linguists and psychologists interested in aphasia.

The most influential linguistic theory of the last half-century has been generative grammar, the code or rules we use to translate thought into language, as developed by Noam Chomsky and his colleagues from the 1950s. Chomsky was a leader of the 'cognitive revolution' of the mid-twentieth century, when, as he puts it: 'there was an important change of perspective: from the study of behavior and its products . . . to the inner mechanisms that enter into human thought and action', at a time when 'advances in the formal sciences had provided appropriate concepts in a very sharp and clear form, making it possible to give a precise account of the computational principles that generate the expression of language'.

Chomsky drew inspiration from a sentence written in 1836 by Wilhelm von Humboldt: 'The language process . . . confronts . . . a truly boundless area, the scope of everything conceivable. It must therefore make infinite use of finite media . . .' Chomsky postulates a 'language organ', an innate template built into the brains of all human beings (but not animals), which accounts for the astonishing ability of children between the ages of eighteen and thirty-six months to grasp:

the property of discrete infinity, which is exhibited in its purest form by the natural numbers 1,2,3, . . . Children do not learn this property of the number system. Unless the mind already possesses the basic principles, no amount of evidence could provide them; and they are completely beyond the range of other organisms.

Similarly, no child has to learn that there are three word sentences and four word sentences, but no three-and-a half word sentences, and that it is always possible to construct a more complex one, with a definite form and meaning.

Chomsky has drawn a distinction between 'competence', the idealized knowledge we all have of our native languages, and 'performance', the way ideal rules and structures are flouted or corrupted when we actually use language. Competence is necessarily the subject of pure linguistics. But, since abstract rules do not describe real behaviour, Chomsky maintains that the investigation of language must also take account of the mental processes that are the subject of psychology. Linguistics and psychology look at language from different perspectives, but the differences between them are differences of emphasis rather than of subject-matter. They cannot therefore be regarded as separate and autonomous disciplines.

Chomsky's transformational-generative grammar, the quasi-mathematical rules that govern the generation of one grammatical structure by another, provided a new conceptual framework for the investigation of aphasic difficulties with syntax and was a major influence on the aphasiology of the Boston neo-classicists. Although Chomsky himself, as far as I am aware, has never concerned himself with aphasia, the new generation of psycholinguists, who gather their material from studying speech errors in normal people, are increasingly informed by the evidence provided by the lacunae of aphasic language. And academic linguistics, since the 1970s, has provided the motivation and the vocabulary for associated disciplines that are concerned in one way or another with aphasia.

Another development of the 1970s is pragmatics, the branch of linguistics concerned with the effect of context on meaning and the way we perform in real time and space when we transmit and interpret non-verbal as well as verbal signals. Depending on the context, you can communicate a lot by remaining absolutely silent. Don de Lillo, in his novel *The Body Artist*, describes a woman trying to make sense of the utterances of a mentally disabled man whose speech is unsupported by 'the code in the simplest conversation that tells the speakers what's going on outside the bare acoustics':

This was missing when they talked. There was a missing beat. It was hard for her to find the tempo. All they had were unadjusted words. She lost touch with him, lost interest sometimes, couldn't locate rhythmic intervals or time cues or even the mutters and hums, the audible pauses that pace a remark. He didn't register facial responses to things she said and this threw her off. There were no grades of emphasis here and flatness there. She began to understand that their talks had no time sense and that all the references at the unspoken level, the things a man speaking Dutch might share with a man speaking Chinese – all this was missing here.

Many aphasics, by contrast, retain the ability to convey precisely those unspoken references. A psychologist specializing in pragmatics might take note of John's normal – indeed gracious – turn-taking in conversation; in the way he can use silence to convey scepticism or surprise; in the way he points his finger when he wants to indicate *here* or *there*, or *this* or *that*; in the body language that looks so normal from a distance and allows people who are on John's wavelength to enjoy his skills as a wordless conversationalist. When John converses he can calculate very precisely the effect of a gesture, the length of a gaze, a pause, the lift of an eyebrow, the position of hand and fingers. He can modulate his vocal tones to convey the full range of crucial sub-texts – extreme courtesy, irritation, humility, sarcasm, irony, menace, and so on – without which spoken language loses much of its meaning.

Our friends have learned, more or less, to interpret his private repertory of hand and arm movements, ironic groans, radiant smiles, wriggling eyebrows, blown kisses, satirical mimickings. He can describe an event, respond to questions, make everyday needs and wishes known. Nor is his non-verbal vocabulary restricted to concrete matters. Some of his drawings and mimes convey abstract, often poetic metaphors: such as a telescope and the sound of the wind to represent the future. Nevertheless it has to be said that his attempts to initiate new ideas or topics of conversation are inevitably frustrated by the lack of a language with a shared symbolic programme.

While pragmatic linguists study context and non-verbal communication, psycholinguists attempt to map the mental events that take place during the long journey that starts with motive and intention and ends with verbal utterance; or, in the case of comprehension, that starts with the perception of speech sounds and ends with abstracting meaning from them. Although the field was dominated until fairly recently by studies of English-speaking subjects, it has always been a fundamental assumption of psycholinguistics that the acquisition, development, use and breakdown of all languages are governed by the same neural/mental processes. Cross-linguistic research in the past decade or so has not challenged the hypothesis of universality. But it has revealed that patterns of impairment do differ according to the way the language 'organ' has been configured by a particular language.

'Psycholinguistics is crucial,' says Alfonso Caramazza, Professor of Psychology at Harvard:

Aphasic patients are the laboratory. Nature has done it for you. She has given you an experiment. She forces us to ask questions that we otherwise would not. And maybe one day a patient will walk in and give you the answer. But to understand it you would have to know something about the structure of normal language.

Professor Caramazza began his academic career as a psychologist specializing in aphasia in the 1970s. For him, as for all aphasiologists of his generation, the terms 'Broca's' and 'Wernicke's' are merely convenient tags, used in quotation marks. 'Broca and Wernicke were giants,' he says. 'But you can't base a modern science of language on them any more than you can base modern physics on Aristotle.' Nevertheless, the old locationist/holistic dialectic, although refined and complicated by modern developments, is not quite obsolete.

The modern discipline most systematically dedicated to identifying the brain parts responsible for language, and to classifying the aphasias accordingly, is neurolinguistics, the goal of which was described by the French neurologist Henri Hécaen and his colleague the linguist Armand Dubois in a seminal paper of 1969 as the establishment of 'a purely linguistic typology' of neurologically caused verbal disorders. Although the neurolinguistic search for a locationist classification system continues, especially on the Continent and in parts of the United States, the relationship between linguistic theories and brain structures remains elusive. And there is continuing controversy about whether any classification system is worth pursuing – at least 60 to 70 per cent of aphasics, when examined in detail, seem to present unique patterns of deficits that cannot be conveniently slotted into any classification system. 'Classification doesn't describe the mechanism,' said Professor Caramazza. 'It creates an illusion of comprehension when there isn't any comprehension.'

Although the new locationists are looking for patterns of neuronal activity as well as for one-to-one correspondences with particular sets of neurones, Professor Caramazza is among those who dismiss efforts to link linguistic behaviour to bits of the brain's machinery as a return to the old phrenology. Dr Wise admits the charge: 'It *is* a bit phrenological. But we are looking at much smaller areas,

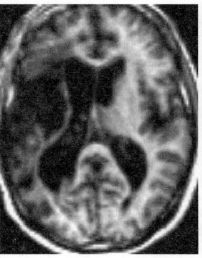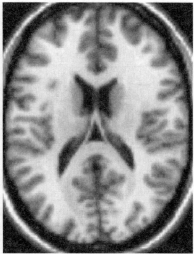

and always on the understanding that messages are arriving from elsewhere in the brain.' Dr Wise is one of the British leaders of the first generation of brain scientists to be in a position to examine the nervous system with computerized technologies that some believe will eventually do for neuroanatomy and neurophysiology what Galileo's telescope did for cosmological astronomy. Imaging techniques that allow scientists to peer into the brain and monitor its activities have meanwhile restored for neurologists the respectability of neuropsychology. Fifteen or twenty years ago very few neurologists took an interest in neuropsychology, and those who did risked their reputation. When the kindly Dr Y advised us that John would regain his language within nine weeks but would never walk again, he was doing what Dr Wise calls 'pronouncing'. Neurologists of Dr Y's generation had no choice but to pronounce on the basis of experience. 'And,' Dr Wise adds, 'they were often right. But imaging has changed all that.'

Magnetic resonance imaging (MRI) creates a three-dimensional virtual brain, which can be sliced and examined from bottom to top or side to side in greater detail than is possible with a post-mortem dissection. Here is a horizontal slice seen from above of John's brain (left) and of a normal brain (right). The dark areas show high levels of water, which replaces brain tissue after damage. In John's brain 'Broca's' and 'Wernicke's' areas, and connections between them, have been destroyed.

Other techniques make it possible to watch the brain in action and see which parts are activated by particular cognitive tasks. Positron emission tomography (PET) charts changes in blood flow, glucose consumption or neurotransmitter uptake. Functional magnetic resonance imaging (fMRI) measures changes in blood flow and oxygen content.

A technique called transcutaneous magnetic stimulation (TMS), which safely disables precise cortical areas by discharging a magnetic current for 300 milliseconds, is sometimes used before surgery for epilepsy to enable the surgeon to avoid the language centres. It can also be used for research purposes to simulate aphasic symptoms. Dr Wise and his team of researchers often experiment on themselves with TMS, 'because nature never gives you exactly the experiment you want'. He has experienced disruption of his reading by this method.

Researchers can follow language unfolding in real time by detecting event-related potential (ERP), electrical signals generated by the concerted activity of groups of neurones as they perform certain tasks. It has been known since the 1930s that the brain emits very weak electromagnetic waves, which can be measured by attaching electrodes to the scalp. Electroencephalography (EEG) has long been used to detect tumours and other brain abnormalities. The signals, which are only one-millionth of a volt or so, can now be amplified and transmitted to a computer, allowing scientists to follow brain activities associated with complex cognitive activity, including, up to a point, language.

The positive voltage P600, for example, is triggered by grammatical errors, and is an indicator of syntactic processing. If I writes a sentence that are ungrammatical, my computer program underlines it in green, and when you read it your brain emits P600. A negative signal, N400, is produced when the brain is confronted with nonwords or real words used in contexts that make no semantic sense. When I write the sentence 'Colorless green ideas sleep furiously' (Chomsky's famous illustration of the dissociation between correct grammar and meaning), my word processor takes no notice, but less than half a second after you read it the event activates in your brain the potential voltage N400. Because ERP does not always reveal the source of the electrical activity, it is often used in combination with imaging. But a promising new development, magnetoencephalography (MEG), which detects the magnetic fields generated by electrical currents, can record both magnetic activity and its source. It is also now possible – although nobody knows quite how – for some people to control their own brain waves well enough to move the cursor on a computer screen.

Experiments using such new techniques indicate that the classical language zone in the left hemisphere – Broca's, Wernicke's and the pathways that connect them – is only part of the picture. Virtually every region of the brain has been implicated in at least one language study. The right hemisphere plays a larger part than was previously supposed; the cerebellum and the sub-cortical thalamic complex and basal ganglia seem also to be involved. An example of the kind of experiment being conducted in laboratories all over the world was undertaken by Dr Wise and three colleagues who used PET imaging to investigate the articulation of single words in the brains of twelve normal people. Their early report on the project, published in the *Lancet* in 1999, concluded that the formulation of an articulatory plan is not, after all, a function of Broca's area but of the left anterior insula and lateral pre-motor cortex.

'There has been much redefining and relocating, and readjusting of old positions,' says Dr Wise:

Someone once wrote a paper entitled 'Where is Wernicke's area?' I've now gone back to a minimal Wernicke's, the original small area in the back part of the superior temporal gyrus. But one has to remember that the classic Wernicke's symptoms can also be caused by damage elsewhere. The problem is that strokes are not that neat. Nature's laboratory is a messy place and millimetres matter in the brain.

Computerized imaging is still too crude an instrument to provide definitive answers about the cerebral universe, one square millimetre of which is capable of making as many as a billion connections with neurones that may be widely distributed across a network that interacts with other networks. It is unlikely that the complexity of brain activity is entirely reflected by measurable increased blood flow and chemical changes, which could be just the tip of the iceberg. It may be that scans are picking up and blurring areas that are engaged in more than one kind of cognitive activity. Language appears to have colonized brain regions that continue to perform other functions: Broca's area, for example, is activated when you watch another human being perform complex hand movements or see a tool that is associated with a particular movement. Certain areas will 'light up' in the same subject when a cognitive task is new; others fifteen minutes later when it has been learned.

The psycholinguist Steven Pinker tells a story that illustrates both the power and the limitations of neuro-imaging experiments. In his book *Words and Rules* he argues that irregular verbs, which cannot be computed by the brain because they are not governed by rules, are necessarily memorized, while regular verbs are computed according to rule. 'Look-up and computation', according to Pinker, are two distinct processes and therefore ought to be represented differently in the brain. While working on the book he discovered that four PET research centres had also been investigating that very question. They used different languages, techniques, designs and tasks that would explain their different conclusions about which parts of the brain do what. Although Pinker's dual-route theory works neatly for English, it is less satisfactory for such languages as Chinese, in which the regular–irregular distinction does not apply in the same way. The significant outcome for Pinker, however, was that all four studies agreed that the past-tense forms of regular and irregular verbs are, just as he had independently hypothesized, processed in different parts of the brain.

In the summer of 1993, six years before Pinker's *Words and Rules* was published, Jane did not need a scan of John's brain to discover that he had less trouble writing irregular words like *knife*, *nought* and *went* than regular words like *spoon*, *zero* and *walked*. It is a fairly common aphasic pattern: John's ability to retrieve words he would necessarily have learned by heart, because they don't follow any computational or phonological rule, was less impaired than his ability to retrieve regular words. But with some other aphasics it happens the other way round.

Psychologists call such complementary patterns double dissociations. If one patient can do A but not B, and another patient can do B but not A, the inference is that because A and B can be damaged independently they are processed by different neural mechanisms. The concept of double dissociation was a starting-point for cognitive neuropsychology, a branch of neuropsychology pioneered in Britain in the early 1970s when experimental psychologists began to test and develop their theoretical information-processing models on brain-damaged individuals. For cognitive neuropsychologists the focus of research and treatment has shifted from groups, syndromes and anatomical explanations to the in-depth study of individual profiles of impaired language. Each brain-damaged patient is regarded as a mini-research project, which may confirm or contribute to models that describe all language processing.

Cognitive neuropsychologists maintain that mental architecture is modular: that cognition is achieved by a system of discrete components, which can break down independently. In normal language the aural and visual signals by which we receive and deliver messages are encoded at different levels: semantic (meaning), lexical (dictionary of words), syntactic (the rule-based structure), morphological (the ways in which words are changed by context and inflection), phonological (the sounds of language). A purist cognitive neuropsychologist would claim that each of these levels can be damaged separately, as can the four modalities, comprehension, speech, reading and writing; and that within each level and modality there are other modules that can be separately crossed off the cognitive map.

Early cognitive neuropsychologists interested in normal and dis-ordered reading discovered what has become a classic example of double dissociation. Research with normal subjects had suggested that people with healthy brains read by way of two parallel mental routes. One is governed by the rules that translate print to sound. Children learn these correspondences when they start reading, and all normal readers can apply the rules to any pronounceable word regardless of whether they have encountered it before or know its meaning. All grown-up normal English readers know that non-existent words like *griff* or *bim* are pronounced differently from *grife* or *bime*.

The second route works the other way around. As we become sophisticated readers we learn to recognize whole words irrespective of their spelling or pronunciation. The irregularly spelled words that make the English language such a nightmare for foreigners are no problem for us because we have filed them away as whole entities in our lexicon. No normal native English speaker would pronounce *yacht*, *knight* or *island* according to phonological print-to-sound computation. (The English brought up in England find it hilarious when Americans do just that with words like Worcester and Cholmondeley.)

The observation of aphasics with acquired reading disorders seemed to confirm the dual-route theory. Psychologists found that some patients who had no problem recognizing letters or real words could not easily read aloud any pronounceable word with which they were not already familiar. This condition was called phonological dyslexia. Those who also made paraphasic mistakes – reading, for example, liberty as *freedom*, uncle as *nephew* or *black* for white – which suggested that the failure of the print-to-sound mechanism was affecting comprehension as well as pronunciation, were called deep dyslexics.

But other patients *could* read unfamiliar words. Their problem was that they could not read any of the many English words, such as *yacht*, *knight* or *island*, that are not pronounced as they are spelled. They were relying mainly on phonological print-to-sound and could not reliably retrieve from their lexicon words that looked different from the way they are pronounced. This disorder was called lexical or surface dyslexia.

The examination of aphasic subjects has revealed numerous dissociations as, for example, between reading and writing, speaking and writing, nouns and verbs, content versus function words, high- and low-frequency words. Although it is not clear how pure the dissociation is between expressive and receptive language, there are aphasics who can speak or write certain words that they can't understand when they hear or read them, and others who can understand some words they cannot produce.

The concept of dissociation would seem to resolve some of the many paradoxes that characterized John's aphasia in its early stages. He could, for example, copy written words but could not repeat spoken words. He could, with some difficulty, write words from dictation; he could understand words, but he could not imagine or generate the sounds written words would make if spoken. Since there are aphasics who present a complementary pattern, there seems to be a double dissociation between accessing the orthography and the phonology of language. John could judge whether a sentence was grammatical and well formed, but he could not write a grammatical sentence. He could, furthermore, correct grammatical mistakes even if he didn't understand all the words in the sentence.

Within two months of his stroke John was able to recognize whole words. But nine months later, when Jane started working with him, he could not always recognize individual letters either by their names or by the sounds they make. He knew perfectly well what a cat was; as time went on he could sometimes write the word from dictation or occasionally from his own mind. But if you asked him to chose the first letter of cat from a choice of seven letters he could not use his knowledge of the word to select the letter 'c'. He had particular trouble with vowels, which he still tends, when writing a word, either to omit or guess at.

The dissociation between vowels and consonants is even more pronounced for an Italian aphasic whose case was written up in *Nature* in 1991 by Roberto Cubelli. The Italian wrote all words accurately apart from leaving blank spaces where the vowels should go. He wrote his name, Fondacaro Ciro, as F ND C R C R . For Bologna he wrote B L GN . But there are other aphasics who find vowels easier than consonants; and still others who can read or write only capital letters or only lower-case letters: John retained both, but Fondacaro Ciro wrote in capitals.

Elizabeth Warrington, one of the pioneers of cognitive neuropsychology, identified another dissociation, which she calls reverse concreteness and which interests me because it applies to John's aphasia. Whereas most aphasics have more difficulty with abstract than concrete words, Dr Warrington described a patient, a former civil servant, who could not understand concrete nouns, such as *hay*, *needle*, *acorn* or *geese*, but had no problem with abstract words such as *supplication*, *arbiter*, *hint* and *vocation*. John's case is less clear-cut, but he does find abstract words like *democracy* or *flattery* easier than concrete words like *dog* or *table*.

Psychologists who disagree with the modular approach argue that on-line aphasic performance rarely reveals clearly defined dissociations. Most aphasias affect more than one aspect of language, some of which may be better preserved than others. Professor Caramazza is one of the modern aphasiologists who believe that the original concept of double dissociation as applied by the pioneering cognitive neuropsychologists was 'Naïve. That's not how the brain works. The brain is a collection of expert individuals, each with specialized knowledge and expertise. If one leaves, the group tries to compensate. If too many leave it ceases to function effectively.'

One of the most fascinating contributions of cognitive neuropsychology has been the discovery of a rare but suggestive condition in which memory for words is disproportionately impaired within certain semantic categories. In the early 1980s Elizabeth Warrington and her colleagues described five such cases, one of whom had problems finding the words for non-living things as opposed to living things, and four of whom showed the reverse pattern. One of the latter, for example, could easily define the words *torch* and *helicopter* but failed to recognize the meaning of *camel*, *wasp* or *buttercup*.

There have been subsequent reports of category-specific deficits. Professor Caramazza has described a patient who can name an *abacus* and a *sphinx* but not a *peach* or an *orange*. Professors Antonio and Hanna Damasio investigated two aphasics who could name tools and utensils better than animals, fruits and vegetables. But they had difficulty with the other non-living entities of place-names and musical instruments. Other cases have emerged in which the names of animals are damaged independently of inanimate living things (fruits, vegetables, plants); fruits, vegetables and plants independently of other living or non-living categories; and non-living things independently of both animate and inanimate living things.

The interpretation of these as of other aphasic dissociations remains controversial. Some psychologists suggest that they signal the existence of distinct, dedicated neural mechanisms or structures for distinct mental operations. Others take the reductionist view that the mind is a seamless, all-purpose computational device and that aphasic dissociations are the product of differences in processing complexity or of damage to the sensory and motor cortices where information is received and action planned.

The original theory of category-specific semantic deficits, as developed by Elizabeth Warrington and her colleagues Rosaleen A. McCarthy and Tim Shallice, took the latter position, that conceptual knowledge is organized not by semantic category but by the way things are perceived: information is relayed to the language system either by the senses (sight, smell, touch, taste, hearing) or by considerations about the way an object might be handled and used. Animals and other living things are perceived through the senses, mainly vision, while inanimate non-living objects are perceived according to their function.

Professors Antonio and Hanna Damasio offer a different perspective on category-specific deficits. They describe the neural organization that drives language as consisting of three separate interacting structures. The first is a large collection of systems in both hemispheres that represent 'anything that a person does, perceives, thinks or feels while acting in the world'. These pre-linguistic concepts are categorized and classified in the ways that permit us to organize our perception of ourselves and the world without resort to language. The second system, generally in the classical language centres of the left hemisphere, represents the fundamental building-blocks of language: phonemes, words and syntactic rules. And there is a third, also located in the left hemisphere, which mediates between the first two, acting as a kind of neural broker which selects the words that will best express the concepts, and the sentences that will express the relationship between concepts.

This tripartite division of neural labour would explain why words and concepts can be independently damaged. The Damasios describe an aphasic patient whose cognition and linguistic skills are unimpaired apart from the loss of concepts for certain unique entities previously familiar to him. Faced with a picture of a racoon he recognizes it as an animal but cannot describe its unique characteristics. Other patients, by contrast, can recognize and define any entity from any conceptual category – by sight, by touch, or by a characteristic sound – but cannot always retrieve the word for it. Shown a picture of a racoon, one such aphasic said: 'Oh! I know what it is – it is a nasty animal. It will come and rummage in your backyard and get into the garbage. The eyes and the rings in the tail give it away. I know it, but I cannot say the name.'

Professor Caramazza, considering the problem from a different angle, asks not how but why it is that most category-specific deficits so far reported involve the category of living things, why it is that no single case has yet been observed in which the living and non-living categories were both damaged, and why the words for living things are more frequently impaired than those for non-living things. His conclusion is that we use different neural mechanisms to process animate and inanimate objects: the brain does not organize conceptual knowledge by categories, but in broad semantic domains, which were determined in the course of evolution by the survival value of recognizing and responding to animal and plant life. The evolutionary adaptations that permitted our ancestors to distinguish between animals that are predators and those that are sources of food, and between plants that are edible or poisonous or medicinal, have provided 'the skeletal neural structures around which to organize the rich perceptual, conceptual, and linguistic knowledge modern humans have of these categories'. Because these structures or mechanisms were more recently acquired and are more concentrated in the brain they are more vulnerable to brain damage.

In Professor Caramazza's view the separate concepts of animal, vegetable and artefact are by now innate, in the same way that language itself, according to Noam Chomsky, is innate. And just as toddlers absorb the rules of the language to which they have been exposed, so infants as young as three or four months know instinctively the difference between animate toys and real animals, between, for example, a toy aeroplane and a live bird with its wings outstretched. As further evidence of his theory Caramazza reports three PET studies which compared the brain activity of normal subjects when naming living things and when naming artefacts. Although the studies differed about the specific areas involved there was some overlap; and, as with the experiments cited by Steven Pinker for regular and irregular verbs, they did show that in all the brains under investigation living things and artefacts were processed by distinct neural areas.

Neurological evidence that each of our brains does things in its own way does not necessarily invalidate the fundamental assumption of cognitive neuropsychology, that the modular codes involved in the processing of language are universal. Unlike the boxes and arrows of the nineteenth-century 'diagram makers', which were intended to represent real centres in the cerebral cortex and the neural pathways running between the centres, the boxes and arrows plotted by cognitive neuropsychologists are nothing to do with the physical brain. They represent theories about how information is processed, which can be tested against normal as well as abnormal language.

In their book *Cognitive Neuropsychology*, Elizabeth Warrington and Rosaleen McCarthy explain the relationship between the neurological investigation of brain biology and psychological theories of brain function:

If evidence is available to show that the doubly dissociated deficits in question are the product of damage, or lesions in different sectors of the brain, then it is possible to infer that these areas differ in their processing. More specifically we can conclude that the neurological correlates of particular types of impairment are different. However, it should be noted that even in the absence of precise anatomical or localising information a double dissociation of function still stands in its own right. The question of 'what is impaired' is quite distinct from the question of 'what are the anatomical correlates'.

Cognitive neuropsychology is therefore essentially a hybrid discipline involving neurology and artificial intelligence as well as psychology. The spread of its influence from its British home base to continental Europe and North America has had the beneficial effect of encouraging collaborative research. Although they have different agendas, psychologists who identify impairments of function and neurologists who search for the anatomical correlates are addressing the same problem. 'Laying boxes on brains doesn't work to the extent that they don't map on to what I see when I look into the brain,' says Dr Wise. 'The brain isn't actually wired up like that. But you don't have to smash a radio to grasp the principle of how it works. And can you describe language only in terms of synapses and molecules? No!'

A century and a half after Broca the disciplines that subserve neuropsychology have multiplied and divided. Specialists in robotics, radiology, computer sciences, pharmacology, as well as aphasia therapy, linguistics, psycholinguistics, neurolinguistics, pragmatics, cognitive neuropsychology and the various branches of neurology, which include molecular biology, biophysics, neuroanatomy, neuro-physiology, are collaborators in the great adventure of exploring and mapping the capacity for language that is humanity's greatest and most distinctive achievement. Psychologists, psycholinguists and philosophers develop theories of mind while brain scientists explore the physical organ responsible for the mind. The bottom-up sciences study the molecules and cells. The top-down sciences look at gross brain anatomy and activity.

One of the most ambitious of many ongoing interdisciplinary research programmes is in progress at the University of California at San Diego, which is the capital of American brain research. Here, at the International Aphasia Project, part of the Center for Research in Language, teams of specialists in cognitive science, computer science, communication disorders, developmental psychology, linguistics, neurosciences, paediatrics and psycholinguistics study the effects of brain injury on language and communication across seven different languages.

Some pieces of the jigsaw puzzle are in place, but the picture is far from complete. It is still not known how and where the cerebral ensemble of molecules, cells, synapses, zones and networks adds up to the unique ability of all normal human beings to talk and write to each other. It may be that what the philosopher Galen Strawson calls 'the basic materialist premise' that 'all reality is physical' is a misguided basis for the quest for 'a clear line between the mental and the nonmental' that Strawson, among other philosophers, considers critical for the philosophy of mind. Science and philosophy are still a long way from solving the mind–body problem, even, as Chomsky has pointed out in a recent paper, for very simple neurological systems for which direct experiment is possible:

One of the best studied cases is the neroatode, little worms with a three-day maturation period, with a wiring diagram that is completely analyzed.

It is only very recently that some understanding has been gained of the neural basis of their behaviour, and that remains limited and controversial.

Some scientists fear that the plethora of specialist disciplines threatens to turn aphasiology into a tower of Babel. Some, like the Damasios, are more optimistic:

Considering the profound complexity of language phenomena, some may wonder whether the neural machinery that allows it all to happen will ever be understood . . . Even the structures that form words and sentences, which have been under study since the middle of the 19th century, are only sketchily understood.

Nevertheless, given the recent strides that have been made, we believe these structures will eventually be mapped and understood. The question is not if but when.

Dr Wise's advice is not to hold our breath: 'Every discipline gives a different view, which is correct but limited. There is an ideal conclusion whereby all theories will add up to the explanation. But we are light years away from that. In the meantime all approaches are inadequate, and all are valid.'

10

The Chances of Recovery

The more atypical an individual and the less common his arsenal of skills, the poorer our success at predicting the effects of lesions in his left hemisphere ... The highly skilled musician, painter, athlete, or chess player may, in some cases, perform at an extremely high level after aphasia, while, in other instances, he is reduced to but a shadow of his former capacity.

Howard Gardner, The Shattered Mind

Most group studies agree that chronic aphasics – those who do not improve significantly within the first six to nine weeks – will not make much further recovery. But group studies of aphasia are usually misleading. Many chronic aphasics do in fact regain language, but not until months or years after they were statistically written off. All brains, healthy or damaged, change with time and experience. Our brains are programmed, within the constraints of our cerebral hardware, by the way we use them; but the changes do not necessarily occur in nine weeks. In a lecture addressed to the British aphasia charity, Speakability, in the autumn of 2000, Professor Steven Small, a neurologist at the University of Chicago, made the point: 'The brain changes with experience and with stroke recovery. Normal experience that we all get every day changes the brain, as does the experience one gets after having a stroke.' Professor Small told his audience about Vicky, who first consulted him when she was forty-two, twenty-five years after she had had a stroke, which had resulted in paralysis of the left limbs and mutism. Vicky had been told by her doctor to 'hang it up': she would never again walk or talk; she must not think of having children. She refused the advice, made a good recovery, and by the time she met Professor Small she was working as a nurse. Although she still found reading difficult, batteries of standardized tests showed that she was no longer aphasic.

After his stroke in 1825 Professor Jacques Lordat endured weeks of sadness and frustration at not being able to read, then suddenly found that he could read the title of a book on his library shelves, *Works of Hippocrates*. From then on his 'education' was slow, but he recovered, returned to an active career as a scholar and writer, and died in 1870 at the age of ninety-eight laden with honours. Douglas Ritchie could not speak or write for a year after his stroke; but was still improving when he wrote his great book five years later, using what he estimated to be 40–60 per cent of his former command of language. Robert Bolt wrote, with help, the script for the film *The Missionary* after recovering from deep aphasia. Sue Gilpin, a head teacher in an English comprehensive school who was severely aphasic after a stroke in 1987, subsequently gained an MA in education and is now an active worker in the cause of aphasia; as is the Marquis of Tavistock, who had a near-fatal cerebral haemorrhage in his forties ... The world is full of recovered aphasics who appear so normal that you would not immediately guess that they have a problem with language.

Aphasia can leave in its wake traces that are merely bizarre. Guy Wint recovered everything except one word: he could never again find the word for hedgehog, which always came out as *chairhorse*. A Norwegian woman, who lost her speech after an injury to her left skull during a bombing raid on Oslo in 1941, was left with severe 'Broca's' aphasia for two years before she recovered – but with a German accent. She had never been out of Norway, and had never met a German, but the accent was so convincing that she was shunned as an enemy alien. In 1999 a Yorkshire woman who had never been to France and spoke no French recovered with a charming French accent. When she gave an interview on the radio even French listeners could not believe she was not a native of France.

Although every recovery seems to differ as much as every aphasia, in most cases language remains difficult, and chronic aphasics come to accept that they will probably never again be entirely at ease with words. The American actress Patricia Neal, after prolonged work with Valerie Eaton Griffith, made a number of successful movies;

but continuing word-finding difficulties obliged her to keep live appearances to a minimum. Sometimes the sense that language is not flowing normally is largely subjective. A recovered aphasic who seems highly articulate in conversation may continue to feel at a loss for words. C. Scott Moss, an American clinical psychologist who suffered a stroke in 1967, made tapes of himself as he recovered which were later transcribed into a book, *Recovery with Aphasia* (1972). Although the transcripts reveal no problems with language Moss insists in them that he is not as fluent as before his stroke.

One of the most moving documented recoveries is described by Alexander Luria in his book *The Man with a Shattered World* (1972), which tells the story of a Russian scientist by the name of Zasetsky whose left brain was extensively damaged by a head wound in the battle of Smolensk in 1943. In the first years of his illness Zasetsky's disabilities were so severe that he could not remember his home town when he returned to it. He lost awareness of the existence of the right side of his body and could not see the right side of any scene or object. He suffered, like Alice in Wonderland, from a shifting sense of his own size, sometimes feeling very tall, sometimes very tiny. He never learned to read without immense difficulty, but eventually discovered, with the help of therapists and friendly doctors, that he could express himself, albeit with effort and only partial success, in writing. For the next twenty-five years he worked every day on a diary in which he portrayed for posterity the extraordinary fragmented world into which he had been plunged by brain damage.

Some aphasics recover within a few days: the episode remains for them nothing more than a passing nightmare. Those as seriously affected as John may never recover. Or they may make better recoveries than aphasics whose symptoms were initially milder. Or they may recover some but not other aspects of language: comprehension often returns before speech; writing has been known to return many years after loss of speech. Usually there is some spontaneous improvement by the end of the second week, as the turmoil in the brain begins to subside and neurones that have been temporarily damaged by swelling and by chemical and metabolic changes throughout the brain begin to revive. Some aphasics will be back to normal, or near normal, by the nine-week deadline. After six months progress will probably but not necessarily slow down. It may, or may not, continue indefinitely; in some cases in fits and starts, in others slowly and steadily.

Recovery depends on a multitude of factors, of which, for adults, the extent and distribution of the lesions is the most significant. Children who lose all or most of their left hemispheres are usually able to learn or regain language to normal or near-normal standards. After adolescence that degree of plasticity declines, but, perhaps surprisingly, there is no evidence that old age is in itself a deterrent, although with advancing years recovery may be compromised by other unrelated conditions. In the majority of right-handed adults the more widespread the destruction of the left hemisphere, and the more numerous the deficits, the less likely is complete recovery. Nevertheless, two strokes that look very similar on a CAT or MRI scan may have very different outcomes. 'Scans don't conform to symptoms,' says Dr Wise, 'because every brain is unique, and because we are unlikely to have a baseline scan of the pre-morbid brain. There are always wildcards. And plasticity is an unknown factor.'

Behavioural and neural plasticity is one of the crucial issues in modern cognitive neurobiology. When I first consulted Dr Wise four years after John's stroke he told me that he had chosen to specialize in aphasia

because language always has the potential for recovery. In 99 per cent of aphasics the processing of language is damaged, but the memory for language is retained. I have seen spectacular late recoveries that could not have been anticipated. Aphasia is neurologically interesting because nobody understands how late recovery happens. The big question is how some patients recover language processing with a hole in their heads.

Depending on the extent and site of the lesion, the brain seems to recover from unilateral injury in one of two ways. Where the damaged area is small and circumscribed, cells that have been stunned but not killed outright may revive, neuronal sprouting may occur around the edges of the lesion, or redundant neurones within the same system may be brought into play. If the lesion is more extensive and deeper the brain may reorganize itself, adopting for language purposes systems or areas outside the language centres, either elsewhere in the left hemisphere, in the right hemisphere, or both.

Dr Wise showed me the scans of an aphasic woman in her forties who had made an unexpected recovery from a very severe aphasia. She was left with only one remaining handicap: although quick-witted she spoke very slowly and took an abnormally long time to take her turn in conversation. Dr Wise's interpretation of her brain scans was that some of her language processing had been transferred to the right hemisphere, and needed extra time to make contact with the semantic system.

Paul Broca and after him John Hughlings Jackson saw no reason why brain damaged adults should not be able to transfer language to the homologous regions of the right hemisphere. (It was after all the appearance of hemispheric symmetry that had made Mark Dax and Broca suspicious of their own evidence of functional assymetry.) Nevertheless, for successive neuropsychologists the left brain, the seat of language and analytical thought that distinguish us from animals, was 'dominant'; and in the absence of any technical means of investigating the brains of recovering aphasics, the right brain was considered to be mute.

Hughlings Jackson was aware that the right brain played a greater role than the left in emotional recognition, emotional language and visuospatial skills. Nevertheless, it was not until nearly a century after Broca had located language in the left hemisphere that the right brain began to come into its own. Thanks to increasingly sophisticated research into the different anatomical and functional properties of the two hemispheres, aphasiologists now have more insight into the role played by the right hemisphere both in normal language and in recovery of language.

The first demonstration that the two hemispheres are not, in fact, anatomically symmetrical was produced in 1968, when Norman Geschwind and Walter Levitsky examined 100 brains at post-mortem. They found, among a number of differences, that the classic 'Wernicke's' area was larger on the left in 65, larger on the right in

11, and equal in 24. The findings have subsequently been confirmed by brain imaging, which has revealed other asymmetries; for example, in right-handers the occipital lobe at the back of the head which receives visual information is usually wider on the left whereas the frontal lobe is wider on the right, while in left-handers the situation is often reversed. Such findings do not, however, explain why more than 95 per cent of us will lose some language after damage to the left language zone, or why some, but not others, may with time adapt to the loss, possibly by involving our non-dominant hemispheres.

The two halves of the brain are connected by nerve fibres, the neocortical commissures, which act rather like telephone lines, carrying messages back and forth so rapidly and smoothly that we are not aware of which hemisphere is doing what. The corpus callosum, which is the main inter-cerebral pathway, consists of more than 200 million nerve fibres – which is at least 200 times as many as the optic nerve. If it is damaged, the patient is likely to suffer from one of the disconnection syndromes. If it is severed altogether the two brains become independent of one another and can no longer communicate and pool information received by the senses.

Scientific evidence that the right hemisphere can, in fact, produce and understand language followed the discovery by neurosurgeons in the 1950s that epilepsy in patients who were unresponsive to other treatments could be controlled by an operation that severs the corpus callosum. Commissurectomy, severing the corpus callosum, provided human guinea pigs for experiments designed to discover how each hemisphere works in isolation. The psychobiologist Roger Sperry, who won the Nobel Prize for his work with split-brain animals and human volunteers in 1981, devised a technique for addressing visual information exclusively to one or the other hemisphere. While the volunteers focused their eyes on a dot in the centre of a screen images were flashed to the right or left of the dot just long enough for the image to be registered but not long enough for a person to shift both eyes in order to bring it into focus, thus sending it to both hemispheres. When the images were flashed to the right eye, entering the left hemisphere, the volunteers could name them. When they were flashed to the left eye, and therefore to the right hemisphere, they denied seeing anything. The inference was that the normal right brain is mute.

But a second wave of experiments with split-brain patients, by Michael Gazzaniga, then at the University of California, and Joseph LeDoux of New York University, led to a different conclusion. Many of their experiments confirmed Sperry's findings: the volunteers could read printed words addressed by the right eye to the left hemisphere but not vice versa. But a few patients showed evidence of linguistic ability in both hemispheres. The most striking case was that of PS, a fifteen-year-old boy who had suffered from neurological problems since early childhood. After his corpus callosum was cut he was still able to understand with his right hemisphere. Two years after the operation he began to use his right brain to spell out words with Scrabble tiles (using his left hand) and for limited speech. When the question of what he wanted to do when he graduated was addressed to his left hemisphere alone, he replied that he wanted to be a draughtsman and was already training for that career. When the same question was put exclusively to his right hemisphere, he spelled out with Scrabble letters the words: 'AUTOMOBILE RACE[R]'. The words – the first verbal message known to have emanated under laboratory conditions from the right hemisphere – indicated that some split-brain patients have more bilateral or reversed representation of language than normal people.

There are now plenty of documented cases of split-brain patients with some right-hemisphere language. And just as PS's right-brained preference for a more dangerous and glamorous career than the one planned by his sensible left brain demonstrated how different were the personalities and aspirations of the two halves of his brain, so the French psychologist Jean-Luc Nespoulous and colleagues cite evidence from split-brain patients that the two brains express themselves in different ways. 'Modalizing' language – that is, language largely confined to describing the speaker's impressions, as when confronted by an abstract painting ('It seems to me . . . I like . . . It reminds me of . . .') – is sometimes retained in the right brain after severing of the corpus callosum, as indeed it sometimes is in aphasia; while 'referential' language ('It is a painting of a horse') seems to be the prerogative of the dominant hemisphere.

The usual explanation for right-hemisphere language in split-brain patients is that critical damage to the left-hemisphere language areas at an early age, when the brain is still very plastic, has encouraged development of language in the non-dominant hemisphere. Some neuropsychologists, until recently, have maintained that 'hemispheric switching' can take place only in children. The good news for aphasics is that there is now multiple evidence that in some adult, even elderly, aphasics the right brain can after all mediate in the recovery of language. Aphasics who make good recovery of auditory comprehension show a significant increase in right-hemisphere blood flow. When the right hemispheres of recovering aphasics are put to sleep with injections of sodium amytal the patients often lose language again for as long as the effects of the barbiturate last. In some patients recovery seems to be a dynamic process in which language that has been transferred to the right hemisphere eventually returns to undamaged areas of the left.

Bilaterals like me are more vulnerable to aphasia, because it can be caused by a stroke in either hemisphere, but are for the same reason better equipped for recovery. Dr Wise, on the basis of scanning experiments with aphasics and normal controls, has concluded that, although most right brains carry only a pale, distorted copy of the neural mechanisms necessary for language, lateralization for language varies more from person to person than was previously supposed. 'Some people', he says, 'are strongly lateralized on one side, others seem to distribute language between the two hemispheres.' Without a baseline scan of the pre-morbid brain, however, it is hard to assess whether recovering aphasics are maximizing pre-existing language capacities in the right brain or whether their recovery is the result of hemispheric switching.

However we lateralize language, the contribution of the non-dominant hemisphere to higher cognitive functions and the expression of meaning can no longer be discounted. While the hand postures of sign language or the tonal shifts and emphases that change meaning in some verbal languages may be lost after left-hemisphere damage, affective language – the prosody and emotional gesturing that are so intact in John – is the prerogative of the right hemisphere. Some researchers have suggested that the functional organization of affective language in the right hemisphere mirrors that of the formal propositional language in the left. The observation that damage to the right hemisphere can cause a range of 'aprosodic' symptoms that seem to parallel aphasic deficits has given rise to the notion of a propositional language of the face, voice and body. People who suffer right-brain strokes are often deprived of the ability to express feeling or underlying meaning that may alter, emphasize or contradict the spoken word.

Howard Gardner, writing in *The Shattered Mind*, has described right-brain patients as 'reminiscent of language machines, automatons responsive to the literal meaning of messages but appreciative of neither subtle nuances nor the non-linguistic context in which the message was issued'. Some, like the patient who, when Gardner asked how long he had been in hospital, said he couldn't tell because he wasn't wearing a watch when he arrived, become alarmingly literal minded: they lose what Goldstein described as 'abstract attitude'. The man in Don de Lillo's novel *The Body Artist* who cannot communicate 'outside the bare acoustics' could have suffered right-brain damage.

The discovery that the right brain is in its way as crucial as the left, and the revelation that we are all split personalities, controlled by two cerebral worlds as different as those on either side of Alice's looking-glass, has not been lost on philosophers, journalists and writers of popular science. Marshall McLuhan, the prolific Canadian pioneer of media analysis – who, ironically, was silenced at the end of his life by aphasia – was obsessed by the differences between the sequential, analytical operation of the left brain and the simultaneous, intuitive grasp of the right. Social anthropologists have been known to blame the communicative and strategic skills of the left brain on our imperialist, materialist, unfeeling, 'logocentric' Western society. There are books and training courses that advise us on how we can get in touch with our gentle, dreamy, emotional, imaginative, artistic, intuitive, more Oriental right-brained selves. (Betty Edwards's book *Drawing on the Right Side of the Brain* is a perennial best-seller.) Some big corporations hire psychologists to test employees for right- or left-brainedness in order to slot them into appropriate jobs. Humourless people like tax inspectors who cannot see the woods for the trees favour their left brains; London taxi drivers have well-developed right brains.

The right brain is indeed, as Hughlings Jackson predicted, better at making sense of the visual world. It is better than the left at making fine colour discriminations, at depth perception, at guessing new patterns from just a few details, at helping you find your way around – all capabilities at which John excels. Anyone who imagines that aphasics are stupid should try the visuospatial test given to John by one of Dr Wise's researchers. John's score, eleven out of twelve, was well above average (and well above mine). While the left brain is programmed to manage the sequenced analysis of familiar material, the right is the source of jokes, metaphor, lateral thinking, Gestalt. It is more intuitive, more perceptive of nuance and non-verbal signals; better at social behaviour. The right brain is essential for the appreciation of music, especially of tone and pitch. Patients with right-brain damage are more likely to suffer from denial or lack of awareness of paralysed limbs. They may lose their sense of direction; their enjoyment of music, poetry, the visual arts; their sense of humour – the qualities that continue to give John and his friends such pleasure.

While patients with right-brain damage can be socially handicapped by their inability to give and receive non-verbal signals, aphasics with intact right brains may become remarkably sensitive to the propositional language of the face. A research project, published in *Nature*, tested the lie-detecting abilities of aphasics whose comprehension was limited to single words. Watching silent films of the faces of people concealing powerful emotions and of people honestly revealing positive emotions, the aphasics were able to detect insincerity 73 per cent of the time, as compared to the control group of fifty-eight normals and ten patients with right-hemisphere damage which identified only 50 per cent of lying faces. This doesn't surprise me. John, who was always observant, is now uncannily perceptive, and can often predict, before they know it themselves, who will marry or start an affair with whom; who, before they have said a word about it, is pregnant, or about to divorce or leave their job. I have given up trying to fool him with even the smallest white lie.

But although music, art and architecture are probably right-brain functions in amateurs, professionals engage their left brains as well

because all complex rule-based disciplines seem to require its partici-
pation. And in the last decades of the twentieth century research by
the California-based psycholinguist Ursula Bellugi and her colleagues demonstrated that all non-verbal languages – whether communicated by the hands, as in American Sign Language, or by rise
and fall of vocal pitch as in 'tone languages' such as Mandarin
Chinese and Taiwanese, which have tone as a property of each vowel
– are processed in the same way as languages that rely on words,
and are equally vulnerable to left-hemisphere damage.

But there is a caveat: hemispheric specialization is not phylogen-
etically fixed. Just as some brains adapt better than others to the
inevitable but gradual loss of neurological tissue that is part of the
ageing process, so some mature brains are more plastic than others,
better able to reorganize, and perhaps regenerate, after sudden focal
damage to either hemisphere. It is well known, for example, that
the blind become more acutely responsive to touch and sound
than sighted people. Ursula Bellugi, working in collaboration with
molecular biologists and radiologists, has found that deaf children
– and the hearing children of deaf parents – who learn sign language
develop special visual skills in a part of the left brain that is normally
used for auditory recognition. They have allocated the zone usually
dedicated to the abstraction of meaning from the continuous flow
of speech sounds to processing instead the interpretation of visual
signals articulated in space. Oliver Sacks describes this outcome of
Bellugi's work as 'one of the most astonishing demonstrations of the
plasticity of the nervous system'.

I would not be surprised if many of us, without being aware of it,
have learned, and then adapted neurologically, to compensate for
some inborn cognitive deficit. I, for example, have no innate sense
of direction. For as long as I can remember I have realized that other
people have an instinct for finding their way around that I lack.
Perhaps my disability may be related in some way to the bilateral
processing of language that Dr Wise discovered? Whatever the
neurological explanation, I finally discovered, while living with John
in Venice, that I could compensate for my embarrassing mental
deficit by memorizing directions and landmarks verbally as I moved
about the tortuous routes of the city. I now do this, almost unconsci-

ously, wherever I am. I remember the way by recalling a sequence of named landmarks: the yellow house, the broken sign, the news-agent on the north-west corner, the sharp bend in the road. I know that I will never be able to find my way around as efficiently as people whose normal right brains give them an instinctive sense of direction. Still, I've learned how to compensate well enough to have written a guidebook to Venice, in which the suggested walks are, I'm told, appreciated for the detail and clarity of the verbal directions.

Some recovered aphasics describe similar compensatory strat-egies, but in reverse: they invent imaginary spaces in which to locate lost words. Nancy Kerr taught herself to picture little boxes in her brain, each box containing a category: colours, numbers, days of the week, body parts, and so on. It did not always work at first: some-times, searching for the word red, she would say yellow or green. Once when trying to compliment a student on his shiny hair, she heard herself saying, 'Your penis is so shiny.' But later in her rehabili-tation, she discovered another visual trick, which helped her with organizing sentences. She began to visualize sentences as diagrams, as she had been taught when learning grammar in school: 'a light went on in the darkest spot in my brain . . . the "picture" part of my brain connected to the "language" part. Now I had a new road to replace the damaged pathways that I had used before.' Within a week she had composed a paper for publication, which contained sentences so complex that she did not try to concieve diagrams of them.

A British aphasic, Robin Jones, has described how he imagined that he was 'standing in the middle of his brain, looking up':

It is a very integrated, complicated mass, it's huge, it's daunting. But some-where in there, there's the bits that make it possible for me to do, or not do, things and some of which is damaged. THIS I know.

I must search in it. I imagine that the mass is now an empty office block with no lights and I am standing at the bottom and have to get in. In my mind I do this, and systematically walk along corridors looking at the doors. I am searching for the room which contains words. After tremendous effort, I find a room where there are hundreds of thousands of words. It is like any office room but has been completely wrecked – the file of words is scattered everywhere, which was why I couldn't find them before. The floor is covered in words. Every word I ever learnt or knew is in that room and I realise that I have to clear them up. I sweep the whole lot down an imaginary hole, then build some imaginary shelves and on the shelf I put the words I used to know. I can still remember them, but not in alphabetical order or anything like that . . .

There was a fine line between sanity and insanity and between imagination and the fact that the strength required to stay on the right side of both was enormous. It was also frightening because in some of the corridors there were doors I didn't want to open. I had a feeling about them . . .

I mean, just imagine the excitement of doing this. Lying there, going through the brain, individual cells! To me this is not imagination but fact . . .

Well, it's funny because you don't read it. You *know* what is in there. None of it is numbered or tagged, you know exactly what is in the file . . .

You know, it's your own thing. You're locked up in your brain with it. But I've always loved work, *loved* work.

For most recovered aphasics language will probably never again be instinctive. They may sometimes or always have to wait for words to come or search for them using mnemonic strategies. The American aphasic C. Scott Moss said that the difference between a normal person and an aphasic is that the normal person thinks mainly about what he wants to say while the recovered aphasic must attend consciously to the task of finding the right words. 'It was so hard to write,' wrote the Russian aphasic Zasetsky in his journal:

At last I'd turned up a good idea. So I began to hunt for words to describe it and finally I thought up two. But by the time I got to the third word, I was stuck . . . What a torture it was . . . Finally I managed to write a sentence expressing an idea I had . . . sometimes I'll sit over a page for a week or two . . . But I don't want to give it up. I want to finish what I've begun. So I sit at my desk all day sweating over each word.

There will be days when the effort to speak or write feels like trying to communicate in an unfamiliar foreign language. But there may be better days when an aphasic can write well enough to describe the experience, scarcely imaginable to those of us who take words so much for granted, of losing and gradually regaining them. For the many who have fallen foul of premature triage it is rarely too late for rehabilitation:

Like any venture, be it playing a ball game, taking advantage of a business opportunity, creating a work of art, or earning a college degree, rehabilitation takes time, effort, support, and stamina to keep on going, even when things get tough. There are no guarantees, but the work can be fulfilling and the rewards great.

That was written by Nancy Kerr, the American rehabilitation psychologist who has been on both sides of the rehabilitation process, five years after her stroke.

The Search for a Cure

Now when thou findest that man speechless, his relief shall be sitting; soften his head with grease, [and] pour milk into both his ears.

An ancient Egyptian surgeon,
the Edwin Smith papyrus, c. 2800 BC

It's easy to smile at the nostrums of previous ages: milk poured by Egyptian doctors into the ears of aphasic patients, grease applied to their heads; the mixture of aromatic carbonate and aloes that Dr Johnson's physician applied, along with a blister-inducing preparation of dried Spanish flies, to the throat of his distinguished patient.

Today the giant multinational pharmaceutical companies spend a large proportion of their budgets on researching and manufacturing chemicals that affect the brain. Drugs have been developed that relieve or delay the symptoms of depression, multiple sclerosis, Parkinson's and Alzheimer's diseases. In the last fifty years or so many drugs have been tried on aphasics: they include caffeine to stimulate the central nervous system, and barbiturates to tranquillize it. Since as many as 70 to 80 per cent of aphasics suffer from depression, particularly in the first weeks and again after the first year, modern anti-depressants can at least help release the motivation that is an important, if unquantifiable, factor in recovery. There is, however, no pill that will restore the flow of language once the damage is done.

Dr Wise believes that a pharmacotherapy for chronic aphasia is, or could be, on the horizon. Clot-busting drugs, which can prevent the damage altogether if administered within three hours, are, as he says, useless for the majority of patients – at least in countries like Britain with rundown public health care – who do not reach suitably equipped and staffed hospitals in time. Under those circumstances it would be better, in his opinion, to focus research on drugs that repair the damage, probably by stimulating unaffected cortical areas. Why then are there no large-scale, well-controlled trials for possible drugs? Stroke, after all, is the main cause of disability world-wide. Apart from the human suffering it causes, it is a hugely expensive burden on hospital and social services.

Dr Wise gives three reasons: animal trials don't work for aphasia because animals don't have language; neurologists and neuro-psychiatrists don't lobby for human trials because they are by and large uninterested in stroke; and pharmaceutical companies are in any case reluctant to mount expensive trials of likely drugs that are old, cheap, or out of patent and would not therefore return a reasonable profit.

In the absence of hard evidence from large-scale trials it is difficult to evaluate the possible risks and benefits of drugs for aphasia; but some do seem to help some patients if combined with intense clinical therapy. Low doses of amphetamine ignite stunned cells throughout the brain and rouse them to forge new connections, combating tiredness and making things seem more interesting. (Rats with induced strokes walk again within twenty-four hours after a single dose.) The downside of amphetamines is that they are addictive for humans and can over-stimulate the heart.

Bromocriptine, which releases stored dopamine, is effective for Parkinson's and may also work for post-stroke motor problems, but the evidence for its impact on language is slight. There is a theory that Aricept, a drug that ameliorates the symptoms of Alzheimer's, might also improve synaptic connections in victims of vascular dementia. Studies since the early 1970s have suggested that Pirace-tam, which seems to restore the fluidity of cell membranes and stimulate microcirculation in the brain, improves reading ability and comprehension in dyslexic children and memory in elderly patients. Piracetam is now popular in Germany and Holland. Specialists in Britain and America are less convinced by it and it is not prescribed in either country. The latest *Cochrane Review* concludes that although it may be of some help there are concerns about its safety.

Although there is no pill that cures aphasia, and none that seems to help at all unless combined with high-level therapy, there are routinely prescribed medications that can actually impede recovery by interfering with neuroreceptors – catecholamine, monoamine and cholinergic – that are concentrated in brain regions involved in language and memory. They include drugs an aphasic patient may be taking for other conditions, such as diabetes, high blood pressure, epilepsy, or sleeplessness. Drugs such as clonidine and prazosin that inhibit the brain's production of noradrenalin, a neurotransmitter important for brain function and the autonomic nervous system that regulates blood pressure, are among those for which substitutes should be found. Research into the negative effects of pharmacology is in its early stages and may not have revealed more than the tip of the iceberg. If so the pharmaceutical industry may after all have a contribution to make to aphasics by identifying products that seem to have baleful side-effects.

Because the behaviour of neuronal cells is better understood than the chemistry of neurotransmission, cellular biology is likely to offer a more fruitful approach to the rectification of brain damage. Since before the discovery of the structure of DNA in 1953 biologists have been tracking the problem of how one fertilized cell divides in nine months into a baby consisting of many million millions of specialized cells that constitute all the differentiated tissues that make up a human being. The decoding of the human genome at the end of the twentieth century will bring the answer closer.

The outcome of the first major trial of implanted foetal cells as a possible cure for Parkinson's disease was reported in 2001. Patients over sixty did not benefit, and 15 per cent of younger patients suffered from disastrous side-effects. The implanted cells appeared to have grown too well and to be producing excessive amounts of dopamine, which caused uncontrolled movements worse than the disease itself. Some patients, however, did benefit. And the discovery that grafted foetal cells seem to have the innate capacity to migrate to a site where they are needed, to differentiate into the appropriate mix of cell types and encourage weak cells to grow or integrate with existing undamaged cells, has implications for the treatment of other neurological diseases, including focal brain damage. Despite the disappointing results of the Parkinson's trial, the theory behind the implantation technique, which is to encourage regeneration by 're-seeding' the brain, remains valid.

In the spring of 2002 the first licences were granted in Great Britain to use early human embryos consisting of about a hundred cells to create 'stem cells', the master cells of the different tissues of the body. The researchers use only 'surplus' embryos – those resulting from IVF treatment, which would have been discarded anyway. Cell lines will be deposited in a national stem cell bank expected to be operational by early 2003. The implications for stroke, Parkinson's and cardiovascular diseases, which are now otherwise untreatable or poorly treated, are particularly exciting.

Until the early 1980s it was a fundamental principle of neuro-science that neurones differ from other cells: that sophisticated animals like humans are born with a supply of brain cells that are never renewed and if destroyed cannot replace themselves. (It is this received wisdom that underlies the pessimistic advice given by so many doctors who insist that significant recovery from stroke is not possible after two years at the most.) The dictum that the brain cannot renew itself was finally successfully challenged in the last decades of the twentieth century, when Fernando Nottebohm, a zoologist at Rockefeller University in New York, observed that some songbirds – the only animals who attempt to communicate vocally in the way humans do – change their songs with each season. He speculated that neurones carrying old patterns were being exchanged for new ones. After bearing much ridicule from the scientific community, he surprised even himself: an experiment that involved labelling the birds' brain cells with a radioactive molecule demon-strated that old birds as well as young ones were indeed producing thousands of new cells each day.

Neurogenesis has been one of the most exciting and controversial areas of scientific research in the last twenty years or so. It is now generally accepted that new neurones are generated continuously in some parts of the adult brain. And there is strong evidence that primitive neural stem cells continue to divide in the human brain even into old age. The existence of small reservoirs of stem cells capable of dividing and differentiating may explain why, under certain circumstances, the brain repairs its own damaged tissue. The challenge now is to find ways of encouraging neurogenesis in brain areas that have been damaged, perhaps by extracting new primitive cells, cloning them and implanting them where they are needed.

Although the prediction of success with implants is now about three decades, and re-implanting of naturally produced stem cells has not yet been tried, other experiments are underway. In February 1999 scientists at the University of Pittsburgh Medical Center reported the first experiments with a pioneering technique of transplanting laboratory-grown neuronal cells into the brains of stroke survivors. The cells were taken from human tumour tissue, which was manipulated in the laboratory to produce differentiated, non-dividing neurones. It was the first time laboratory-grown adult cells had been transplanted into human brains, and the first attempt to treat stroke with a nerve-cell implant. The trial was besieged by volunteer human guinea pigs. Its purpose was to determine only whether the procedure was safe, which it seemed to be, although patients did not report much benefit in the short term.

In the autumn of 2001 a group of scientists based in Oxford and London announced, in a letter to *Nature*, the discovery of a gene, FOXP2, 'involved in the developmental process that culminates in speech and language'. In an article in the same issue Steven Pinker wrote that 'the discovery of a language gene is among the first fruits of the Human Genome Project for the cognitive sciences'. Science is still a long way from translating genetic codes into practical ways of implanting progenitor cells that will repair or replace damaged or dead neuronal tissue. Nevertheless, the identification of a 'language gene' allowed Pinker to 'imagine unprecedented lines of future research'. And the editors of *Nature*, a journal not given to irresponsible speculation, illustrated his article with a cartoon of a pig speaking to a farmer. The pig says, 'What's for dinner? . . . Not me, I hope?' The farmer says: 'That's the one that received the human gene implant.'

Implanted hardware – electrodes or microchips – is another line of research. Parkinson's patients already show benefit from an operation that introduces electronic probes deep into the brain. A battery installed in the chest like a pacemaker sends a low-voltage current into the surrounding tissue. The stimulation seems to simulate the effects of dopamine, in ways that are not entirely understood. Parkinson's, however, is an easier subject for implants than the complications of stroke because it is known exactly what has gone wrong in the brains of Parkinson's patients, and where. Stroke is an altogether messier condition. The full extent of the damage cannot be determined even by the most up-to-date technology. Computerized imaging can locate focal damage very precisely; it can indicate the sites that are activated by cognitive tasks. Imaging, however, is not yet nearly sophisticated enough to chart all the circuits that are generated by the thousand million synapses in every tiny pea-sized piece of cerebral cortex.

Brain circuits can, however, be simulated by artificial neural networks, which model the brain like a computer according to binary mathematics. Neural nets can already do a lot of what the living brain does, and much faster, although not in the same way. They can, for example, learn as a child does that English has rules that have exceptions. The implantation of silicone chips programmed to take over the jobs of lost or interrupted circuits is theoretically possible – if the technical problem of integrating them with the electrical-chemical system of the living brain can be solved. That won't happen in John's lifetime, which is perhaps fortunate, because I am not certain what I would decide if faced with the possibility of trading in my husband, brain-damaged and all, for a cyborg.

Just as Broca didn't know about cell division, which wasn't discovered for nearly forty years after his discovery of the language centres, we don't know what's coming. One day surgeons will be able to reach into the brain and re-seed damaged areas or switch on genes capable of re-growing lost cells or replace them with spare parts more easily than they can now transplant skin or internal organs. Whether it will take years, decades, or centuries nobody can be sure.

Meanwhile, there are a few certainties about the treatment of aphasic patients. Aphasics whose brains are challenged and kept active do better than those who are left sitting in front of the television. Nottebohm has discovered that animals living in the wild, whose brains are continuously challenged by the problems of survival, produce more new neurones than animals in captivity. And it seems likely that the mental stimulation of coping with the problems of ordinary daily life encourages neurogenesis in humans also. An aphasic who takes part, as far as possible, in normal social activities, daily responsibilities, planning and decision-making will be better able to rebuild morale and self-confidence, better motivated to devise alternative ways of communicating; and may have a better chance at regaining at least some language. Music and art can be therapeutic as well as promoting well-being; and aphasics can learn about managing and improving their condition from one another.

The temptation to treat an aphasic patient like an incompetent child is very great, and it is a mistake made by many well-meaning friends, relatives and nurses. Another is to fill embarrassing silences by doing all the talking. Aphasics, like everybody else, will learn better from trying than listening. However senseless an aphasic's utterances or apparently limited his/her comprehension of words, aphasia is not the same thing as deaf-mutism: shouting won't help. Most aphasics are if anything more intuitive than normal people. Those with reduced comprehension of language are able to understand the gist of what is being said, and quickly become extremely sensitive to tone of voice and body language.

To expose an adult whose ability to answer back is trapped in an otherwise intact mind to sarcasm or condescension is a form of bullying. People who address aphasics in baby talk or in a falsetto voice or in the first person plural – as in, How are we today? – may have the best of intentions, but can provoke justified rage. Here is Douglas Ritchie remembering his reaction to a well-meaning motherly nurse when he was speechless and physically helpless in hospital after his stroke in the 1950s:

[One of the nurses], a middle-aged woman whose heart was over-flowing with love and kindness towards me, I could not bear in the room, even for a moment. In the first days in the nursing home I was grateful to her for her constant waiting on me. But she got into the habit of talking baby-talk to me. I think that was the beginning of it. Every time there was a knock on the door, her head peeped sideways and she would say 'Peep-bo' or something like that. If I left a tray of food with some cakes on it or a plate of tapioca – which to me has a disgusting taste and a more repulsive appearance – she said: 'Naughty boy! He must finish his tapioca. It's good for him.' Once she even tried to make me eat some custard, holding the spoon. My sickly smile refused to come on my face on this occasion and she said: 'Temper, temper!' . . .

I went madder still because I could not express myself. I waved towards the window – and I must now have given the nurse the feeling that I was going to throw her out of the window if she gave me the chance to get hold of her – and she shot out of the room . . .

Of the other nurses, one was my favourite because of her efficiency and because her sense of humour appealed to me; and next to her was a good-looking woman – alas, I did not get her normally – and a temporary nurse, who was very kind and did not embarrass me because I could not speak.

Arthur Kopit, who in the 1970s spent months in an American rehabilitation centre researching his play *Wings*, must have seen similar scenes there:

Through the screens, upstage, we see a nurse bringing on a tray of food.
NURSE (*brightly*): Okay ups-a-girl, ups-a-baby, dinnertime! Oo Open wide now, mustn't go dribble-dribble – at's-a-way!
Mrs Stilson screams, swings her arms in fury. In the distance, upstage, the tray of food goes flying.
MRS STILSON (*screaming*): Out! Take this shit away. I don't want it! Someone get me out of here!

Robin Jones, in an interview published in *Speaking Up*, the newsletter of the charity Speakability, gives this advice:

It must be very frustrating for those caring for patients like me to watch them try to make sentences that are meaningless. But by talking in a natural way you help them to fit words together again. It is the best thing you can do even if it doesn't seem much good at the time. It reassures the patient that they are not insane and gives them a sense of normality . . .

The worst thing for me was when people treated me in a different manner and kept repeating things as though I was an idiot.

Many aphasics prefer one-to-one conversation with a full view of the other person's face. But everyone is different – John, from the beginning, was entirely at ease in chattering groups of friends. Like Douglas Ritchie he was frustrated by his own inability to keep conversation going with subtle jokes and was grateful to people who didn't curb their sense of humour. This is one of John's favourite passages from Douglas Ritchie's account of his own stroke:

It was the little things, the jokes that are legitimate but should not go on too long, the interruption that must be made but not so that the narrator loses track of his story, that were annoying me. A visitor would tell me of his adventures . . . I had a great desire to say something, either asking something or being rude in a jolly way or being congratulatory, and my wife, seeing that, would start 'Twenty Questions'.

Amateur volunteers – and, alas, some older or inexperienced speech and language therapists as well – often make the mistake of assuming that childish tasks must be easier for aphasics than more complex cognitive challenges, or that an aphasic who cannot repeat *ma* or *da*, or write a three-letter word for a domestic animal beginning with 'c' must be stupid, uncooperative or too badly brain-damaged to be worth further treatment. There used to be a school of thought that the re-education of aphasics should progress from easy to more difficult tasks. The 'didactic school' of aphasia therapy (rather like the French education system) emphasized repetition, copying out written texts and learning by heart. But aphasia is not like a return to infancy, and most professional aphasia therapists have abandoned the more naïve tenets of the didactic method, one of which is that there is a hierarchy of difficulty that applies to all aphasics.

Another school of therapy that has now been largely abandoned was derived from behaviourist psychology. Carrot-and-stick methods were used with the intention of modifying 'bad' language behaviour and reinforcing 'good'. An extreme example of behaviour modification is described by Pat Barker in her novel *Regeneration* when a mute shell-shocked soldier is 'persuaded' to speak by a psychologist who applies electric shocks to his tongue and throat. I hope there are no psychologists today who would resort to such brutality. It would not in any case work for aphasia, which is an altogether different condition from traumatic mutism.

Nevertheless, the right kind of challenging situation, even one that provokes what Kurt Goldstein called a catastrophic reaction, can be therapeutic. Frustration, even to the point of emotional collapse, usually indicates favourable progress because it means that the patient is fully aware of his/her situation. John's even good temper is for that reason one of the more worrying aspects of his condition.

Douglas Ritchie explained why strangers were better able to elicit words from him than his wife or close friends:

This is because strangers are frightening to me and fear ranks above tiredness or lack of concentration as a stimulus. If I get into a bus, something makes me say 'Sixpence' to the conductor, and the something is fear. Fear of the other passengers, who may think me dumb or mad, of the conductor, who won't know where I want to go.

Sometimes aphasics stumble by chance on what works for them. The Russian aphasic Zasetsky discovered – on the advice of a friendly doctor – that he could often write a word more easily by not thinking about it than by trying to build it syllable by syllable. Douglas Ritchie was helped by reading aloud the plays of Chekhov. Some right-handed aphasics who can't write with their left hand find that they can write more easily, or only, on a computer. Those, like John, whose problems accessing language go deeper than the motor mechanics of writing (John in any case has always written by hand and never learned to touch-type) may find computers useless. There is now a good choice of teaching machines and computer hardware and software designed specifically for aphasics. John didn't respond to those we tried. Nancy Kerr, however, benefited from audiotapes with accompanying manuals that allowed her to match, at her own pace, the look of written words with the sounds of their spoken equivalent.

A new and much more sophisticated augmentative communication device, still in the experimental stage, is a Sentence Synthesizer, developed by Marcia C. Linebarger and her colleagues at the Unisys Corporation, Malvern, Pennsylvania; and by Moss Rehabilitation Research Institute, Philadelphia, Pennsylvania. The programme compensates for short-term memory loss – the inability of agrammatic patients to hold the elements of a sentence for long enough to assemble and monitor them – allowing aphasic subjects to put together narratives 'with the clock off'. I hope one day to try it on John.

Another new technique, 'Fast ForWard', has worked well with children who have problems with auditory comprehension. Certain speech sounds that normally have very short durations are slowed down to enable the patients to recognize and discriminate among them. Nina F. Dronkers tried Fast ForWard on twelve adult aphasic stroke patients and found that it improved severe-to-moderate auditory comprehension patients with lesions in the temporal and parietal lobes but not those with more extensive damage involving the frontal lobes.

Some stroke or aphasic charities, hospitals and rehabilitation units issue leaflets giving advice, which is necessarily simplified and unlikely to describe any one individual's pattern of impairment. I found well-intentioned generalizations alarming, because John's symptoms didn't seem to match descriptions of different types of aphasia. The voice of an expert prepared to listen and answer questions over the telephone would be more reassuring than printed advice, which is bound to be wide of the mark because each case of aphasia is unique. I believe therapy by telephone is available in some remote parts of the United States. If it exists in Britain I've never come across it. But the English Stroke Association offers a service of amateur volunteers prepared to work one-to-one with aphasics; and publishes books of puzzles, exercises and games devised by Valerie Eaton Griffith for the benefit of Alan Moorehead and Patricia Neal.

University psychology, communication, rehabilitation or speech and language departments can be good sources of information, and some may be willing to treat an aphasic, as Jane did John, as part of a research programme. There are also neurological research projects actively seeking aphasic subjects at, for example, the International Aphasia Project at the University of California, San Diego, and the

National Hospital for Nervous Diseases, Queen Square in London. Jane treated John at no cost as a research project for the National Hospital's College of Speech Sciences investigating how volunteers can best be used to help aphasics. John and I also took part in a British Medical Research Council project supervised by Dr Wise at Hammersmith Hospital in London.

I believe, although I can't prove it, that John's first signs of real progress were stimulated by the guidance of Jane, an experienced professional therapist who specializes in aphasia. We learned from Jane that breakdown of language is as complex as language itself, and that common sense, puzzles and kindness are not the most efficient means of identifying and addressing the many counterintuitive problems that characterize chronic aphasia.

It is notoriously difficult to diagnose, describe and treat aphasic symptoms. They change, sometimes from one day to the next. In the acute stage side-effects of the brain damage may confuse the pattern. Later, compensating strategies may obscure essential problems. Each aphasic has a unique personality, history, intellect, educational background, set of interests and values. John was able to write the names of obscure artists before he could write *cat* or *pen*. His lifelong preoccupation with art may seem an obvious explanation: he has thought about art and artists in so many different contexts over so many years that their names must be represented in far-flung corners of his brain.

It does not follow that another aphasic, equally intelligent, equally committed to his/her subject, will necessarily retain its specialized vocabulary. Nevertheless, the unquantifiable state of having one's heart in something should never be underestimated. The conductor Herbert von Karajan was once persuaded by Austrian psychologists to take part in an experiment. He allowed his autonomic responses to be measured while he performed various activities: conducting in a recording studio, listening to the playback of the recorded piece, landing his private jet at Salzburg airport. While performing, his pulse rate went up more dramatically during emotional passages than during those that required physical exertion. The same profile emerged when he listened to the playback. When he landed his plane, and was told after touchdown to make an emergency takeoff at a steep angle, his pulse rate was increased far less than by the music.

Some neuropsychologists consider that the problem of identifying aphasic symptoms is exacerbated by anecdotal, incomplete and perhaps subjective case reports by clinicians who lack a sophisticated database by which to describe and classify their patients' deficits. In the course of the last century many batteries of standardized tests have been devised – by, among others, Pierre Marie in the 1910s, Henry Head in the 1920s, Weisenburg and McBride in the 1930s – with the aim of bringing order to the diagnosis and treatment of an unruly, elusive condition. Modern standard aphasia tests that are used to assign patients to one or another of the classical syndromes include the Boston Diagnostic Aphasia Examination, Western Aphasia Battery, the Porch Index of Communicative Ability and the Aachen Aphasia Test. Tests designed to assess aphasics' ability to communicate in everyday life include the Functional Communication Profile, Communicative Abilities in Daily Living and the Edinburgh Functional Communication Profile. The Psycholinguistic Assessment of Language Processing in Aphasia tests are widely used in Britain by adherents of cognitive neuropsychology and psycholinguistics.

The most famous part of the Boston Diagnostic Aphasia Examination – designed in 1972 by Harold Goodglass and Edith Kaplan – is the 'cookie theft picture', a line drawing of a chaotic kitchen where a woman is absent-mindedly drying a dish while the sink overflows and a child reaching for a jar of cookies on an upper shelf teeters on a stool. Patients who describe the picture in abrupt telegramese, using content words – *mother, sink, boy, cookies* – but few grammatical words, are classified as 'Broca's' aphasics suffering from damage to the anterior left hemisphere. Those whose descriptions are fluent, grammatical, but windy and full of neologisms and wrong words – *That boy is going to spin off the spool if he doesn't wash out. It seems to me and his brother doesn't seem to notice that the blink . . . ship . . . the rink, yes, the rink is stimbling* – are designated 'Wernicke's' aphasics, with damage to the posterior left hemisphere.

The cookie theft test is of course not appropriate for those aphasics who, like John, cannot speak any words at all. Nevertheless, I tried it on him one rainy day when I was researching different methods of therapy for aphasia. From his expression of extreme distaste I gathered that he found the drawing banal. But then, always anxious to help, he entered into the spirit of the game. He took the part of the mother – *da woahs, da woahs, woahs, da woahs* in a falsetto voice with American accent: she is tired, or perhaps fed up with a life of poverty, or perhaps having an affair (Italian accent, narrowed eyes, lustful panting) and thinking about her lover. Then the boy – American child's voice – who is hungry because he missed lunch at school and is now about to break his leg. Enter the plumber (Irish), followed by the doctor (German), the Italian lover, the estranged father of the boy, the social worker. The play then turned into an opera with sung dialogue in the style of Giancarlo Menotti – a composer John used to enjoy parodying when he wanted to communicate a thought too silly for words alone – and concluded with a septet, each member of the cast *da woahs*-ing in character. By this time both John and I had ceased to notice that he hadn't actually used a single word to tell his story. I said, You are ridiculous. He gave me a look that reminded me of the way he used to call me 'Vassar' when he thought I was being too American-earnest.

Which parts of John's brain were lighting up, which neurotransmitters activated as he performed this elaborate mime in order to lighten my spirits on a dreary afternoon? One of the experimental psychologists I've been reading says that 'ludic behaviour' is characteristic of left-brain strokes, because, as I understand him, the jokester right brain is no longer kept in check by the sensible but humourless left brain. Maybe. But John's cookie theft opera was invented and acted by the same person who, as a schoolboy, had delighted his school audience with his rendition of Shakespeare's Feste the Clown (and who seemed to know the whole of Shakespeare by heart by the time I met him), whose acting at Oxford had nearly led him to Hollywood. He chose instead to use both sides of his brain to communicate his fascination with Renaissance Europe to television audiences and to successive generations of grateful students – and to entertain his friends and me with the wild sense of humour that has survived his appalling predicament.

12

A Voyage of Exploration

MRS STILSON (an aphasic patient): *Where do you get names from?*
AMY (an aphasia therapist): *I? From in here, same as you.*
MRS STILSON: *Do you know how you do it?*
AMY: *No.*
MRS STILSON: *Then how am I supposed . . . to learn?*
AMY: *I don't really know.*
Mrs Stilson stares at Amy. Then she points at her and laughs.

Arthur Kopit, Wings

Professor Steven Small has a controversial vision of what aphasia therapists might be able to do for their patients in the future, when medical science has the power to restore damaged brains. Far from being made redundant by scientific progress, therapists could in his view be empowered by it. Even now, drugs that seem to stimulate cortical connections are ineffective unless combined with intensive behavioural therapy. It is as though the reawakened brain needs guidance about what to do and how to do it. When scientists have discovered how to introduce hardware, tissue or cells into damaged brains,

What connections are those cells going to make? Are random connections going to help? Or do we want to have those cells make connections that are going to promote the right kind of recovery? I claim that we want those cells to develop in a certain way. Do you think we can go in there with a microscope and wire up those cells? No, the approach is going to be to have therapy that reinforces the right kind of connectivity patterns of these new cells and avoids maladaptive connection patterns.

If Professor Small is correct, therapists may one day be as powerful as scientists and doctors, and, like scientists and doctors, they will have the power to do harm as well as good.

Not everybody agrees with Professor Small that therapy has, or ever will have, the ability to change brain function. Nevertheless, he can claim evidence that supports his vision. He cites the case of Vicky, the aphasic nurse who came to him with a reading disorder, which, although it had not shown up on standardized aphasia tests, was preventing her from studying for a Master's Degree in Nursing. Vicky suffered from what cognitive neuropsychologists call phonological dyslexia. She couldn't read non-words or words that were unfamiliar to her. She also had trouble with function words, which can make all the difference to the meaning of a sentence. Professor Small's team in Chicago decided to try to overcome the problem by giving Vicky examples of individual words: real words she could understand, unusual words she didn't know, non-words and function words. They avoided explanation in favour of asking her to focus her attention on each individual word. Eventually they taught her to read by decomposing sentences into their component words, rather than just reading the words she recognized, as she had been doing. It isn't, as he says, a very efficient way of reading, but it did in the end improve Vicky's understanding of what she read.

Professor Small was interested to know whether Vicky's brain encodings of the reading process had been altered in the course of treatment. He found that in the period from before treatment to its successful conclusion her brain activation in the angular gyrus, the area just behind 'Wernicke's' which links hearing with vision, had declined from about half of all brain activation while reading to just over 5 per cent. At the same time, a region in the occipital lobe that had shown zero activation before treatment had increased to about half of the total. The scans indicated that her brain function had altered as she learned to interpret written words visually rather than relying on their phonology. 'We saw that behavioural interventions actually changed the functional anatomy of the brain. For me, that's very profound. We can intervene with therapy and have effects that are biological in nature.'

In the first months after John's stroke the only specialist we came across who strongly recommended that professional aphasia therapy could improve his condition was Dr Schapiro, an American speech-language pathologist practising at one of the best-funded hospitals in New York. Dr X, having declared John a hopeless case, had banned him from the hospital's rehabilitation programme. Dr Y had advised us that volunteers would do just as well as professional therapists. Dr Z had employed a highly qualified aphasia therapist, but when she took another job shortly after we arrived he didn't replace her for as long as John was in his geriatric ward. White Coat, who had pronounced John incurable, didn't seem to have much faith in the efficacy of her own profession. And when I met Dr Wise on 12 July 1996, four years after John's stroke, he confessed to being 'agnostic' about the value of clinical therapy, which in his opinion was at best probably better than nothing.

There have never before been so many aphasics alive in the world, or so many aphasia therapists, or so much research into the efficacy of clinical treatment for aphasia. But it is probably harder for an aphasic today to find adequate therapy than at any time since the Second World War, when the aphasic population was inflated by young, healthy, brain-damaged veterans wounded in action. In the 1950s the National Health Service referred Douglas Ritchie as a matter of course to the Medical Rehabilitation Centre in Camden Town, then one of the exemplary institutions of its kind. At first he hated it. The physical exercises made him feel ridiculous. The speech therapy irritated him. He thought of the doctors and therapists as witch doctors. He resented the hard work:

Who would ever think that I had had cerebral thrombosis, seriously at that, and that, so far from being an invalid in bed with hot-water bottles, I worked harder than I ever used to in my life?

A year later,

this grousing was like the skin of an onion. Underneath I had a new kind of confidence . . . Dating from the summer before, when my morale hit rock bottom . . . I became better co-ordinated, more in tune with myself. I had got into a virtuous circle. I had confidence in myself and was grateful to the doctors, the instructors, the physiotherapists, and the speech therapists.

Half a century later an aphasic as severely affected as Ritchie would be lucky to get a few months of intensive rehabilitation. An unsatisfactory compromise has been struck between those who have faith in the value of rehabilitation therapy and those who sit on the fence or would rather not fund a treatment that is labour-intensive, more often called for by geriatric patients than by the young, and that can't be guaranteed to work. Many, perhaps most, aphasics who seek more than one opinion will receive conflicting advice about what to do about it. Some never even learn that their illness has a name: a telephone survey of a thousand people conducted by the English charity Speakability in 2000 found that 3 per cent had heard of aphasia. When it was explained to them 21 per cent recognized that they did in fact know someone with impaired language following brain damage.

Most aphasics in Britain will probably be offered some token therapy, but it is unlikely to go deep enough or last long enough. After meeting Dr Schapiro I assumed that the grass must be greener across the Atlantic in my native America. But it seems I was mistaken. Professor Small runs a rehabilitation clinic for aphasics at a hospital in one of the poorest neighbourhoods of Chicago where each patient is funded for no more than six sessions in total with a speech and language pathologist. He has tried in vain to persuade insurance companies that aphasia is a chronic illness – more like diabetes mellitus than heart attack – which needs ongoing treatment. The University Psychology Department donates two evaluation sessions a month, because the hospital would otherwise be required to pay for their services. 'Medical care in the United States,' says Professor Small, 'is in need of some urgent care.'

It is true that not everything that calls itself speech and language therapy, or speech-language pathology, is worth funding. Dr Nancy Kerr, as an aphasic rehabilitation psychologist, was in a good position to pick and choose. She found nine or ten therapists through a variety of sources, including hospitals and the Speech Department of the University of Arizona; and concluded that some of it was useful but too much of what was available was a waste of dollars.

While all group trials indicate that some intervention is more beneficial than none at all, many conclude that low-level non-specific treatment by professionals like some of Nancy Kerr's therapists (and like White Coat) is not superior to generalized stimulation by amateurs. But single-case and crossover studies, which compare the results of identifying and treating specific deficits with not treating them, indicate that informed, professional focused therapy does, as it did for Vicky, have the power to remediate aphasic impairments.

Nevertheless, in England the profession is widely regarded by the medical profession as a suitable career for pleasant young women who prefer helping people to grappling with intellectually challenging ideas. (Ironically, students seeking to study speech and language therapy at the University of Newcastle, which has one of the most popular courses in England, need better A-levels than those wishing to study medicine.) It's scarcely surprising that surveys suggest that many aphasia clinicians suffer from low morale and consider themselves marginalized by health-care providers and doctors. Without sufficient training or retraining it is difficult for practising therapists to keep up to date. There is no lack of published research about communication disorders, but it is scattered among journals specializing in medicine, linguistics, education, psychology, behavioural sciences and engineering. In 1990, according to a review published for the American Speech and Language Hearing Association, there were sixty-seven journals devoted to communication science and communication disorders. Since few practising aphasia therapists have the time or motivation, or in some cases the fundamental knowledge or access to good libraries, to take advantage of such a plethora of complex information, they continue to use untargeted methods of re-education which are not much better than harmless.

Aphasia therapy was not always the Cinderella it is today. Until the First World War, few people who were not doctors were involved in therapy. Broca regretted that other commitments prevented him from spending more time with aphasic patients. Hughlings Jackson, and Freud while he was a practising neurologist, gained many of their insights from clinical engagement with patients. The tradition of combining medical practice with therapy persisted in Russia, where Alexander Luria ran a rehabilitation centre for aphasic soldiers during the Second World War. But it has largely died out in the West as medicine has become more specialized, more dedicated to acute illnesses that can be diagnosed and treated with technology, drugs or surgery; and where the medical profession, which is good at creating hierarchies, has relegated clinical therapists to the bottom of the pecking order.

Specialization may be an inevitable result of scientific advance, but it is not always in the best interests of progress or of patients who suffer from illnesses that cannot be cured by taking a pill. Professor Small has recognized the problem of the pill-culture for many years. 'You go to the doctor and you get a pill. And this has translated in American society into trying to take a pill for almost every problem that arises.' He advocates 'a more biopsychosocial' approach to the treatment of aphasia. His impoverished rehabilitation centre in Chicago is modelled on American comprehensive centres for epilepsy and Alzheimer's disease where patients are cared for by teams of doctors, nurses, psychologists and social workers. At Professor Small's centre, speech and language pathologists, neuropsychologists, neurologists and other specialists with relevant skills 'sit around and talk about the patient in terms of language behaviour, psychology, in terms of cognitive neuropsychology, in terms of affective disorders and neurological function, brain function . . . we talk about all these things and then we recommend different approaches for intervention . . . Comprehensive models now, in an era where we cannot eradicate aphasia, are the way to do things.'

But while epilepsy and, increasingly, Alzheimer's respond to medical treatment, it remains impossible to prove definitively that a particular dose of a particular brand of therapy taken over a particular period of time, with or without a pharmacological agent, will have the same measurable beneficial effects on all aphasic patients. The decision-makers about health expenditure today demand just that kind of evidence. The purse strings world-wide are no longer held by clinicians, as they were in Douglas Ritchie's day, but by bureaucrats, in charge of budgets strained by ever more expensive technologies, who demand proof of value for money.

In their book *Aphasia Therapy* David Howard and Frances M.

Hatfield plead that the heterogeneity of aphasia renders the question of whether therapy does or doesn't 'work' for all aphasics inappropriate, as wide of the mark as asking whether aspirin cures a headache: 'if a treatment for a headache is being studied it is important to establish that all the subjects have the same sorts of headaches; if some have migraines, others cerebral tumours, and the rest tension headaches we would not expect one particular treatment to have the same effect on all the patients'.

Nevertheless, the more necessary it becomes to satisfy the paymasters with certainties, the more money is diverted from treating aphasic patients to evaluating the efficacy of the only treatment that exists for aphasia. And as far as the bureaucrats are concerned the jury is still out. Two recent meta-analyses of research evaluating the success of aphasia therapy reached diametrically opposite conclusions. In 1999 the British-based *Cochrane Library Review* by Jenny Greener and her colleagues argued that there is insufficient evidence to justify a decision one way or the other. But in 2000 an American review, which analysed the same studies as the *Cochrane Review*, argued that the evidence is so convincing in favour of therapy that it should be considered a 'practice standard' for the treatment of aphasics.

Most experts agree with Professor Small that 'There is no question in anyone's mind any more that aphasia therapy helps.' The controversial question is whether it 'works' to the extent that it has the power to change brain function permanently. Professor Caramazza, when I spoke to him in 1999, was not convinced that it does: 'There is no evidence that it "works". The evidence is that it helps. What there is not is a fundamental change. But people are better off with therapy. Some people are able to function independently after treatment. It maximizes ways of dealing with the problem, and the smarter you are the more it helps. That is different from recovering what you had.' Chris Code, Professor of Psychology at the University of Exeter and editor of the standard textbook *The Characteristics of Aphasia*, is more optimistic:

Alfonso Caramazza does not believe therapy has the ability to change cognition, or rather the little we know about it. But he's wrong I'm sure.

The 'literature' says it does work – whatever that means. There are some bad studies which claim it doesn't, and some bad ones that claim it does, but most good ones confirm that it does work. The real issues today are who will benefit, for how long, when therapy should begin, how long it should continue.

For aphasics and those close to them, however, the most pressing question is what they can do about it, not in some visionary future when scientists have come up with a cure that satisfies the bureaucrats, but here and now. Aphasia, as Howard and Hatfield say more than once in *Aphasia Therapy*, 'is a problem that *demands* a response'. More than a decade after the publication of *Aphasia Therapy*, David Howard, Professor of Speech at the University of Newcastle, dismisses arguments about what 'works' means as 'rather silly'. There is, as he says, 'a very real benefit, which should not be underestimated, in just meeting someone who is able to talk about and understand that communication is difficult, life is hard, explain, and help to understand the nature of the problem'. In his lecture given in 2001 for Speakability, Professor Howard challenged the usefulness of randomized control trials for the effectiveness of aphasia therapy. 'RCTs for aphasia,' he said, 'are politically important but scientifically unsound. What *is* aphasia therapy? There is no general answer. It's not a thing, like aspirin. What matters about it is what is done with whom and how.'

When John's language did not return after months of intensive work with our friends, we both knew that we had to find somebody who knew more about what was wrong with him and could do something about it. In England at that time most professional therapists were educated, as Jane was, in the school of cognitive neuropsychology. Had we been in a different place at a different time we might have found a therapist with a very different approach. As A. Basso and colleagues have written: 'It is very difficult to know what aphasia therapy is ... What occurs under the heading of aphasia rehabilitation in one place may have nothing in common with what occurs in a different place except for the fact that a speech therapist and a patient interact with each other.' Despite evidence that domain-specific treatment is more successful than general language stimulation, therapists tend to polarize at one of the two approaches. Some therapists are more concerned with counselling than curing. (Some, like White Coat, counsel acceptance of what they regard as irreversible tragedy.) Some would define a major part of their job description as requiring them to teach social workers, doctors, nurses and the immediate family to understand and adapt to the appalling predicament of being aphasic. There is a politically correct movement that places as much emphasis on castigating the defects of a society that marginalizes disabled people as on treatments that might help the disabled to re-enter society.

Psychosocial support is important, particularly for the majority of aphasics who are further disabled by depression and for the many who lack family or community support. Sympathetic and knowledgeable counselling can encourage motivation – just as insensitive advice handed out by ignorant social workers or therapists can be counter-productive. But counselling and campaigning, important though they are, can distract from the direct mediation in the recovery of language, which is, after all, what most aphasics most keenly desire.

John and I rejected psychosocial support – especially in the condescending and discouraging way it was proffered by White Coat. But we were luckier than most aphasics. John was not depressed. He considered suicide. He was frustrated, sad, bewildered. But depression is different, and he has all his life been blessedly free of it. We adapted to his aphasia in our own no doubt idiosyncratic ways, with the help of friends and family attracted by the courtesy and charm that made his apparently paradoxical condition seem all the more fascinating. Surrounded as we were by so much warmth and encouragement, the decision to go all out for recovery was easier for us than for many. Given the severity of his condition, it may have been a naïve and reckless choice, and I have no doubt that we were both in a state that a psychotherapist would call denial. We certainly had no idea of where we were actually going or how we might get there. And we would not have got very far without the guidance of professional therapists who showed us that searching for lost language is one of the most difficult, exciting and rewarding open-ended adventures it is possible to undertake.

Howard and Hatfield explain the scientific approach that distinguishes informed therapeutic procedure from generalized, hit-or-miss stimulation. Trained clinicians begin, as Jane did with John, by trying to find out in detail what is wrong and why. They will then formulate a hypothesis, which is tested by the patient's response to therapy. If in the course of treatment it is proved wrong, the hypothesis will change.

But observation, hypothesis and experiment will take a clinician only so far, because the relationship between identifying impairment and treating it is not straightforward: 'Knowing what is wrong does not in any simple way determine what to do about it.' Some of the most successful therapists say that what they do is as much art as science: when it comes to treating an aphasic patient they have to trust their own gut feelings. Many would agree with the clinician in Dr Z's geriatric ward who told John and me that treating every aphasic patient was a great voyage of exploration.

There are many strategies, but only three options: impaired elements of language may be restored; language may be reconstituted or reorganized by teaching the patient to find ways around deficits using intact abilities. Finally, encouraging the use of whatever abilities remain may lead to the restoration of function or it may, in the worst cases, help the patient to compensate for irretrievable loss. 'Restoration therefore is intended to enable the patient to operate normally by normal means; reconstitution that the aphasic performs normally using unusual methods. Compensation is aimed at the patient performing abnormally but optimally.'

The clinician may decide to treat a deficit directly (a patient who is anomic, for example, would practise word retrieval); or indirectly, focusing not on the deficit itself but on what seems to be the underlying cause (word retrieval may be impaired by a semantic or phonological problem). Or an intact ability or modality may be used to support and help to reorganize disrupted performance (singing, rhythm, gesture, reading might elicit spoken words).

If the problem is anomia, cueing with the first letter or sound of a word often produces gratifying results, which don't, alas, seem to last. Some therapists might try to prompt the word by giving the patient its 'address', say, a large mammal that inhabits Africa and India and has a trunk. Both strategies worked well for John. But the next day the elephant would be as elusive as ever, and we would have to start hunting it all over again. Word finding, in any case, was only one of John's many problems. Even if he could write a word he couldn't say it, and he couldn't put written words together to make a sentence.

Aphasia therapists today tend to gather under one or another of a number of umbrellas, or schools, according to the discipline in which they have been trained or the theory they believe provides the most reliable insights. There is no single metatheory of aphasia therapy, no evidence that one school works better than the others, and considerable disagreement about how far any theory or model can guide treatment. Many would probably say that all theoretical models are underspecified but can provide useful frameworks for diagnosis. Many therapists combine methods from different schools to suit particular patients.

The stimulation school was formulated by the American therapists Joseph Wepman and Hildred Schuell in the 1940s and 1950s, a time when the brain-damaged population was swollen by wounded veterans of the Second World War. Two of its founding principles were that aphasia is a unitary disorder varying only in severity, and that it is a disorder of access to language rather than loss of language. The original strategy was to facilitate the retrieval of other lost components by exposing the patient to intense bouts of spoken language, the theory being that speech is the primary modality and listening to it is the way we learn language in the first place. This simplistic application of regression hypothesis was abandoned. But the stimulus–response approach, which remained prominent in America and Britain until the late 1970s, later inspired more subtle techniques, which make use of other intact modalities or attempt to progress from involuntary utterances elicited by the therapist to language that is under the patient's control.

Even for its time, the notion that aphasia is only one kind of disorder and that exposure to oral language is the key to recovery was naïve. But it does not seem to have prevented the stimulation therapists from achieving results, and many of the techniques they developed are still used by therapists who adhere to more sophisticated schools. Wepman and Schuell's idea that just the right kind of stimulation given when the patient is in the right frame of mind can restore the language system to normality may be vague, but it does describe what all therapists who subscribe to the theory that lost language is ultimately recoverable hope to achieve.

Clinicians of the *neo-classical school* use many different strategies, which have little in common apart from the influence of certain shared assumptions derived from the Boston neo-classicists' rediscovery of the nineteenth-century classifications and from an interest in disordered syntax, inspired by Chomsky's generative-transformational grammar. Like the stimulation school, the neo-classical school regards aphasia as a failure of access to intact language rather than a loss of language. The goal of therapy is therefore to re-access rather than re-educate. Patients are treated according to the syndrome to which they have been assigned by the results of testing with the Boston Diagnostic Aphasia Examination.

Melodic Intonation Therapy (MIT) uses expressive prosody, or the ability to sing words that is sometimes preserved in aphasia, to support access to oral language. The technique goes back as far as the eighteenth century, and is the single therapy to have the approval of the American Academy of Neurology. We tried using rhythm and singing to unlock John's words soon after his stroke, and again after Dr Schapiro suggested it. It didn't help him, but that could be because we were experimenting without professional guidance, or because his apraxia was too deep to permit articulation.

Visual Action Therapy (VAT), another of the battery of methods used by the neo-classical school, begins by associating representational drawings and gestures with real objects and actions, and proceeds to more symbolic gestures, and in some cases pantomime. John's talent for expressive gesture and pantomime is in the class of Marcel Marceau, but it has not elicited spoken words, possibly for the same reasons that MIT didn't work for him.

Voluntary Control of Involuntary Utterances (VCIU) tries to support semantic and phonological recovery by utilizing the reading capabilities that are sometimes preserved by otherwise severely afflicted aphasics. If patients say a word involuntarily they are given that word to read. If, when reading aloud, patients make a paraphasic error, reading, for example, *chair* for *table*, they are immediately given the word 'chair' to read. The idea is to reintroduce the connections between the sound of the words patients can articulate and their spelling and meaning. Once or twice I wrote down the only two – meaningless – syllables John could utter, and gave them to him to read. He laughed. He was amazed. He was insulted that I should suggest that *da* and *woahs* represented the messages clamouring in his head. He was quite certain that he was not making those sounds, nor could he make them at will when I asked him to read them aloud.

The Helm-Elicited Language Program for Syntax Stimulation (HELPSS) aims to recover access to syntax in agrammatic – 'Broca's' – aphasics. Patients repeat the concluding sentence of a story read out by the therapist. They are then asked to devise their own final sentences, at first using the grammatical constructions that are considered easiest for Broca's aphasics and progressing to those regarded as more difficult. Intransitive commands are followed by transitive commands, then questions beginning with *who, what, where, when* (the *wh*-words that John could not understand), and finally intransitive and transitive declarations. There are claims that HELPSS helps some patients; and counter-claims that it cannot help all 'Broca's' aphasics because there is no hierarchy of difficulty with grammatical constructions that applies to them all.

The rationale of yet another method, Language Oriented Therapy (LOT), is that language is lost or impaired at one of three levels: phonological (the sound of words), semantic (the meaning of words), or syntactic (grammar and morphology). The four modalities of language – auditory comprehension, reading, speaking and writing – plus a fifth, gesture – are regarded as independent of one another. Within each modality there are 'areas', which are also mutually exclusive. Therapy is about identifying and treating impaired areas. Cueing is used to elicit correct responses and to encourage patients to devise their own cueing strategies. As with all methods, there is evidence that LOT is more beneficial than others, and evidence that it is not.

Therapists of the *pragmatic school* aim to improve communication by whatever means – drawing, gesture, primitive gestural systems like Amerind. (Real sign languages as used by deaf mutes are not available to aphasics because they are rule-based systems of agreed symbols that are processed in the same way as verbal language. Deaf mutes are as vulnerable to aphasia as speaking people.)

Some pragmatic therapists try to suggest meaningful gestures, others encourage their patients to invent their own. There is always the hope that control over gestural communication might facilitate the return of verbal language. (Evidence from research with primates indicates that just watching another animal move the right arm stimulates parts of the motor cortex, which, in humans, are very close to 'Broca's' area.)

In some cases aphasic communication by means of drawing as well as gesture shows patterns of deficits similar to those that have affected verbal language. Elizabeth, the therapist who took over John's case from Jane, showed us that this was part of John's problem. In one of their first sessions she asked him to complete a picture of a man painting a house. The man was standing on what was obviously a ladder, although it had no rungs. John knew that something was missing, but he could not fill in the rungs. He showed us that he knew what a ladder was by climbing with his fingers. But, Elizabeth explained, he did not at that stage have a complete enough representation of the concept of a ladder to draw one. Later, when a physiotherapist asked him to draw the outline of a human figure John did it perfectly, but left out one hand. When, six months later, I asked him once again to draw a human figure, he cunningly drew it with one arm bent and the hand concealed as though behind the figure's back.

A pragmatic method known as PACE – Promoting Aphasics' Communicative Efficiency – tries to tackle the chief limitation of non-verbal communication, which is that it is better at responding and describing than initiating new ideas. Practitioners of PACE eschew formal exercises in favour of tasks that require the patient to convey new information by any available means through interaction with a clinician. This is what our friends and I instinctively did with John from the beginning. I'm sure it helped, up to a point. But although his gestures and drawings became more complete and explicit, we still had to resort to Twenty Questions when he wanted to introduce a new topic of conversation.

The fragile thread that unites therapists who subscribe to the *neurolinguistic school* is a shared faith in the use of linguistic parameters to classify aphasic patients. The early neurolinguists were silent about therapy, and built their typologies (there were many, depending on which linguistic theory was adopted) on reported case studies rather than observation of real aphasics. Thoughts about the treatment of aphasia are more recent and are still diverse. According to Howard and Hatfield, neurolinguistic theory guides treatment in continental Europe and some parts of the United States, and the best representatives are in Bonn and Aachen. It has never made an impact in Britain, and I have never met a therapist who subscribes wholeheartedly to its tenets. Some I've asked say they are informed by neurolinguistic theory. Others say that attempts by neurolinguists to relate linguistic theory to brain structures are at an impasse and can go no further until the neuropsychology of language is more developed.

I am more familiar with the *cognitive neuropsychology school*, because Jane, who treated John as part of a research project in the summer after his stroke, was a disciple. She was the first person to provide us with a plausible demonstration of what had gone wrong with his language machine and how we might go about trying to fix the broken parts. She made no attempt to fit his symptoms into some preconceived category of aphasia, and told us that John's case was making a contribution to knowledge about aphasia. It was certainly better for our morale to be part of a research project than it would have been to have been treated as part of a group.

Jane addressed John's problem of not recognizing individual letters by the direct method, giving him sheets of randomized single letters arranged in rows of seven. Row by row, he had to choose one of the seven letters when we said its name, made the sound with which it is usually associated, and said a word that begins with it. He improved at letter recognition, but very slowly. When, however, she tackled his loss of the meaning of prepositions, the result was spectacularly successful. One week he could not begin to respond to a request to put one object *in*, *on*, *next to*, *under*, *over*, *behind* another, or to judge from pictures which of a choice of prepositions described the relationship in space between two objects; the next he was wondering why we were wasting his time with such simple exercises.

Jane diagnosed two related causes of John's inability to enunciate any word, even if he had just heard it, could understand it and write it to dictation. He suffered from severe articulatory apraxia, a loss of the ability to organize the vocal muscles for speech sounds. Some aphasiologists regard apraxia as mainly a failure of motor control. Jane is among those who believe that it is also related to purely linguistic disorders. John's inability to judge whether words, written or spoken, did or did not rhyme indicated that his apraxia was either caused or exacerbated by inability to generate the sounds of language in his head.

Jane tried to address the problem with exercises that required him to make conscious judgements about the way words sound. In one task he had to identify which of four words, spoken or written, was the odd one out: *man fan mad van*, *pin tin sit sin*, and so on. He tried and tried, but he couldn't do it. Other tasks used pictures to reinforce the words. Given a picture of, for example, two bees and a row of peas in a pod he had first to point to the right drawing when we said the word for each. Then we said *bees-peas* – do they rhyme? Or we said *bees-wasps* – do they rhyme? If that didn't work – and it never did – we were to put the words into a couplet that either rhymed or didn't: Fresh garden peas/Are attractive to bees (or wasps). It was while doing this particular task with John that I lost control and heard myself screaming: BEESPEAS PEASBEES WASPSBEES PEASWASPS FOR FUCK'S SAKE JOHN YOU *MUST* BE ABLE TO HEAR THE DIFFERENCE.

Everybody, especially John, was happier working with proper poems, with the rhyming words blanked out and a selection of semantically plausible distracters, as, for example:

> Edward the Confessor
> Slept under the *(table, desk, dresser, stove, bed)*.
> When that began to pall,
> He slept in the *(parlour, hall, bed, garden, hammock)*.

The poem task appealed to our literary friends, and it was gratifying for us all because he never failed it. The friends moved on from clerihews, nursery rhymes and limericks to any rhyming poem they happened to like and think John would enjoy. Over the months that Jane was supervising them, they brought dozens of poems for John to consider:

> The art of losing isn't hard to master;
> so many things seem filled with the intent
> to be lost that their loss is no *(problem, disaster,*
> *tragedy, hassle, trouble)* . . .

John always made the right choice.

> Say that thou didst forsake me for some fault,
> And I will comment upon that offence.
> Speak of my lameness, and I straight will *(cease, stop,*
> *desist, halt, turn),*
> Against thy reasons making no *(excuse, defence,*
> *argument, answer, apology).*

He didn't know what a rhyme was. He couldn't hear it, imagine it or understand the concept – except, for some reason that nobody can explain, in the context of a poem.

I experimented with a couplet for which all the choices rhymed, all were equally possible semantically, and two suited the poet's rhythmic scheme. I chose it because he could not have chosen the correct word unless he knew the lines by heart:

> In the room the women come and go
> Talking of *(Fra Angelico, Leonardo, Bellotto,*
> *Donatello, Giotto, Michelangelo).*

The poet's choice had lodged in John's brain. Nor was this the first or last sign that John's memory for language is intact.

Alas, those psychologists who subscribe to the theory of dissociated modules would not necessarily maintain that the language skills John has retained indicate that he will ever regain those he has apparently lost. Unlike members of the stimulation and neo-classical schools, cognitive neuropsychologists are divided about the question of whether aphasic deficits as stubbornly resistant to time and treatment as John's speech and ability to write sentences are disorders of loss or of access. The original proposition by Elizabeth Warrington was that some are disorders of loss and some of access. Now, so Professor Butterworth tells me, the division of opinion is between those who think what is lost is lost for ever and those who are not sure. If there are two lexicons, one for reception and one for expression, then John's expressive lexicon for writing is evidently not totally abolished. But if writing single words and writing sentences are dissociated functions, then he may never be able to combine single words into meaningful sentences. And since writing and speaking are massively dissociated, it could be that speech has been ripped out of his head altogether. Alternatively, the disposition for speech and for the syntax necessary for sentence composition may be hidden somewhere in his brain, like buried treasure.

A year after John's stroke we had a piece of rare good fortune. We were introduced by a friend to an aphasia therapist who is regarded by her grateful patients and her professional colleagues as one of the most successful and talented clinicians working in England. Elizabeth, as I will call her, takes the view that in most cases of aphasia nothing is permanently lost.

PART III

JOHN'S APHASIA

'Pantagruel suddenly jumped to his feet, and took a look around him. "Can you hear something, comrades?" he asked. "I seem to hear people talking in the air. But I can't see anything. Listen" . . . So as to miss nothing, some of us cupped the palms of our hands to the backs of our ears . . . the more keenly we listened, the more clearly we made out voices, till in the end we could hear whole words.' Greatly alarmed, Pantagruel's party was told by the ship's captain that what they were beginning to hear were the sounds of a great battle which had been frozen over by winter and were now beginning to thaw. Some, indeed, fell on deck; where they 'looked like crystallised sweets of different colours . . . when we warmed them a little between our hands, they melted like snow, and we actually heard them'.*

A story from the fourth book of François Rabelais's
Gargantua and Pantagruel, *as told by John Hale,*
The Civilization of Europe in the Renaissance

13

Cambridge

My mind may have skated over many things that day, for
instance: What an idiot that instructor is – A pretty girl
she is . . . Who will they put in my place at the BBC? . . .
But these ideas, or fancies, or reveries, were not contained
in words: for one reason, the words were not fast enough.
The upper stream of consciousness can be fabricated; I
think it can never be truly written down.

Douglas Ritchie, Stroke: Diary of a Recovery

We met Elizabeth in the early autumn of 1993, just over a year after
John's stroke. The introduction was arranged by Barbara, whose
husband Oliver had recently died many years after a cerebral haemorrhage had destroyed his sense of balance and most of his memory.
From the safe distance of my own normal life I had admired the
graceful way Barbara kept Oliver in touch with his interests and
friends. She took him in his wheelchair to parties and theatres. She
entertained as elegantly and apparently effortlessly as ever. But I
never left their company without thinking how lucky John and I
were that such a thing as had happened to Barbara and Oliver could
never happen to John and me.

When it did happen Barbara sympathized in a way that is more
difficult for those who have never had close personal experience of
stroke. One day she telephoned to say that she had been telling a
friend of hers, Lord Tavistock, about John's aphasia. Lord Tavistock
was also aphasic, following a massive near-fatal cerebral haemorrhage. But he had made a good recovery, which he and his wife
attributed to an aphasia therapist called Elizabeth. They wanted John
and me to come to Woburn, their country house in Bedfordshire, to
meet Elizabeth over lunch. Barbara said they couldn't promise that

Elizabeth would agree to treat John but were sure that if she did she could work the same miracle on him that she had on Lord Tavistock.

We drove north out of London on one of those brisk late August days that herald the coming of a new season: John, in the red cashmere cardigan and his least shabby tweed jacket, looking eagerly forward to the glamorous outing. But as we drew up to Lord and Lady Tavistock's famous country seat I was aware that I had accepted their invitation because it would be fun for John, not because I had any illusions left that John could be cured. In spite of all the hours our forty friends had spent working with John under Jane's supervision, he could still not write more than a few words and they were still mostly the names of artists, and he could not even make a start at composing a sentence. It was as though he didn't know what a sentence was.

Lady Tavistock made a great fuss of John and put him on her right at lunch, which was served in the Canaletto room. She said she felt privileged to entertain a man who had done so much for Venice in a room that must mean so much to him. (She later admitted that she had looked him up in *Who's Who* that morning.) John was indeed in his element. We talked about Venice, and then moved on, for some reason, to Jerusalem. I told them that John had once made a television programme about Easter in Jerusalem. But it was a long time ago, shortly after I met him, and the tape had now faded. John began to re-enact the programme: the different religious rituals, the clamour of exotic voices and accents, the ringing bells; John's voice-over solemn, donnish; John to camera in the Garden of Gethsemane quoting from the Gospel According to St Matthew: Then cometh Jesus with them unto a place called Gethsemane . . .

Elizabeth, who sat quietly on John's right during the performance, later told me that that was when she resolved not to take him as a patient. An aphasic, she said, who is lacking in self-consciousness to that extent – and who can communicate that well without words – wouldn't be motivated to make the enormous effort it takes to recover. But after lunch, sitting next to John on a sofa in the corner of the drawing-room, she lifted up his limp right arm and said, What is this John? John said *da woahs*. Elizabeth said, No, John, listen to yourself . . . Now listen to me: *ahm*. John said *ahhhm*. No, John.

You're saying *ahhhhm*. It's not quite right, is it? What is it? This is my . . . ? John said *ahm*.

I doubt if that minor triumph was the reason Elizabeth offered to see John at her house in Cambridge for a few trial sessions. I think she recognized the effort he put into succeeding at whatever he tried: 90 per cent perspiration had always been his own explanation for his successes. That would give her a handle on what she later described as the most difficult case she had ever encountered. She said then that she would continue to treat him only as long she felt she could help. She warned him that she was very persistent, that regaining language would be the hardest challenge he had faced in the whole of his career. He might give up before she did. She suggested making the sessions two days in a row, on Tuesday afternoons and Wednesday mornings, so we would only have to sleep over one night. Could we find a place to stay? The next day Robin and Catherine, old friends of John who commuted between houses and jobs in London and Cambridge, sent us the keys to their Cambridge house. They said it would be fun to have dinner together when they were in Cambridge, and when they weren't we should just make ourselves at home.

John loved our Tuesday morning drives to Cambridge through the quiet, open farmland of west Cambridgeshire: the patterns of the fields, the hazy English colours that change slowly with the seasons; the black clapboard barns hugging the sides of narrow old roads; tiny farming villages and church steeples punctuating gentle vistas from low hills. As we crossed the Thames he blew it a kiss goodbye. Then he allowed himself one mint humbug, and tried to make it last through the boring stretch out of London. We argued about whether or not to switch on the car radio. I said I deserved the diversion; he said the sound of music and voices disturbed him. He won. At Ashwell we stopped for a drink in a pub then drove to the magisterial fourteenth-century wool church of St Mary where John gazed up at the west tower marvelling each time as though this was the first time he'd ever seen it.

As the months passed we developed new rituals. When we passed a field of horses, I would say, What are they? What are those animals called? John would flash his most Puckish smile, shake his head, put his finger over his mouth; and just as I had given up – he always knew precisely the moment – he would say *hawwwse*, horse being one of the words Elizabeth had taught him. From Ashwell John pointed the way through one of the several indirect routes. I said, I hope you know where you're going John because otherwise we'll get lost. At the crests of certain hills I had to stop so that he could admire the view and I could say, It looks just like one of those feeble English watercolours you like.

As we entered Cambridge I could feel his mood shift. In the old days, when words came cheap, he had liked to make exaggerated play of the famous differences between his own university, Oxford, and the other place, Cambridge: Oxford magnificent, convivial, worldly, connected by the Thames to London; Cambridge provincial, isolated in the Fens, inhabited by joyless scientists and statisticians. But from the way his eyes followed the students and dons bicycling to and from libraries, laboratories and lecture theatres I knew that any great university was for John a kind of home.

And Cambridge recognized John as a person who belonged: forty years of university teaching had left its imprint on his style. If I tried to enter a college when it was closed to visitors I was turned away. If John was with me the porter at the gate waved us through with a respectful nod. One sunny afternoon we found the side entrance to the Great Court of Trinity College barred, and a sign in five languages instructing visitors that entrance was strictly forbidden without a ticket which could be purchased during certain hours at the main gate. John raised the barrier, entered. The brown-hatted porters ignored him until he waved his stick at the nearest, saying *woahs? da woahs?* The porter said, I'm terribly sorry, sir, but the library is closed until tomorrow.

We walked along the Backs, across a bridge, through a meadow so thickly planted with crocuses and scillas that it looked like a Mediterranean sky, to visit the chapel of King's College. We often attended Evensong there: John was beginning to enjoy music again. On summer evenings, when we hired a punt, there were always a few students who came forward to help him in and out of the boat. But if John had had a bad session with Elizabeth, it had to be the Fitzwilliam Museum: looking at works of art was the only diversion that would take his mind off his despair.

Elizabeth lives in a small village a few miles to the west of Cambridge, where she shares her bungalow with a cat and her garden with a large and various population of birds attracted by the feasts she lays out for them summer and winter. When she is not treating aphasic patients or researching aphasia or giving lectures about aphasia, she fills what is left of her days with reading, gardening and bird watching – interests, as it happens, that she shares with John. Even now, when I write to her with some question about aphasia, her replies bring news of her garden – 'My lawn is now totally moss and bird droppings because every morning I've put out Belshazzar's Feast . . . so far 29 different species in one morning.'

She trained at the Central School of Speech and Drama in the 1950s, before degrees came in for speech therapy. But after qualifying, she went on to take a degree in Human Communication Disorders at London University; and began her career as a clinician in a hospital where she treated everything from pre-school voice disorders and stammering to swallowing disorders and aphasia. She was offered a post teaching trainee speech therapists in London, where she gradually took over the aphasia course, 'being one word in the book ahead of my post-graduate students'.

In the late 1970s she began to take an interest in psycholinguistics, which was just starting to break into the aphasia literature. She told John and me that although she didn't understand it at all initially it began to feel like something that addressed the paradoxes of aphasia. She thought academic psycholinguistics might have application in the clinic, but when she started teaching it she felt a cheat because she'd not had the opportunity to see if the theories really could be usefully applied to language rehabilitation. In order to find out, she returned to clinical work, taking the position of head of speech and language therapy at a hospital where she worked mainly with aphasics, developing methods that proved remarkably successful. When we met her, she had recently retired from the hospital job and was treating patients privately, charging what they could afford to pay.

Although she has been claimed by cognitive neuropsychologists as one of their own, she continues to find psycholinguistic theory more relevant to clinical practice. Psycholinguists, like cognitive neuropsychologists, require models of information processing to be compatible with data from normal as well as pathological language. But psycholinguists maintain that their models are more specific than those informed by cognitive neuropsychology, which, in their view, are not sufficiently detailed, dynamic or sophisticated to describe the realities of on-line processing or to provide adequate explanations of those apparent paradoxes that cannot be explained by double dissociations.

Elizabeth, however, has found no existing research-based model that conforms well enough to her clinical observations to guide treatment. She believes that the clues to what has gone wrong and how to put it right are more likely to be found by exploring interconnections between modules than by identifying dissociations. After many years of clinical experience – and a remarkable record of successes – she feels strongly that therapists would benefit from more research into the ways the components of the language system interact and affect one another; and that data provided by therapists who observe the realities of disrupted performance could inform research more than they do.

It is the by the associations, rather than the dissociations, between encoded modules and levels – in the ways they seem to map on to and affect one another – that Elizabeth seeks to explore the symptoms of her patients. She says she has never treated an aphasic whose symptoms matched any one categorization: there are always associated problems, although they may not be immediately obvious.

Although she has devoted most of her professional career to studying aphasia and treating aphasics, Elizabeth says that even now she often feels with a patient like the blind leading the blind. It is only retrospectively that she begins to understand why one strategy worked, or why another didn't. Although she is in the camp of those who are certain that lost language can be unlocked in most cases, given persistence and time, she admitted to us from the start that sometimes the damage is just too great; there are aphasics who will never be able to re-access their language. I knew without her having to say so that she thought John might be one of the untreatable cases.

John wanted Elizabeth to tell him why when he sat down to write, knowing perfectly well what he wanted to say, it was still so difficult to find words. Why, when he did write a few words, could he not string them into a proper sentence? Why could he read books in German, Italian and French as well as English, but not write a sentence in any language? Why, when it felt to him as though he was speaking normally did people fail to grasp his meaning? Elizabeth answered him with metaphors.

It is as though the road between Naples and Rome had been blown up. You can still travel between the two cities, but you have to make your way through the rubble or find an alternative route.

In your brain, John, there is a brilliant concert pianist. He is playing away, listening in his head to the music. But the instrument has no strings.

When you try to talk or write you are like an old railroad signal man. You keep making the signals that will keep the trains running on time, but the connections from the signal box have been severed.

The British Library has been shaken by an earthquake. The books have been hurled off their shelves. They're all mixed up and the catalogues can't be found. The books are like your words: they are there, but you have no means of finding them.

For you, it's like learning a foreign language that has no rules.

Jane had passed on to Elizabeth her notes and the results of the PALPA tests she had given John. They indicated that his semantic understanding of words and pictures was 100 per cent, as was his ability to read and copy upper-case as well as lower-case letters. He could also recognize reversed letters (although he often reversed letters when writing them), distinguish between real and non-real written and spoken words, match synonyms, and match written and spoken words to pictures. Tests of 'inner voice' – judging whether words did or did not rhyme – had shown that he had no ability at all to generate the sounds of language in his head.

What seemed to Elizabeth the most significant test result was John's problem with what she called phonological segmentation. If he was shown a three-letter word, for example *gap*, spelled with Scrabble tiles, and heard that word and then heard *map*, he could not point to which letter had changed. He knew that *map* was not

eel

frog

pie

lemon

shell

skate

cage

honey

parrot

the same word as *gap*, and he could demonstrate that he knew the meaning had changed. But he could not indicate which letter of the word had changed to change the meaning. The problem evidently did not always affect his comprehension, but Elizabeth guessed it might be significant in terms of his lack of spoken output.

Elizabeth was able to elicit single written words from John more successfully than Jane, me or any of the volunteer helpers. In a measured, mesmeric voice – I can hear it, and John can imitate it to this day – she required him to *think*: think about everything to do with that word, focus his entire attention on its colour, shape, use, habitat, where it would come in a sentence. Was it a verb or a noun?

She soon found that he could usually indicate with dashes the number of letters in the target word: so he did know something about the structure of words. Sometimes, however, he would go for a close semantic distracter – a paragraphia. If the target was *chair* and he made four dashes and began the word with '*s*' she might say, Yes, it's for sitting on; but for only one person. Then she would draw a sofa and a chair. Sometimes he started on the right track – *ch* – lost his way, and wrote a word that had nothing to do with the target – for example, *cheer*. She reminded him over and over that he must keep on thinking about the meaning of the word and hold on to it; if he stopped thinking about it for a second, his mind would trick him into writing a different word. Vowels remained a matter of guesswork. And he often made dysgraphic mistakes, writing *b* or *g* for *d*, for example. But although he sometimes misspelled words, or wrote words that were off-target, he never wrote a word that was not a real word.

RICARDO WENT OUT SHOPPING TO BUY SOME FRUIT. HE BOUGHT A POUND OF _pears_, AND A LARGE JUICY WATER _melon_. HE ALSO WENT INTO THE OFF-LICENCE AND BOUGHT THREE BOTTLES OF _wine_. HE WALKED HOME ALONG BY THE _river_ AND WATCHED THE MEN ROWING THE _boat_. A VERY BEAUTIFUL _girl_ WAS SITTING ON A _bench_ SO HE SAT NEXT TO HER. SHE HAD LONG BLONDE _hair_ AND BIG BLUE _eyes_. RICARDO SAID 'GOOD _morning_ IT'S A

LOVELY *day* ,' SHE TURNED TO HIM AND *smiled* SHOWING
LOVELY WHITE *teeth* . RICARDO OFFERED HER ONE OF HIS *pears*.
THEY TALKED HAPPILY FOR HALF AN HOUR AND THEN RICARDO
ASKED HER OUT TO *dinner* SHE AGREED AND THEY MET OUTSIDE
THE *restaurant* AT 7.30PM.

After a few months he was able to label many of the objects in
her drawings of shop windows, grannies' attics, street scenes. And he
could usually fill in most of the blanks in the stories she wrote for him.

John and I were elated by his progress. Knowing very little about
aphasia at the time we both imagined that once he had re-accessed
his vocabulary – his lexicon – he would be equipped to communicate
in writing. Then Elizabeth showed us something about John's
aphasia that surprised and alarmed me more than it did John. One
Tuesday afternoon she wrote the verb *ride*. On its left she drew a
picture of a boy and on its right a bicycle. John wrote *boy* under the
boy and *bicycle* under the bicycle. She said, Very good. So who is
riding the bike? John pointed to the verb *ride*. She did the same thing
with a girl flying a kite, an executioner chopping off the head of a
prisoner, a dog chewing a bone, and so on. In each case John pointed
to the verb or the object or shrugged helplessly: he didn't understand
what she wanted him to do. She wrote sentences, such as *The men
bought ham in the supermarket*, and asked John who did the buying
and what they bought. He drew a picture of two men carrying a
ham in a shop. Evidently he understood the sentence. So why could
he not answer simple questions about it?

Elizabeth explained that John could not unravel the discrete
elements of a sentence. The kernel of a sentence is its verb. Every
verb has a number of arguments; it begs certain questions, which
must be answered to complete its meaning. The verb *to put* for
example is a three-argument verb: its meaning is incomplete without
a subject that does the putting, an object that is put, and a place
where it is put. *I put the bananas . . .* is not a sentence until you
indicate where you put the bananas. The words *who, what, where*
and *when* are empty traces that stand for verb arguments. John
had lost the concepts of these *wh*-words because he could not unravel

– or 'disambiguate' as she put it – the elements of verb arguments.

That, at least, was Elizabeth's theory. And looking back on the gestures and drawings with which John had communicated since his stroke, I could believe that in John's mind the world was now represented not in sequences of abstract signals but in images that stood for aggregations of the elements of sentences. For him the packaging in which he had seen a pair of socks displayed in a shop represented the way I would see the socks when I went to buy them for him. If he wanted to refer to friends, he would draw an accurate map of the way to their house from ours. If he wanted to tell me that the doctor had come while I was out he drew a picture of a man taking another man's blood pressure. He could probably, with effort, have written the words *sock* and *doctor*; but the words, for John, had less significance than the totality of the scene, which he could not describe in a sentence because – like the American aphasic psychologist Nancy Kerr – he had no idea of what a sentence actually was.

I often wondered, and still do, whether John's lifelong absorption in the visual world – his rejoicing in birds, butterflies, art, beautiful objects, beautiful women and their clothes – had predisposed his brain to register experience in images. John has always regretted that he could not paint – he has a profound respect for artists and for his daughter Charlotte's skill as a restorer of paintings. All his life he has been driven to interpret and describe visual experience indirectly in words. But he knew the translation was second best: his gift for spinning words about pictures was a poor substitute for the creative act of painting pictures. When we visited galleries with the children, we would all grow impatient with his habit of standing for half an hour in front of a picture, which had stolen his attention from us. We were jealous. It was as though he had gone away from us. We plagued him with questions: why do you love that picture so much? He would try to explain, but the children grew bored and wandered off. Matthew would say, Dad is still in front of that picture, oohing and aahing. Sometimes words failed him. I remember looking with him at a painting of the Park at Château Noir in an exhibition of late Cézanne at the Museum of Modern Art in New York. John said, There is nothing to say about this picture. It's too great. It is what it is. It's beyond words.

Elizabeth said she had never before come across an aphasic whose semantics were so intact but who was at the same time so unable to disambiguate the elements of language. She laboured with him on the problem for more than two years. I have a file of the exercises she gave him for homework. There are hundreds of pictures showing activities – a man putting a ring on the finger of a bride, a horse jumping over a fence, a woman stirring a cup of tea – followed by the words *who* and *what*. There are lists of verbs around which John must build a sentence, and notes reminding John that the order of the words is VITAL: REMEMBER THE EARTHQUAKE, JOHN. THINK BEFORE YOU WRITE. There are sentences followed by questions: *Who stole the purse? Who peeled the orange? What did the man climb?* As he made progress, she gave him paragraphs to read and introduced the concepts of *where* and *when*: *When did the princess see the frog? Where did the bird fly?*

On a large card she drew him a guide to sentence structure. It looks like a board game. VERB (= How?) is in the centre in red. The game starts at the top-left-hand corner with WHO (stick figure of human below it)/WHAT (picture of an animal) = Actor or thing that affects the action and a red arrow pointing to VERB. The other arguments are arranged in a circle around VERB and connected to it by blue dotted lines: WHO/WHAT? (= Object or thing that is affected). WHEN? (picture of a clock). WHY? (reason for . . . because). WHERE? (= place, picture of a house).

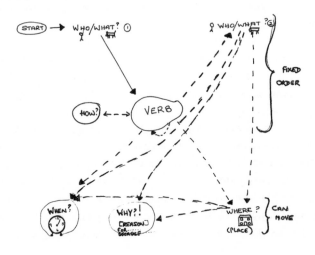

Just as Elizabeth had warned, the work was so difficult for him that it was sometimes too painful for any of the three of us to bear. Re-learning what a sentence is was harder for John than any book he had written in the years when sentences came automatically. But after eighteen months or so he had pretty well grasped the idea. Under a picture of a woman wearing a crown tapping with a sword the shoulder of a kneeling man John wrote the sentence: *The queen knights John.* Under a picture of a cow butting a man is the sentence: *The cow butts the man.* A picture of a girl painting a picture is described with the sentence: *Charlotte paints picture.*

Then there are pictures of single objects – a horse, a book, a bell, a car. John must use his syntactic board game to construct a sentence about the objects. Under a picture of a bicycle John has written *Dr Hale rides home yesterday.*

On an evening in December 1995, at about the time John had begun to grasp the meaning of *who*, *what*, *where* and *when*, he picked up a novel, took it to the chair where he liked to sit by the fire before dinner, and began to read. Although he had never lost the ability to read for information, this was the first time he had showed any revived interest in reading fiction for pleasure. The novel was *Turning Back the Sun*, by Colin Thubron. I remember the title well because when I called John for supper he didn't answer and he didn't come to the table. I found him so absorbed by the end of the novel that he refused to budge until he had finished it. From then on John has been reading at the rate of three or four books a week. Sometimes he gets stuck in the middle of a long or complicated sentence. (He describes the block with a screech-of-brakes sound and a bewildered look.) But he reads with what he judges to be about 90 per cent of his former concentration. Although I can't prove that the return to reading for pleasure was related to Elizabeth's treatment it does seem reasonable to suppose that an understanding of the rules of sentence structure might enable reading.

John wanted Elizabeth to teach him to speak. (This was puzzling because much of the time he seemed to think that he *was* speaking.) Elizabeth's first idea was that a way round his apraxia might be to utilize the apparently intact prosody that convinced everybody that his reiterated *da woahs*es represented real words, sentences and paragraphs. Elizabeth knew that this was unlikely: if he could not access words or syntax when writing, it would be surprising if he could do so when speaking. She did hope, however, that he might at least know something about the syllable structure and stress of individual words. She thought this might be the case because he could recognize if a spoken word was incorrectly stressed.

She gave him a list of seventy-two written words, and asked him to tap out how many syllables each one had and where the stress would fall. He was totally unable to do either of these tasks. Nevertheless, she remained curious about the prosodic 'chunking', as she called it, of his output, which continued to suggest to her that at some level he was planning what he wanted to say. She gave him a set of simple subject-verb-object pictures and asked him to 'talk' about them. His vocal response was as fluent as ever. But it was in no way appropriate to a description of the pictures.

Elizabeth performed this experiment on a day when I was not sitting in on her session with John. She didn't tell me the results until much later, because she knew very well that at that time it was for both John and me an essential article of faith that John's voice reflected a deliberate intention to convey meaningful messages. If I had allowed myself to believe that his voice was not expressing anything, the golden thread that bound me to him might have snapped. I had often said to Elizabeth that if John had Alzheimer's rather than aphasia I might not have been able to cope.

But even she was not entirely persuaded by her own evidence. His spontaneous output, which seemed so relevant in conversation, must be conveying something. There must be some metalinguistic intent. She began, occasionally, to teach him to speak words, employing the same method for speech as she had for writing. She did not insist, as many speech therapists do, that he should master individual speech sounds. Instead she bullied and cajoled him into *thinking* about the word, and refused to let him give up. '"On . . . ?" Are you trying to say *enough*, you slimy toad?' 'I don't think you are clear in your thinking. I don't mean your intellectual ability. I mean that for words your head is like a sieve. Hold on to them.' '"*I*?" Did I hear you say *I*? Well, I love your snooty upper-class accent.' 'Who's that? Is it *my* wife? No? Then whose wife is it?

It's mm ... Mine! Yes, John, that's right!' 'Who's thick as two planks around here? Did I hear *ooooooo*? Do you mean *you* by any chance? Say it then, come out with the truth. Who's thick as two planks?'

Towards the end of the third year John had a reliable spoken vocabulary of the following words: haaaloo, bye, I, fine, wine; bus, bow, bell; more, my; house, horse. Sometimes, when trying for one of his words, he would say *arm* instead: he was stuck on the first spoken word Elizabeth had taught him. Sometimes he confused *haaaloo* with *bye*. Otherwise he used his little vocabulary reluctantly but appropriately. Elizabeth tried him once again with the seventy-two written words, asking him to tap out how many syllables each had and which part of the word would be stressed if he could say it. This time he got 85 per cent of the syllable structures and was 100 per cent correct in indicating the correct stress syllable. He had also improved in the phonological segmentation task, and was more often than not able to tell Elizabeth which letter had been changed, even of four-letter words. When she showed him a four-letter word, such as *bake*, but said *cake*, he pointed to the first letter; when she showed him *blot* but said *blob*, he pointed to the last letter. He was, she said, getting closer to the phonological form of words.

Nevertheless, Elizabeth had very gently, without ever insisting, begun to persuade me that John's prosodic flow, however apparently in tune with a subject under discussion, did not actually represent real words or sentences. The fact that he thought they did was part of his problem. He wasn't 'monitoring' his output. Sometimes, when people confessed that they could not understand what he was saying, he would react by slowing down, speaking more emphatically as though to rephrase and clarify his point. But sometimes, when they guessed at his meaning, and he agreed with their verbalized interpretation, I suspected that he had done so mainly in order to please them and keep them talking.

John, in any case, never used any real words, written or spoken, unless Elizabeth or I insisted and guided him – or unless there was an emergency or a special occasion which demanded words. Once, when there was a plumbing crisis in the house, he wrote: 'Cd help boy', meaning JJ might help. For my birthday on 11 April 1994

John wrote this message, without help, on the back of a postcard of Romney's painting of a shepherd girl:

I knew exactly what this meant: I was to spend £70 on a large terracotta pot in which to keep our hostas safe from the snails that infest our garden.

For my birthday in 1996 he chose a postcard of van Gogh's *Portrait of Trabuc*, with a message for me written on the back:

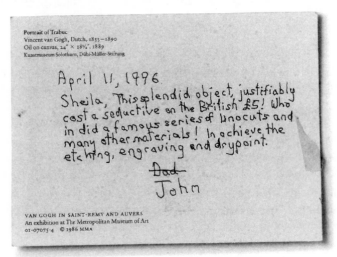

That was a big improvement, although I suspected that he had copied some of the words from a book about printmaking.

That Christmas he gave me a scarf, specially hand-painted by Christina, with a postcard of a mysterious seascape by Caspar David Friedrich and another message written on the back:

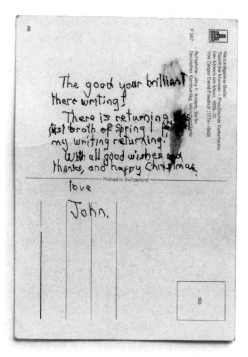

Elizabeth rejoiced with me. She said that if he could compose one complete sentence, on his own without help, he would write more. But he did not write another spontaneous sentence. And in October 1996 he told me he wanted to take a long break from therapy. Elizabeth agreed: she said she was getting stale; John had one of the most intractable problems she had ever come across. In the new year I reminded him that it was time to go back to work. He pushed the idea away. He had lost the desire to write or speak. Now that he could read to his heart's content his life and his mind were full enough. Our friends seemed to accept his way of talking, so why couldn't I?

Without stopping to think, I did something that I instantly regretted. I said: *Da woahs, da woahs, da woahs.* That's what you say, John, but we want to hear what you are actually thinking and we can't do that if you won't try to write or speak to us in real words. John was shattered. What was this nonsense I was speaking? He was fully aware that people didn't always understand him, but surely he didn't sound like that? But, as always, he rallied. He stood up and recited, hesitantly and awkwardly, the real words that he only ever spoke to humour Elizabeth and me: *haaaloo, fine, bye, horse* . . . He pulled them out of his mouth and flung them on the floor. Then, arms open in his most histrionic manner, he said: '*Da woahs, da woahs, woahs, ach ga ga da woahs.*' You see how eloquent I can be if you will just leave me in peace.

14

John's Days

I get up in the morning with the sun and go to a spring, and from there with a book under my arm, Dante or Petrarch, or one of the minor poets, Tibullus, Ovid or someone like that . . . Then I move along the road, to the inn, talking to passers by, asking news of the places they come from, hearing about this and that, and observing the various tastes and fancies of mankind . . .

When evening comes, I return home and go into my study. On the threshold I strip off my muddy, sweaty, workaday clothes, and put on the robes of court and palace, and in this graver dress I enter the antique courts of the ancients and am welcomed by them, and there I taste the food that alone is mine, and for which I was born. And there I make bold to speak to them and ask the motives of their actions, and they, in their humanity, reply to me. And for the space of four hours I forget the world, remember no vexation, fear poverty no more, tremble no more at death: I pass indeed into their world.

From a letter by Niccolò Machiavelli written to a friend while he was in exile from Florence, 1513, translated by J. R. Hale; from J. R. Hale, The Literary Works of Machiavelli

In the two years since John gave up therapy with Elizabeth our life has settled into a routine that suits us both. John wakes me up earlier than I would like with one of his new words: *uuuuup!* He studies the newspapers over breakfast, pointing out articles of particular interest that I might otherwise miss. John used to say that anyone who reads a newspaper after breakfast will get brain rot, so this is his only chance. He reads every word of every obituary, whether he knew the deceased or not. Then he scans the evening's television and marks programmes about wildlife or art. After breakfast I tell John that I cannot possibly write this book. It started as an article for the *London Review of Books*, but I can't really remember when or why I considered turning the story of John's aphasia into a book. I think I was talked into it by friends who are charmed by John into wanting to know more about his condition; and, of course, by John, who continues to believe that anyone who can write at all is happier when writing.

I remind him that he is the writer of books in our family, not me. I may have grasped something about some *theories* of aphasia. But he is the one who knows what it is to *be* aphasic. One day he will write a book about his stroke even better than Douglas Ritchie's. But for someone like me who has never experienced the inconceivable, trying to understand aphasia well enough to write about it is like running in circles around a hydra. One head tells me one thing, the next says the opposite; I chop them both off and they are replaced by more heads suggesting more hypotheses. The subject is too big, I say: it straddles too many disciplines; there are too many unknowns. If I read all the books in all the libraries in the world I still would not know what is going on in your head. John points his index finger in the direction of my study.

At about ten Anie arrives. She is supposed to work with him on his physiotherapy exercises, but I think they spend more time chatting about Poland and her problems with her boyfriend. She helps him in and out of the bath. He dresses himself in old clothes, straps on his splint, stows his house keys in one pocket of his jacket and in the other a card issued by Speakability, on which I have written his name and our telephone number and address. If Anie and I can catch him before he escapes one of us ties his shoelaces and I bargain with him about when he will return: I say lunch at two, he puts up three fingers, we settle for half-past two. But sometimes he is so eager to be off that he slips away without our noticing. I know he will soon find someone to tie his laces. But I have repeatedly told him that if I don't know exactly when he's coming back I will get anxious and run around the neighbourhood searching for him.

I run to the dry cleaners: the two large middle-aged women behind the counter, who have known and loved him since long before his stroke, did or did not see him limping past: how fast he goes now, they say. I ask the ferryman if he has rowed John across the river that morning. The ferryman says yes or no, and how wonderful it is that John is so independent. I try the antique shops: since *The Civilization of Europe in the Renaissance* began to bring in royalty cheques I show them to John and leave it to him to decide how much he wants to spend of his earnings. As always, he wants to spend, rather than save, and he now haunts the local antique shops, where he bargains ferociously using his fingers to indicate his bottom-line price. So far he has bought two paintings, three eighteenth-century prints of our stretch of the river and a Victorian armchair; he has also designed and paid for new curtains to replace the shredded ones in the drawing-room.

On my rounds, I might run into a friend who has just had a drink with John in the pub. Usually somebody has seen John. If not I telephone Camilla and we drive in different directions further afield: she to the garden centre where John has befriended the boring lady who replaced the Scholar; I to the second-hand bookshop, which is closed on weekdays but has made an arrangement for John to come in by the side entrance whenever he likes. The chances are that I will find him there, among the shelves in the basement bookstore, with a cup of tea and a plate of fairy cakes by his side, as provided by the owner.

On most days John returns from his walks with a book or two tucked into his shirtfront, presumably – now that I've had to stop him buying new hardbacks – by a friendly librarian or one of the assistants in the second-hand bookshop, who are happy to search for old editions of anything John requires and notify him when it is found:

Dear Sir John,
You were asking for a copy of 'The Journals of Dorothy Wordsworth', – ed Mary Moorman, Oxford 1971.

I have come across the Journals, but an earlier edition. It is edited by William Knight, 1st edition (2 vols) 1897 . . .

I have put it aside for you, in case you are interested: if I'm not in, Rose (Friday) or Jeremy (Saturday) will know where to find it.

Looking forward to seeing you soon, and I hope you're keeping well!
Roland

He receives less personal notifications from the public library:

'Art 2 Ritual of Childbirth in Renaissance Italy' JM Musacchio. We are still trying to obtain a copy of this.

That was how I discovered that John had joined the public library. Didn't the librarian think you a bit strange, John? John nods and shrugs. How did you do it? John mimes himself miming reading a book. How did they know who you were or that you are a resident of the borough? John shows me his identity card from Action for Dysphasic Adults, which has our address on it. Of course.

Before returning books to the public library John copies out their titles and puts them in a desk drawer.

Over lunch he tells me about his morning. *Mmmmmmm* means John walking along minding his own business. *Arrrr-up!* with his left hand describing an arc means that he has crossed a bridge. He meets a friend: broad smile, greeting gestures; they go into a pub: mime of conversation – *bahbahbahbahbah* – and drinking. Or John gets on a bus: sounds of changing gears, starting and stopping. John's adventures in our very ordinary neighbourhood are tremendously dramatic. Raw, everyday experience seems to have become even more intensely interesting for him now that he is unable to describe it in words. Many people comment on how strangely happy he seems. He is not happy. But he has an enlarged capacity for enjoying small pleasures – the company of friends, food, wine, a beautiful day; capable, too, of what I can only describe as moments of transcendent bliss. Watching John studying a map or great painting, or watching a bird in flight, I glimpse the ecstasy 'behind the ecstasy', the 'thrill of gratitude to whom it may concern' that Vladimir Nabokov tells us in his autobiography that he experienced when standing among butterflies.

In less transcendent moments he prefers reading, looking, thinking, walking, listening to what others have to say and figuring out what they really mean to resuming the painful struggle to recover his own words. He has, I suppose, given up. But I haven't. I find it significant that if I ask him *who* it was that he met or *what* they drank or *where* he went, he now understands the questions

A Classical Education
Richard Cobb
Chatto and Windus, 1985.

Samuel Johnson
Walter Jackson Bate
Chatto and Windus, 1978

Elizabeth Gaskell: A habit of stories
Jenny Uglow
Faber and Faber, 1993

The Life of Charlotte Bronte
Elizabeth Gaskell
Penguin Books, 1997

Henry James: the imagination of genius
Fred Kaplan
Hodder and Staughton, 1992.

France 1848-1945: Volume I: Ambition, Love,
Politics
Theodore Zeldin
Oxford, 1973

Sir Robert Walpole
J.H. Plumb
The Penguin Press, 1956

Vanessa Bell
Frances Spalding
Weidenfeld, 1983

and will even have a go at writing a name, a drink, a place. If I insist.

Three friends still visit John, each once a week, to help with his correspondence and try to coax the retrieval of some language. Monday at noon is Anthony's slot. Anthony is an opera producer. He directed many of the plays in which John acted at Oxford, and they have been friends ever since. On Fridays Susan, a journalist

who has known John longer than I have, comes at midday; and in the evening, Ann, the journalist who invented the Sloane Rangers when she was features editor of *Harpers & Queen* in the 1970s, comes by train, after she has sent off her column.

Until recently, John's nephew Chris (the son of John's sister Joan, who had put aside the colander of peas for the photograph of the three Hale children in their garden in the 1920s) used to drive up from his house in Worthing on the Sussex coast. Chris was unremittingly enthusiastic about John's progress. John was 'in great form', they had had 'an extremely pleasant hour', and, as always, 'a lot of laughs'. Since Joan died Chris and his wife Sally have been free to spend more time sailing. He comes less frequently now. We both miss him, but he writes to John from ports in Greece, Spain, Sicily – the most recent letter was from north Africa – on blue paper stamped with a picture of the boat. His letters say that he and Sally have never been happier. They wish John could join them. Perhaps one day he will? Ann or Susan helps John to express his desire to be on that boat, sailing on unpredictable seas to exotic destinations.

Sometimes I worry that we are abusing the loyalty of friends who have other problems and other demands on their time. But the truth is that John's days would be greatly impoverished without them. By making it possible for John to write and receive letters they have become a lifeline. Thanks to them he carries on as before, corresponding with absent friends, family, professional colleagues. They help him reply to all correspondence, including crazed letters from lonely old ladies who have misunderstood his books, questions from professional colleagues who have not heard about his stroke. He insists on replying to notes on Christmas cards, even if it takes him and the friends until the following summer. John also initiates his own letters, which is of course more of a problem for the friends, who may know nothing about the recipients or what John wants to say to them.

Part of the fun of acting as John's secretaries, they say, is the detective work. When they have finished their hour or two with him, they write a note to me in a desk diary explaining how, when John wished to write a letter to a person unknown to them about an unknown subject, he managed to convey a message. Later or the next day I catch up with the diary entries and help John with the draft they have prepared, which he then copies on to one of his buff-coloured correspondence cards printed with his name, Professor Sir John Hale, and our address.

Ann's diary notes mark the seasons:

First day it was still light when I arrived at 5:15.
Daffodils out in the park.
Magnolias blossoming in the street.
Roses out. J still answering Christmas cards!
Many varieties of roses out in Sheila's garden.
Dark by 6:30. Clocks put back this Sunday.
Found towpath flooded when I tried to walk along the river from the
*   station.*
Snow!

Occasionally there are comments about public events. John votes for Blair, but a year later he is disillusioned (he writes the word by himself). Sheila votes for Clinton and celebrates his re-election. But the diary notes are mostly about the letters John receives and writes. The friends are getting to know the most regular correspondents: Eva in Prague, David in Los Angeles, Jill in Boston, Miriam and Jean-Pierre in Paris; Charlotte in New York; Niss, his old nanny, who is in a retirement home in Kent; Pauline, who is stuck in her cottage in Lincolnshire because she can't drive any more on account of her bad knees.

27 Oct. 1996.

Darling Polly,
    I am glad Joan is all right.
I am sure she was better
for these three weeks. Sheila
and I are well. We went to
St. Petersburg with friends
for a week.
                    Love,
                        John

10 February 1997

Dear Polly,
    You are so good to Joan. I am
glad your family are spending July
in England. I send you much love.
Keep on keeping your mouth shut!
                With love,
                    John

5 April 1997

Dear Polly,

I am very sad to think of you being discouraged and overburdened. Thank goodness your family is coming in June. I am writing to Joan. At least she is safe in the Nursing Home!

Lots of love,
John

2 November 1997

Dear Pauline, We are very much hoping that you are going to be able to come to J.J.'s wedding.

We were so sorry to hear about the death of your dog.

Sheila and I have just returned from a very enjoyable visit to Venice.

I do hope that you have good news about Gillian

With love from,
John.

7 April 1998

Dear Pauline,

It will be 3 months since Sheila and I saw you. How are you?

We had a wonderful holiday in Egypt. We stayed 3 days at the Pyramids and then went on to Luxor and Thebes. I went into 4 tombs. I managed to do so much because the Arabs were so helpfull

With love from, John.

11 November 1998

Dear Polly,
    You will miss Joan dreadfully
— I do too. She was a fantastic
sister and I loved her very
much. I treasure you!
        With love from,
                Joan

19 December 1998

Dear Polly,
    How are you? I am thinking of
you. Sheila and I are going to
Morocco for Christmas! We are
getting back just before the New
Year.
        With love from,
                John.

After lunch John sleeps for exactly one hour, just as he has ever since I met him. At sea in the Merchant Navy he taught himself the trick of banging his head on the pillow for each hour he intended to sleep, and it has never failed him. When he wakes up he makes himself tea, drinks it in the kitchen reading the latest *Times Literary Supplement* and copying out the titles of books reviewed that he wishes to read, then he goes up to his study at the top of the house. He sits at the desk in the window where he pores over his art books or studies the *Oxford Atlas of the World* planning our next trip; he watches the sun set over the garden, and waits for me to give him a chapter of this book, which he reads with great care, putting little ticks on passages he likes, and crosses against those he doesn't. At exactly seven o'clock John changes into a silk shirt and cashmere cardigan, pours himself a glass of red wine, and settles down in the drawing-room to the best part of the day, which is reading books about great men and women who lived in the eighteenth, nineteenth and early twentieth centuries.

The day after he finished Colin Thubron's novel *Turning Back the Sun*, he came home with a paperback edition of Alexander von Humboldt's *Personal Narrative of a Journey to the Equinoctial Regions of the New Continent* tucked into his shirt. A week later it was two biographies of Charles Darwin. In the subsequent three years he has bought so many biographies that we've run out of shelf space. On one shelf there are recent biographies of Turgenev, Dickens, Tennyson, Balzac, Trollope, Lewis Carroll, William Morris, Thomas Mann, Picasso, Wordsworth, Jane Austen, Coleridge, Michelangelo, Caravaggio, Thomas Hardy, James Joyce, Daphne du Maurier, Aldous Huxley, G. M. Trevelyan. And that is one of six shelves holding John's purchases. It was when they were full, and I told him we couldn't afford to go on buying books at this rate, that he joined the public library from which he now borrows his biographies. John is seventy-four. I used to think that his compulsion to read about completed lives was related to his own unrealized ambition to write another biography. Now I think it is a way of coming to terms with the shape of his own life, which has entered its closing chapters.

Like many aphasics John is rigid about his daily routine. Unlike most he is even happier when the routine is broken. When we travel abroad, which we do quite often now, he is much less bothered than I am about the inevitable delayed flights, punctured tyres, uncomfortable hotel rooms, irregular meals. At the end of our first return visit to Florence, our friends put him on a train to Pisa while I was checking in the luggage. In the confusion, the train pulled out with John on board, leaving me standing on the platform, wailing and poised to throw myself on to the tracks. This is the kind of behaviour Italians understand, and I was soon surrounded by comforting voices while someone went off to telephone Pisa explaining that a man who spoke no language but understood Italian would be arriving by the next train. I found John on a bench at the airport station, reading. In Mantua we lost him, then found him outside the city walls leaning comfortably on his stick, gazing at the fortified castle. In Venice he walks so much that he has found a shop that replaces the worn rubber ferrules of his stick. I thought I knew every shop in Venice, but I've never come upon this one. When I ask him where it is he puts his finger over his mouth: it's his secret.

In Madrid, our first venture to an unfamiliar city, Lauro, a Renaissance historian who shares John's love of pictures, was exhausted by John's insistence on spending entire days without a break in the Prado. In St Petersburg we lost him altogether in the galleries of the Hermitage until he got stuck on the curving marble staircase and was rescued by an attendant. He wanted to see St Petersburg from the water. Cynthia hired the nearest boat, which stank of diesel

fumes and could only be reached from the embankment by way of a wobbling slippery plank. I closed my eyes while the frail old boatman helped him across. In Egypt, when the rest of us climbed down into underground tombs by way of steep steps that John couldn't manage, he sat in the sun talking to old Arab men about how many children and grandchildren they had.

In New York, where I don't allow him out and about on his own, we walk from my mother's apartment on East 63rd Street to the Frick, the Museum of Modern Art, and best of all the Metropolitan

Museum, where Charlotte shows John the pictures she is restoring. John cannot hear enough about the minute, crucial decisions involved in Charlotte's restorations of the Metropolitan paintings.

Of all his children, she is the most like him and the only one who shares his interest in art. And now her intimate acquaintance with masterpieces – some of which John has loved all his life, or described in his books and articles – has brought the two of them closer than ever.

In London we go often to the opera and the theatre. Shakespeare and Oscar Wilde keep him on the edge of the seat. But if it is a play he doesn't know I book seats towards the front because he has trouble following the lines if he can't see the actors' faces. At meetings of Speakability, of which John is a patron, he talks to recovered aphasics who tell him their stories; and to aphasia therapists, who say they cannot really answer his questions without a thorough assessment of his particular case.

We are still invited to dinner parties, big parties and, recently, to a ball. No sooner have we arrived than he leaves me in search of interesting conversations, hopping eagerly along on his stick straight into the centre of the room, greeting friends and strangers alike. He used to abandon me like this at parties in our early years together, when I was new to London and didn't yet know many people. Now, for a different reason, I lurk anxiously on the outskirts of the chattering crowds. There is nothing I can do about his gregarious social behaviour short of putting him on a leash. The best I can do is try to keep track of him by the uncannily bright white hair that has replaced the tongues of fire. And more often than not I find him surrounded by laughing people. They insist that he is as good a conversationalist as he ever was; but they want to know more precisely what he is talking about: is it something about war? – or is it walls?

Some, inevitably, are uncomfortable in John's company; but they are in a minority. People who loved John before his stroke love him now all the more. There is something about his eyes and voice and body language that seems to speak more directly to their hearts than all the words with which he charmed and taught throughout his speaking life. Strangers are fascinated by this sociable stranger with the donnish manner who listens so intelligently but replies in an unrecognizable foreign language.

Occasionally Willy takes him to a dining club, of which they are both members, for people associated with the arts who also enjoy good conversation. After these dinners, Willy puts John in a taxi and he arrives home very late smelling of good wine, with food stains on his dinner-jacket, laughing to himself at some joke he has heard at dinner. The other night when he hadn't come home by several hours after midnight I was frantic. I telephoned Willy, got the answering machine. I called the police, who said they couldn't search the whole of London for a disabled man who shouldn't be out by himself in the first place. John arrived after four with the wind in his hair. He had stopped the taxi several miles short of our house, apparently because he felt like a walk. I said, or rather screamed, You are seventy-four not fifteen. You can't talk. You are lame. You can't use your right arm. And now on top of everything else you are behaving like an adolescent boy. I'm too old to bring up another adolescent boy. And so on. John made himself very small, but I could tell that he could tell that I was as proud of his ridiculous feat as I was outraged by it. He had heard me often enough in the past reacting in exactly the same way to JJ's adolescent behaviour.

When we are at home in the evenings we sometimes listen to music after dinner. John puts his chair in the middle of the room between the two speakers and conducts. No expert on the brain has been able to give me a certain explanation for the pain music caused John after his stroke, or for the intense joy it gives him now. Professor Butterworth's hypothesis is that the stroke might have temporarily affected his auditory cortex in such a way that he heard notes off-pitch. The recovery of pleasure in music, in any case, happened as though overnight at about the time he started reading for pleasure.

On other evenings we eat our supper in front of the television. Recently we watched a programme about the life of the albatross on the island of South Georgia. John smiled in a friendly way at the penguins and seals that congregate on the island. But whenever the albatross flew on to the screen he made great swooping movements with his good arm. I could see that he was swooping through space with the bird: he *was* the bird, just as when he listens to music he *is* the music. Why should he want to talk or write about music or birds when he can become them? Does this ability to identify belong to some primitive evolutionary level? Some children enjoy the same power to become the object of their attention. Perhaps animals do too? Is it a gift the adult human brain traded in when its left hemisphere was adapted for language?

Once a month, on Fridays, the doctor visits John. His house calls have got him into trouble with the other doctors in the practice. They have seen John out and about and say that since he is so independent he could just as easily walk the mile from our house to the surgery. They suspect our doctor of liking John, and I think they may be right. When the doctor arrives he says, How are you today, Sir John? And John says, *Fffffffine!* The doctor says, Very good! That's progress. You're doing very well. They have been performing this routine since Elizabeth taught John to say *fine*. The doctor takes John's blood pressure while I wait in an agony of tension for the result. Anything above 160/90 is worrying. Usually, though, it's lower, sometimes as good as 140/80. The doctor renews John's prescription for the blood pressure medicine, and spends another half hour chatting to John about his wife, a former nurse who thinks he works too hard, and his problems at the practice where the doctors are underfunded and overburdened by the load of unnecessary paperwork required by the government. When he leaves John sometimes says *haaaloo* instead of *bye*. The doctor waits while he corrects himself.

Twice since his stroke John has been taken ill. The first time he collapsed with pain in his right knee on a Saturday evening. Our doctor, who happened to be on call that night, summoned an ambulance. It came within five minutes and took us to what I still think of as Dr X's hospital, except that this time it was the orthopaedic ward, which is in a different building and managed by a different consultant. This ward was clean and the nurses were efficient and kind. The consultant diagnosed a recurrence of osteomyelitis and ordered injections of antibiotics in his knee; three days later John walked cheerfully out of the hospital.

The second time John was ill our doctor was on holiday, and no other doctor from the practice would visit us. John was screaming in agony from a pain in his right calf and was unable to stand much less crawl to the loo. When I was eventually allowed to speak to a doctor on the telephone I said I simply couldn't nurse him in this condition. She said that was my problem, why didn't I call an ambulance? The ambulance took us to Accident and Emergency at Dr X's hospital. John lay moaning on a trolley for eleven hours until a junior doctor glanced at him, said he had no idea what was wrong with him, and sent us home. A nurse, who was trying to be kind, explained that the hospital couldn't accept old people, unless they were critically ill, because it was so difficult to discharge them.

John's daughter Sophie came up from Brighton to help me nurse him. A woman doctor from the practice eventually arrived, glanced at him, said she had no idea what was wrong with him; it could be a deep-vein clot. I should make an appointment with a consultant. What sort of consultant? Where? How would I get John to the consultant? She said she had no idea, but that if I continued to make such a fuss she would expel John from the practice. I turned to a private doctor, who called in one of the physiotherapists who had treated John at the Star & Garter. It took her half an hour to diagnose referred pain from a pinched sciatic nerve in John's back. She explained that if a limb is uncontrolled due to brain damage, pain in that limb is also uncontrolled; pain of this kind has no ceiling and is probably more terrible than any normal person can experience or imagine. She treated his back with ultrasound, gave him exercises to do. Gradually he was able to sit up, then stand up, then walk. Three weeks later we went to Italy for a holiday.

On Thursday mornings Anie takes John to Ellie's stroke group. Ellie is a Scottish physiotherapist who clings to the subversive conviction that all neurologically damaged patients should receive professional rehabilitation and advice from the onset of their condition to the grave. The Stroke Association has refused to help her, and our doctor is the only one in this part of London who funds her treatment of his neurological patients. With very little money, and with the help of a retired occupational therapist, Ellie gives stroke, multiple sclerosis and Parkinson's patients of all ages a chance of receiving long-term professional help with the management of their illness.

She holds her groups wherever she can find a free room, usually a dingy church hall or the common room of an old people's home.

She is an advocate of the Peto doctrine of rehabilitation, which is different from the Bobath method, which John got used to at the Star & Garter. Whereas the Bobath method aims to retrain individual groups of muscles, the Peto approach is more holistic, emphasizing movements of the whole body that are as normal as possible. The stroke patients are instructed to recite and count as they do their exercises: *I raise my arms up. One two three. I bring my arms down.*

One two three, and so on. The rationale is that movement will encourage words and vice versa. This is how John learned to say *uuuup*. But it took him three weeks, with much extra coaching from Anie and me, and unfortunately he has never mastered *down* or the counting.

John is bored by Ellie's classes. He prefers the company of normal people. But I make him go because I admire what she does for people who are less privileged than us. She has got an eighty-five-year-old thrombosis patient out of the wheelchair in which he was sitting for fifteen years. Thanks to Ellie he can take two or three steps on his own, which means that his wife, who is older than he is, no longer has to lift him on to the lavatory. I remind John that it was after he had been working with Ellie for a few years that he accomplished the great physical feat of walking the plank in St Petersburg. I give her credit for a lot of the freedom of movement he is beginning to take for granted. I can't prove it, but, as I tell John, we must support anyone and anything that gives stroke victims a chance of independence.

15

Myths and Metaphors

As they went out, behold, they brought to Him a dumb man possessed with a devil. And when the devil was cast out, the dumb spake, and the multitude marvelled, saying 'It was never so seen in Israel.'

Matthew 9: 32–3

As the news of John's stroke spread we received letters – some from people who knew him only from his books and television programmes – reporting a dream. In this dream John suddenly speaks, quite normally and naturally, as though nothing special is happening. In one version of the dream everybody present exclaims and rejoices. In another, the dreamer is the only person who notices. The other people in the room ignore John. Either they have not heard him, or they don't understand what an important event they have witnessed.

I've dreamed both versions, as has John's daughter Charlotte. Evidently it is quite a common reaction to aphasia. After an earthquake in Turkey in the summer of 1999, an aphasic woman who had not spoken for twenty years was buried alive in rubble. On the sixth night her son dreamed that she called out to him, 'I'm alive. Come and save me.' The dream was so vivid to him that he insisted on a search. She was one of the few victims of the earthquake who were found alive. But of course she had not in fact called him, and she never did regain her speech.

People also told us stories about the sudden emergence of language in childhood. There is, for example, the one about the child T. S. Eliot. His fourth birthday has passed and he has not yet said a single word. One day he is sitting silently in the kitchen when his mother hears his voice – the same monotone with which he would later read his poems aloud – speaking: 'Mother. Why. Is. The. Refrigerator. Constantly. Dripping.'

Such parables, no doubt invented to soothe anxious parents, were intended to reassure John and me that just as some children seem to find their tongues suddenly, so might John. Two of our closest friends imagined they actually heard John speak. To Betsy, during a conversation about Broadway musicals, John said 'On Your Toes'. Lauro, a fellow historian of the Renaissance, invited John into his study and heard him comment, 'So this is where you work.' I have never, alas – except in my dreams – heard John speak a phrase or sentence. But the myth that language can be suddenly given or taken away, as though by some higher power, goes very deep.

In the earliest surviving debate on the nature of language, Plato's dialogue between Hermogenes and Cratylus, Cratylus argues that 'a power greater than man assigned the first names to things', while Hermogenes maintains that language is an arbitrary set of symbols that have evolved by 'usage and custom'. Socrates toys for a while with Cratylus' view before agreeing with Hermogenes. But, although Hermogenes won the argument, the 'creationist' myth of language as the gift of some higher power was not so easily quashed. In the Bible the Old Testament God is enraged when Moses confesses to fearing that he might not be sufficiently eloquent to deliver His commandments: 'Who hath made man's mouth? . . . have not I the LORD? Now therefore go, and I will be with thy mouth, and teach thee what thou shalt say' (Exodus 4: 11–12). In the Gospel According to St John, the Word is not only with God, it *is* God.

I know of only one direct biblical reference to stroke: 'If I forget thee, O Jerusalem, let my right hand forget her cunning. If I do not remember thee, let my tongue cleave to the roof of my mouth' (Psalm 137: 5–6). But it is surely possible that some of the dumb men cured by Christ from one minute to the next in the gospels were not deaf mutes but aphasics.

In the twentieth century theoretical linguistics has demonstrated that, as Shakespeare put it, a rose by any other name would smell as sweet. And the congenitally deaf and dumb have proved the case by convincing sceptics that, if left to their own devices, they will always evolve a system of arbitrary hand signals that work as well as verbal language. Nevertheless, although the deaf have finally triumphed over him, Cratylus continues to haunt unconscious attitudes to people who suffer from aphasia. Nobody knows as well as an experienced aphasia clinician that regaining language is a slow and painful process that is not, unfortunately, in the gift of any higher power. And yet I've met several therapists who say they regularly dream the dream of sudden restoration, and that the dreams are so real that when the patient comes for the next treatment the therapist half expects to hear that patient talk normally.

Some of John's friends and admirers also have a waking dream that the miracle of restitution will be performed through the intervention of a computer. I've lost track of the number of conversations I've had with people who *insist* that I must buy John a computer, preferably one like Stephen Hawking's. If Stephen Hawking, who is so much more physically disabled than John, can talk through a computer . . .

The notion of the machine as a metaphor or a model for the brain has a distinguished provenance, which goes back to the beginnings of modern science. In the seventeenth century the discovery by Copernicus, Kepler and Galileo of the physical laws that govern the heavenly bodies persuaded some thinkers, including Descartes, that the nervous system could also be described in mechanistic terms. In *The Treatise on Man*, Descartes compares the nervous system to the musical fountains that were popular wonders in his day, and the brain as the fountain-keeper, 'who must be stationed at the tanks to which the fountain's pipes return if he wants to produce, or prevent, or change their movements in some way'.

Today we use other mechanistic metaphors – engines, telephone exchanges, diagrams of boxes and arrows. It is difficult, even for neurologists and psychologists, to describe the stupendous complexities of the physical brain and its functions without comparing it to some other complex but more comprehensible system. Here, for example, is Noam Chomsky, the most influential linguist of our time: 'We can think of the initial state of the faculty of language as a fixed network connected to a switch box; the network is constituted of the principles of language, while the switches are the options to be determined by experience.'

Douglas Ritchie frequently described his aphasia as like a machine that needs fixing:

It was like starting a motor car. The engine ticked over and speeded up, but the moment one sought to put the car into gear, something went wrong with the clutch, the gear crashed with an ugly sound and the engine stopped.

I thought, three or four months ago it was all currents and switches; now it is motor cars. Why don't I do something about my speech instead of mixing metaphors?

Some aphasics today compare their condition to computer overload. Nancy Kerr writes of hers as like a computer on the blink:

Sometimes, you know that a file is in the computer, but you can't see the open file in your mind's eye just as when your computer's screen is blank. At other times, you can see what is on the screen (which is your mind), but the printer does not work. You get an error message that you should check the connections to the printer (which is writing or speaking).

The computer certainly works better than the motor car as a metaphor for language. But that doesn't explain the faith that a personal computer could somehow act as prosthesis for verbal communication – that the word is not only with the computer, it *is*, somehow, the computer. Before he was himself stricken by aphasia Marshall McLuhan, the visionary philosopher of communication, taught that computers would eventually *replace* language: computers of the future would be extensions of the nervous system, able to communicate consciousness without the fragmentations and misunderstandings attendant on verbal language. He foresaw the computer as bringing a new Pentecost, a new revelation of Holy Spirit without the multiplicity of languages.

It is true that sophisticated digital computers can be trained to model brain function. But the idea, popularized by artificial intelligence researchers, that the brain behaves like a computer is misleading. Brain connections are not necessarily more efficient than artificial neural networks, but they are more labile, dynamic, and far more complex. This is not to say that our planet will not one day be inhabited by a master race of robots with silicon brains that communicate by plugging into one another. But the intelligent and well-meaning friends who insist that John's aphasia can be cured by a personal computer are not thinking about robotics, much less about Marshall McLuhan's vision of a computer-driven Pentecost. Our friends, who would no doubt reject the Cartesian notion of the mind as located outside the body, seem actually to believe that John's lost language could be recovered like a lost file from the hard disk of his Toshiba. Why?

Is it because most of us who rely on computers know as little about them as those of us who rely on language know about language? We take both on faith. The computer arrives in a box and transforms the way we communicate in the few weeks it takes to master it. Language arrives unbidden and without the slightest conscious effort on our part by the time we are three or four. You don't have to understand the first thing about binary mathematics in order to acquire and use a personal computer; or about neural anatomy and linguistic theory to acquire and use language. But the comparison ends there. Computers are mysterious only to people who are not computer scientists. Language is a mystery for everybody, and not only because scientists have not yet cracked the problem of how the brain produces it. Language is mysterious because however much we know about it and however brilliantly we use it to explore our own brains, we cannot ever directly know the unconscious disposition for language.

In the Renaissance some writers liked to play with the idea that words could be transmuted into palpable, visible physical objects. Five centuries later Chomsky has settled on an invisible organ: 'in the sense in which scientists speak of the visual system, or immune system, or circulatory system, as organs of the body'. He argues that the 'language organ is like others in that its basic character is an expression of the genes', and that like other biological organs it develops in a child like the growth of other organs: 'it is something that happens to a child, not that the child does'.

A more simplistic, materialist recent analogy, that the brain secretes thought and language the way the liver secretes bile, is perhaps less convincing. Steven Pinker, at any rate, like Darwin before him, prefers to call language 'an instinct'.

In addition to the prophecy that John will speak suddenly, when we least expect it, or if not suddenly then eventually, through the intervention of a computer, John's aphasia inspires other fallacious certainties. One is the Freudian fallacy, according to which John is suffering from a psychological trauma, which a psychoanalyst or sensitive friend could resolve by discovering the 'key' to his problem. Another is that John is speaking in a code, which could be cracked either by a computer or by me. John obviously intends to speak, knows what he wants to say, and, indeed, thinks he is saying it. It is one of the more poignant characteristics of aphasia that intentionality – which Dr Wise locates in the pre-frontal lobes – usually does remains intact in aphasics. But the intention to communicate is not the same thing as communicating, whether in words, sign language or code. Nevertheless, John's manner and voice are so obviously pregnant with meaning – and he so obviously believes that he is communicating meaningfully – that even Elizabeth found it hard to credit her own evidence that his voice was not describing real words and sentences. She continued to believe that his spontaneous speech patterns must be motivated by some 'metalinguistic' intent, even though when he pretended to read aloud his voice did not map on to the structures and stresses of the words on the page.

Our friends also read meaning into his gestures. The eyes of a distinguished recital pianist, who had been discussing Beethoven with John over dinner, were drawn to the fingers of John's left hand, which were playing on the table while they talked. The pianist insisted that he recognized the opening bars of the *Diabelli Variations*. John, who can read music – but scarcely play the piano, and has certainly not ever attempted to play Beethoven – nodded pleasantly, as he usually does when people give him the benefit of the doubt.

John has begun to attract a reputation for vatic wisdom. An article about his aphasia in the *Evening Standard* was headlined 'The Silenced Sage'. We attended a friend's lecture, which was followed by silence from the audience. John, who had listened intently, stood up and began to ask a long question – perhaps he really wanted to know something, or perhaps he hoped to help out his friend by breaking the silence. He got in quite a few strings of *da woahs*es before I managed to pull him back down on to his seat. The learned audience seemed no more puzzled by his discourse than they had been by the lecture that prompted it. No doubt they were being courteous or kind. But the distinguished academics who came up afterwards to discuss John's interpretation of the lecture seemed really to want to know what he had been trying to say about it.

Why, I wonder, am I so anxious to root out harmless fallacies about aphasia, especially as John rather enjoys being taken for a prophet or a pianist; and is always happy to discuss battles and fortified buildings with people who believe he is talking about wars or walls. It is after all perfectly natural to invent plausible hypotheses for the unexplained or inexplicable: it is that drive that underlies all religions, and all science. Before I began trying to understand what little is known about aphasia I was as superstitious about John's loss of language as the next person.

It also goes without saying that unchecked superstition can be the cause of profound and persistent human suffering. In his remarkable book *I See a Voice*, Jonathan Rée charts the history of the appallingly cruel treatment of congenital deaf mutes, who, until very recently, were classed as sub-human brutes or at best childlike beings whose only salvation lay in their learning how to speak properly. Even great philosophers were not immune to what Rée calls the folk metaphysics of the human voice. Immanuel Kant, for example, wrote that the dumb could never attain the faculty of reason, only at best an 'analogy of Reason'. It was not until towards the end of the twentieth century that deaf mutes were finally liberated from misguided folk metaphysics. The delayed recognition that deaf-and-dumb sign languages are as good at representing thought as verbal languages was achieved by their own concerted political action supported by modern linguistic theory.

If the story of aphasia has had no such happy ending, the reason is that most of us can't help judging the quality of thought – of our own thinking as well as that of others – by the language in which it is expressed. By what other means can you know what another person is thinking? How, without language, can you know what you yourself are thinking? The folk metaphysics of expressive language as a prerequisite of thought has been embedded in philosophy at least since the ancient Greeks used the word *logos* to signify both thought and language and was generally accepted even throughout the

Enlightenment – although some eighteenth-century philosophers had doubts or regrets. In the early twentieth century influential linguists continued to preach the doctrine of linguistic determinism. The structural linguist Ferdinand de Saussure was categorical: thought and language were inseparable, interdependent and simultaneous. The anthropological linguist Edward Sapir taught that language is shaped by the environment in which it develops, and that language dramatically shapes and restricts the scope of thought. The neurologist Hughlings Jackson wrote that:

The speechless patient has lost speech, not only in the popular sense that he cannot speak aloud, but in the fullest sense. We speak not only to tell other people what we think, but to tell ourselves what we think. Speech is a part of thought.

Hughlings Jackson compared aphasics to dogs. Bertrand Russell argued that just because a dog cannot tell you that its parents were honest but poor you cannot conclude that a dog lacks consciousness. But Wittgenstein, who maintained that misuse of language was at the root of all philosophical problems, said that a dog could not have the thought 'perhaps it will rain tomorrow' and therefore did lack consciousness.

And Dr X treated the 'infarcts' in his care with a careless brutality that he probably would not have meted out to a dog, while the speech and language therapist in the white coat treated John as though he were a sub-normal child. John, thanks to his charm and the support it has attracted, has on the whole avoided such treatment. But many aphasics who might otherwise have made some recovery are humiliated and cowed, and come to believe that the pundits are right: they are hopeless, useless. It is hardly surprising that so many aphasics suffer from severe depression.

Nobody can deny that consciousness and language are intricately interwoven. But are they really one and the same? Clinical evidence suggests that they are not. Even the most profoundly amnesic patients on record have not lost language, from which one can infer that there is a strong dissociation between language and semantic-episodic memory. Alzheimer's patients in the last stages of their dementia, when they may no longer know who or where they are, often retain the ability to speak in well-formed sentences.

Nevertheless, only a few decades ago, Antonio Damasio, now Professor of Neurology at the University of Iowa College of Medicine and at the Salk Institute in California, was taught in medical school that any creature without language was lacking a conscious mind. But when he began to observe real aphasic patients he realized that the relationship between consciousness and language was in fact less straightforward:

As I studied case after case of patients with severe language disorders caused by neurological diseases, I realized that no matter how much impairment of language there was, the patient's thought processes remained intact in their essentials, and, more importantly, the patient's consciousness of his or her situation seemed no different from mine ... In every instance I know, patients with major language impairments remain awake and attentive and can behave purposefully.

Many of Damasio's teachers would have been students themselves in the decades when the theory that intellect is diminished by aphasia prevailed, encouraging medical practitioners to assume that garbled or absent language was the product of a garbled or absent mind. Unfortunately not all of Damasio's contemporaries have bothered to observe aphasic patients closely enough to re-think the old doctrines, and so they continue to trickle down from medical schools to practising doctors, to nurses and to some speech and language therapists, to the families and friends of aphasics, and to aphasics themselves. Dr X was fiftyish in 1992. If he attended medical school when in his twenties, in the 1960s, he would have been taught by doctors who had been educated by the theories of Hughlings Jackson.

Dr Wise locates rational thinking and the sense of self outside the language zone in the pre-frontal cortices, which occupy one third of the human brain and which are not usually damaged in aphasia. 'The pre-frontal cortices', he says, 'are the privileged parts of the brain, responsible for planning, decision-making, ruminations, problem solving – which is why aphasics with undamaged fore-brains don't normally lose what we call top-down thinking; and why aphasics with good pre-frontal brains often make better recoveries than those with less good ones.' If Dr Wise is correct – if it is in the pre-frontal cortex that we formulate intentions, lay plans for achieving them, imagine what it is like to be another person, and regulate our social behaviour – then it is John's intact forebrain that explains his undiminished ability to play chess, plan a day or a journey, behave appropriately in social situations and compensate strategically for his disabilities.

Because there are many kinds of high-level thinking that bypass words altogether – master chess players, mathematicians, physicists, painters, architects and musicians do not usually have the need or the time to translate their thinking into words – not all philosophers have been entirely comfortable with the identification of words with thought. Leibniz, in his *Dialogue on the Connection between Things and Words*, was greatly troubled 'that I can never acknowledge, discover or prove any truth except by using in my mind words or other things'. Diderot wrote in 1751 that although our souls experienced many impressions within one 'indivisible instant', we had only one mouth and could say only one thing at a time. Language, which requires us to divide (Elizabeth used the word 'disambiguate') and regiment the 'tonal impression' in our souls, permits great clarity and explicitness, but it also conceals much of the warmth and richness conveyed by more primitive forms of expression. Increasingly, Diderot wrote, we were hanging up our souls in 'chains of syntax'. Berkeley was more categorical: words were the great impediment to thought.

When John could write, he envied artists because they could create images, while he could only envisage images in his mind's eye or describe them second-hand, in words. He told me that in the early Renaissance some humanists compared poetry to painting, and showed off their powers of description by praising, for example, the painting of the great court artist Pisanello. But Pisanello won the competition by demonstrating that he could capture the effects of nature without a single word.

Aristotle believed that images, as well as words, must play some part in thinking. And there are some people who insist that they think not in words but in images. The geneticist and psychologist

Francis Galton maintained that his own thought, whether he was calculating the course of a billiard ball or considering more abstract problems, was *never* accompanied by words, only, occasionally, by nonsense words, 'as the notes of a song might accompany a thought'.

Einstein famously described solving problems 'before there is any connection with logical construction in words or other kinds of signs which can be communicated to others', by imagining himself riding on a beam of light and looking back at a clock, or dropping a coin while standing in a descending lift.

It often happens that after being hard at work, and having arrived at results that are perfectly clear and satisfactory to myself, when I try to express them in language I feel that I must begin by putting myself upon quite another intellectual plane. I have to translate my thoughts into a language that does not run very evenly with them . . . That is one of the small annoyances of my life . . .

The words or the language, as they are written or spoken, do not seem to play any role in my mechanism of thought. The psychical entities which seem to serve as elements in thought are certain signs and more or less clear images which can be 'voluntarily' reproduced and combined. There is, of course, a certain connection between those elements and relevant logical concepts. It is also clear that the desire to arrive finally at logically connected concepts is the emotional basis of this rather vague play with the above mentioned elements . . . [which are], in my case, of visual and . . . muscular type. Conventional words or other signs have to be sought for laboriously only in a secondary stage, when the mentioned associative play is sufficiently established and can be reproduced at will.

Elizabeth used to say that John's problem in finding expressive language was related to an inability to tease out the discrete linguistic elements of images. At that time I believed that his tendency to represent the world in unpacked images – the socks in their display boxes, the floor plan of a friend's house to signify the friend, a drawing of his study with the desk on which we would find the bibliography of his book – was related to the unusually vivid and well-trained preoccupation with images that had moved him to write the word *Vermeer* before he could write more ordinary words. But it may be – as Aristotle, Francis Galton, Einstein, John before his stroke and many others who have tried to analyse their own thought processes believe – that images are as necessary a part of translating thought as words. The thought may start as an image. Or it may be that some people think more in images and some more in words.

Steven Pinker refutes the 'hypothesis of linguistic determinism', maintaining that the thought–language problem has been resolved by new ways of 'thinking about thinking' – and about language – that were set in motion in the late 1950s by Noam Chomsky's revolutionary linguistics, which have demonstrated to the satisfaction of his disciples that thought and language are dissociated faculties:

The idea that thought is the same thing as language is an example of what can be called a conventional absurdity: a statement that goes against all common sense but that everyone believes because they dimly recall having heard it somewhere and because it is so pregnant with implications . . . People do not think in English or Chinese or Apache; they think in a language of thought.

Most of us, as Pinker points out elsewhere in *The Language Instinct*, know all too well what it is like to say or write something we didn't mean, or to have a thought we can't quite express in words.

Willem Levelt, in his book *Speaking: From Intention to Articulation*, argues that

there is no *single* language of thought . . . The cognitive system communicates internally by means of a number of conceptual codes: propositional ones, spatial ones, kinesthetic ones, and probably others. There are procedures for going from one code to another, and there is no reason to assume that the propositional language of thought is the one that should mediate between all others.

A pre-verbal message, according to Levelt, can be in any mode of thought. It is only the message by which we communicate thought to others that must be cast in the propositional mode, 'that, at the same time, meets conditions that make it expressible in natural language'. Levelt's analysis, although not accepted by all psycho-linguists, seems to me to resolve very well the apparent paradoxes of John's aphasia. John's spatial and kinaesthetic thought processes are obviously intact. The fact that he believes he thinks in language may mean that his propositional thinking is also intact. If so, his problems are not in the pre-verbal message but in the processes by which it is translated into communicative language.

Some prefer to describe the relationship of thought and language as a loop: a sequence of control operations in which each depends on the result of the previous one; thought determines language and language determines thought. Einstein, like the linguist Edward Sapir, believed that the language in which it is expressed determines the form of the thought. And after thirty years of working with aphasics, Elizabeth is certain that aphasics do represent the world differently from people with whole brains: not less rationally, or less perceptively; but differently. And after nearly seven years of living with an aphasic, I would agree.

Some of the most compelling descriptions of the interface between thought and language are to be found in the accounts of recovered aphasics. When Dr Johnson after his stroke prayed to God, he composed his appeal in Latin. He concluded that his faculties had been spared because he could judge that the lines were not very good. Although Professor Jacques Lordat was aware that the people around him now regarded him as stupid, he had no difficulty in reflecting on such complex ideas as those relevant to the mystery of the Holy Trinity. 'Be assured,' he wrote after his recovery, 'that there was not the least change in the functioning of the innermost intelligence.'

John insists not only that he thinks as before, but that he thinks in language: that is why he's so surprised when people fail to under-stand his meaning. Dr Wise has no problem with this claim. John, he says, hasn't lost his language: he's lost his language *processing*. Professor Butterworth suggests that John is thinking at the 'abstract level', which Butterworth defines as a kind of interface midway between the message John wishes to convey and the words. But Douglas Ritchie observed 'a wide difference between thinking about words and actually thinking in words about words. I could think, actively, without words . . . but . . . the minute I rehearsed speaking with my tongue, even though I kept silent the words would not come.' Dr Nancy Kerr forgot altogether what language was: the concept was as foreign to her as colour would be to a blind child. And yet she could understand language. Other aphasics say they know perfectly well what language is, but that it is as though their brains are 'talking too quickly'.

People often ask John if he is working on his next book. For those who know nothing about aphasia it's a reasonable question. He always *was* writing some book or other. His mind and left hand are intact. So what else does he need, apart of course from a personal computer, to be getting on with his work? Perhaps one day he will write a book, and if he does I hope it will be about what it was like to be aphasic. Meanwhile I trawl the literature of aphasia, searching for clues. Anyone can imagine what it would be like to be deaf or blind – children play games that mimic such physical disabilities. But to think without language is unimaginable. You cannot really know what it would be like until you have been there, and few who have been there have described it as well as Douglas Ritchie and Nancy Kerr.

Perhaps the most bizarre of all attitudes to aphasia is my own desire to share the experience with John, to know at first hand what it is like to be him. And I was surprised to learn that I am not entirely alone in this wish. Robert, an adventurer, boulevardier and writer ten years older than John, who has been everywhere, seen everything, tells me that he longs to be aphasic – just for a month or two. Robert says that at his time of life there aren't that many new experiences. It would be a last adventure. And from a glint I sometimes notice in John's eyes, I would guess that sometimes it is. In the prelude to *Wings*, Arthur Kopit tries to enter the mind of his aphasic character Mrs Stilson: 'To her, there is nothing any more that is commonplace or predictable. Nothing is as it was. Everything comes as a surprise.' Later in the play he has her say, with delight, 'What a strange adventure I am having!'

16

John's Voice

When anyone speaks to me, I listen more to the tonal modulations in his voice than to what he is actually saying. From this, I know at once what he is like, whether he is lying, whether he is agitated or whether he is merely making conventional conversation. I can even feel, or rather hear, any hidden sorrow. Life is sound, the tonal modulations of human speech.

From letter written by Leoš Janáček, 8 March 1928

When John talks he feels at ease, as though he were communicating perfectly well. His conversational behaviour is so natural that many people are persuaded that his voice, although evidently naked, is somehow also clothed in meaning. Some say they understand him, more or less. Friends are always reporting that John 'said' this or that. I have been known to tell him to shut up for a minute and let me get a word in edgewise. Strangers often give him the benefit of the doubt, assuming at first meeting that he is speaking a rare foreign language. People tend to blame themselves for their failure to understand him. John's charm and thespian qualities, underscored by his expressive voice, make him not just socially acceptable but an object of fascination. But his confidence is also the most worrying of his symptoms. Specialists, from Dr Schapiro to Elizabeth, have advised me that John will never regain his speech until he recognizes that he is speechless.

Can he not hear himself repeating his repertory of *da woahs*es? He is not deaf, after all. He hears and understands the speech of others. He is also if anything abnormally sensitive to other people's reactions, and can see all too well from our blank faces and games of Twenty Questions that he is not getting his message across. About this most bizarre manifestation of John's aphasia our friends admit they have no theories – apart from some form of Freudian denial. You could argue that John is defending his ego by subconsciously denying that his voice, the most salient projection of his personality, is crippled. But why then should John, who always regarded himself as primarily a writer – who was convinced that he couldn't think properly unless he was writing – accept that his writing is impaired but deny his loss of meaningful speech?

He does not, in fact, deny it. When you mimic his voice or play it back to him on tape he recognizes it. Far from denying or attempting to rationalize the evidence, he is horrified by it. Apparently what he hears, or believes he hears, when he is speaking is different from what he hears when he listens to other voices or his own voice off-line. When we discuss this problem, as we do frequently, he sighs, *Ah, oh, ach ga woahs, da woahs*: if only you knew what it is like to live in this ghoulish nightmare.

So he knows. In the years when he engaged eagerly in therapy with Elizabeth, it was more his idea than hers that they should work on his speech. He heard, understood and appeared to accept her instruction that he *must listen* to himself, that he *must* learn to monitor his spoken output. He can in fact monitor the tiny vocabulary that she taught him. He uses those words appropriately, but reluctantly because he is dismayed by the clumsy, and to his mind unnatural, sound of his voice enunciating real words; what he imagines to be eloquent sentences and paragraphs come more easily than single words. If he wants something for which he can sometimes say the word – wine, for example – he will avoid speaking it unless I insist. Then he will say it, but in the spirit of humouring me with a party trick.

I know he knows when, during a meal with friends, he remains silent, perhaps picking up a book as a sign that we needn't make the effort to involve him. But if we invite him to join in and his interest is aroused, or if he judges that a social situation requires a suitable contribution, off he goes – *da woahs, woahs, da woahs*: aware that we can't follow him, and yet not aware that he is not making sense; resigned to our failure to follow his meaning but also puzzled by our obtuseness. He knows exactly what he wants to say and when he speaks his mind he is abnormally fluent. Unlike normal people John rarely hesitates as though reaching for a word. The slight stutter that he had before his stroke is gone. The eloquent rhythms of his voice do however serve a purpose. Like the faint question marks he pencils in the margins of this manuscript, his pauses make us reconsider. And he makes us laugh.

A Freudian, insistent on denial as the explanation of John's paradoxical condition, might invoke his undiminished sense of humour as an attempt to placate the terror that would overwhelm him if he confronted his situation directly. And it is true that some aphasics with John's problem develop an exaggerated and sometimes aggressive sense of humour. But the style of John's wit is identical to what it was before his stroke. The mixture of wildness and gentle irony is unchanged, as are the expansive gestures and amused eyes. Our Italian friends used to say that John, even when speaking English, was more like an Italian. He still is, even when speaking no language.

The clinical term for John's failure to recognize his loss of speech is anosognosia. The cumbersome name – from the Greek *nosos*, meaning disease, and *gnosis*, meaning knowledge – was coined by the French neurologist François Babinski in 1908 to define a disturbance of specific awareness not associated with generalized impairment of either consciousness or intellectual function. Anosognosia is one of the most eccentric, counterintuitive and elusive of neurological conditions. Although it has been observed in brain-damaged patients since the 1880s it continues to generate a range of competing and increasingly complex theories. Almost nothing is known about it, except that it is probably due to a disruption of cross-talk between separate brain regions responsible for sensory perception and for awareness. Something similar happens in conditions that affect vision, such as blind sight in which patients can see but are not aware that they can see; and prosopagnosia – the subject of Oliver Sacks's *The Man Who Mistook His Wife for a Hat* – in which patients can see but cannot recognize what they see.

Anosognosia for paralysed limbs is seen in patients whose left body is affected by right-brain damage but not in those with paralysed right limbs caused by left-brain damage. For this reason some neurologists have concluded that structures in the right hemisphere, probably in the parietal lobe, are responsible for conscious awareness of the body. (Although John in the first weeks after his stroke forgot the existence of his right arm, and still leaves out one hand when he draws a human figure, patients with damaged left hemispheres do not suffer from severe or chronic anosognosia for their right limbs.)

Anosognosia, however, is not confined to paralysed limbs: there are patients who are oblivious to their own blindness, deafness, incontinence, impotence, extreme pain; as well as their own voices spouting nonsense. It varies in severity. Some anosognosics may show an implicit knowledge of their disability, as John does, without feeling that it is real or relevant to themselves. Or they may concur that their limbs, for example, don't move, but invent rationalizations, ranging from plausible (they are too tired to make the effort) to outrageous (the limbs are machines that don't happen to be working that day, or they belong to another person, perhaps a phantom child with disabilities similar to their own). In extreme cases, they may deny that anything at all is wrong with them.

Anosognosia for garbled or non-existent speech affects some patients with jargon aphasia or with aphasias like John's in which articulation is restricted to a few reiterated meaningless utterances. Most jargon aphasics have as much difficulty understanding the speech of others as they do recognizing their own garbled or wordless speech. Mrs Stilson in Kopit's play *Wings* suffers from jargon aphasia. Kopit imagines what she might hear when listening to doctors examining her:

WHAT WE HEAR (*The Components*): Are we moving you too fast? / Mustlian pottod or blastigrate, no not that way this, that's fletchig gottit careful now / Now put your nose here on this line, would you? That's it, thank you, well done, well done.

Mrs Stilson's stroke would probably have damaged or isolated the posterior branches of the left middle cerebral artery. This is where Karl Wernicke hypothesized that brain damage would destroy the link between the auditory images of words and their semantic representations. No doubt he would be delighted to know that modern scanning experiments indicate that he was correct. Self-monitoring of speech also seems to take place in this area. And yet, there are 'Wernicke's' aphasics who have difficulty understanding external speech but are acutely aware of their own garbled speech – although they can do nothing to correct it. And there are aphasics, like John, who can understand external speech but cannot monitor their own.

Evidently there is what a cognitive neuropsychologist would call a double dissociation between auditory comprehension off-line and on-line, which raises the question of how aware any of us is of our own overt speech. It feels, when we talk, that we are listening to ourselves in the same way we listen to other voices. But it may be that we are partly listening to an unvoiced voice, an imagined pre-articulatory plan, which is not the same as the sounds our vocal organs are making. This may be why most people are surprised by the sound of their own voices when they hear themselves on tape.

When I asked Dr Wise for a neurological explanation of John's failure to recognize his speechlessness he replied that self-monitoring of speech is one of the hottest topics in neurological research today:

Do normal people monitor before or after articulating? How do we monitor our internal speech, and how aware is any of us of speech mistakes others can recognize? What is certain is that the monitoring of speech on-line and off-line are two different neurological processes. As you talk your speech is fed back into the auditory system. Listening to your own voice on tape is totally different.

Puzzling over John's problem in the spring of 1997 I came, by chance, on an article in the London *Times*, about the work of Dr Linda Wheeldon, a psycholinguist at the University of Birmingham who specializes in the investigation of 'inner voice', a concept I had previously skated over when I came across it in my research. After reading the article it occurred to me that John's inability to generate the sounds of words and letters in his head might be due to a failure of 'inner voice'; and that it might also be related to his lost ability to monitor his own voiced non-speech.

After she received a substantial grant from the Economic and Social Research Council, Dr Wheeldon's research caught the imagination of the media, apparently because some journalists thought it might be about spiritualism and psychic phenomena. 'I've had a lot of phone calls from people hoping to summon the voices of their dead relatives,' she said warily when I telephoned her. She was relieved that I was asking about language rather than ghostly voices, and invited me to spend a day with her in Birmingham. She emphasized that she is not an aphasiologist – 'because I'm a wimp and can't face the tragedy' – but said she was interested by John's case.

I found her, six months pregnant with a second child, in her cramped office in the Birmingham University Psychology Department, where our conversation was frequently interrupted by students knocking on the door. She seems to be a popular teacher; and she certainly has all the enthusiastic commitment it takes to breathe life into what some might regard as an abstruse academic subject:

People take language for granted. They have no *idea* of its complexity. Just because most people can do it should not obscure the fact that it is one of the most *awesome* achievements ... I'm afraid my field got off to a bad start with Chomsky. He built a psychological model that is procedural: he provided us with theories to test. What interests us today is not that kind of intellectual masturbation, but how we do it, how we actually produce language.

Speech production, said Dr Wheeldon as I took notes, involves four stages:

The pre-linguistic stage is called 'the message'. People are very skimpy about what this might actually contain, i.e. what kinds of units; but it is a psycholinguistic assumption that it precedes the other stages. The second stage is grammatical encoding: you retrieve the lexical items that best match clusters of concepts (these will be different in different languages); and build a syntactic structure that puts them in the right order. The third stage is to generate phonemes, the sounds that make up spoken words. We don't just go and find spoken words. It is not a holistic procedure. We regenerate them in quite small sound chunks. That is why people often accidentally transpose the first sounds of two successive words. The phonemes of the word are assigned to a prosodic frame, syllable by syllable, probably from left to right.

(Dr Wheeldon was not surprised to learn that John is able to generate the prosodic frame but not the sound chunks: 'Unimpaired speakers suffering an aphasic blip can often tell you about the prosody – syllables, stress – of the target word. And normal speech errors will always retain correct syllable structures.') Finally, the vocal muscles are primed to articulate the finished phrase or sentence.

Dr Wheeldon's special interest is in the role played by inner voice in the pre-articulatory stages: 'I used to think it happened at the last stage. Now I think it occurs at one or two earlier levels, that we are monitoring an internal, abstract speech code.' So might John's monitoring problem be at the second or third stage?

Possibly. The pre-linguistic message level is evidently intact. He has a clear idea of the message but seems to have a major low-level word construction deficit, which prevents him from building its full prosodic representation. He may suffer from an overload problem: focusing on what he intends to say uses up all his resources. All his capacity is being allocated to generating meaning, but he's filling all those prosodic frames with only two syllables. It could be a case of focus, a selective attention problem. Monitoring speech requires resources extraneous to processing capabilities. It's like proof-reading: you can read for the meaning of a text or for spelling and punctuation, but it's hard to do both at once. It's *effortful* to monitor your own output; some normal people have very little monitoring capacity.

Before long she was at the blackboard describing the experimental techniques she uses to map the time course of this process in milliseconds: 'The more inventive we are in the lab, the more we can learn. The challenge is to find ways of simulating a concept to be translated into language.' Trials involve twenty-five to thirty-five volunteers, usually students, and last for about an hour at a time. One example of an experiment that requires volunteers to generate and listen to their internal speech involves giving them a target sound, say hard 'c'. They are then shown pictures of objects and asked to press a button as soon as the first letter of an object, say a candle, generates that sound in their heads. The experiment is repeated for consonants that appear later in the word. That experiment, however, only identifies the moment the subjects are actually aware of the sounds.

The main way psycholinguists study language production is via unintentional speech errors in normal subjects. 'People make all sorts of mistakes, without necessarily knowing it. They garden path themselves often, getting halfway through a sentence then changing course.' Slips of the tongue are examined in laboratory conditions for types of error that do and don't occur; how often they occur; the factors that influence their occurrence; how long it takes to repair, or 'pre-pair', mistakes. An example of pre-pairing is demonstrated by experiments that show one role of inner voice to be the censoring of slips of the tongue that might inadvertently produce vulgarisms. Subjects asked to repeat teasers like 'tool kits' or 'duck fate' are much less likely to fall into the trap if the mistake would be rude than if it would be an innocent Spoonerism.

Normal speech mistakes, even though they may result in words that are meaningless, always retain the phonological rules of the speaker's language. I asked Dr Wheeldon whether the orthographic rules that govern written language are also always retained: John's writing, even in the early days when he wrote only strings of non-words, always obeyed the orthographic rules of English. True to the boundaries of her academic specialization she said writing was not her field, but, 'Orthography and phonology must be so entwined that we can't sort them out.'

Does John have inner speech? 'No.'

Now that I have been alerted to the concept of inner voice – and the probability that John doesn't have it – I come across it more often, or perhaps I just notice it when I do. The broadcaster and journalist John Diamond became acutely aware of his pre-articulatory inner voice after losing his speaking voice to throat cancer:

In the milliseconds before I spoke I would hear the words in my head, sounding quite normal, very John Diamond, and I'd open my mouth to say them and what would come out would be somebody doing that honking impression of Charles Laughton in a bubbly, underwater version of *The Hunchback of Notre Dame* . . .

Most of us, under certain circumstances, can hear our inner voices in our heads. But the internal, abstract speech code hypothesized by Dr Wheeldon would be monitored at a deeper, unconscious level. The Russian linguist Lev Semyonovich Vygotsky compared inner speech to 'the other side of the moon'. Inner speech, he said, was 'speech almost without words . . . it is not the interior aspect of external speech, it is a function in itself . . . While in external speech thought is embodied in words, in inner speech words die as they bring forth thought.' (Vygotsky considered that inner speech evolves out of the social speech of early childhood and is essentially predicative in character. His disciple Alexander Luria maintained that the ungrammatical telegraphic speech of non-fluent – 'Broca's' – aphasics was due to a failure of inner speech. I've had different opinions from different experts about whether John's aphasia could be characterized as 'Broca's' or 'Wernicke's'.)

Most of us consciously use silent speech when, for example, we repeat in our heads a telephone number until we dial it or find a piece of paper and write it down. John, who has no problem writing numbers – who can remember historical dates, estimate costs, calculate distance and time, add and subtract – cannot hold a heard telephone number in his head long enough to dial it or write it. All aphasics suffer to some degree from loss of short-term memory for language. It seems that inner speech is necessary for the short-term memory that acts as a buffer, holding words until they are ready to be used. When some aphasics say that their brains 'talk too quickly', that the words are there but they can't catch them, they may be describing an impairment of that pre-articulatory buffer.

A standard test for aphasic comprehension requires the patient to follow instructions to move tokens of different sizes, shapes and colour, e.g. 'pick up the large red square and put it under the small green triangle'. If you give John these instructions orally he can follow them perfectly. But if you write them he has much more trouble with the task. Presumably he cannot hold the written instructions in his short-term memory because he cannot rehearse them sub-vocally. Elizabeth says this problem has less to do with comprehension than with his failure to articulate words.

Dr Wheeldon subscribes to a theory of self-monitoring proposed by her mentor and colleague, the Dutch psycholinguist Willem Levelt, who has produced one of the most highly specified models of speech production. Dr Levelt envisages a double 'perceptual loop' in the language system, by which inner speech and external speech are 'perceived and parsed'. Both loops involve the comprehension system (which, in John's case, works for externally perceived speech but not for inner speech.)

Dr Levelt cites experiments with delayed auditory feedback (DAF) as evidence, but not proof, of the intimate connections between listening and speaking. The experiment requires a normal speaker to listen to his/her own voice through earphones. When the speech is amplified and delayed by about 200 milliseconds, speech is severely disrupted. The speaker immediately begins to stutter, hesitate and drawl. The perception of speech interferes with its production because, Dr Levelt infers, the connections between the two systems have been short-circuited. (Some neuropsychologists consider that congenital stuttering may be caused by a neurological fault that delays auditory feedback in a similar way.)

Although an abstracted view of the two classic poles of aphasia – 'Wernicke's' and 'Broca's' – suggests a dissociation between comprehension and speech, Levelt's connectionist approach posits that audition and production of language are part of the same chicken-and-egg process. And Dr Wise has found physiological evidence 'that the mental representations for the structure of sounds in words used in speech perception are shared with the system involved in speech production'. By this analysis John's lack of inner voice, compromised short-term memory for language, inability to speak, and failure to perceive that he is not speaking are not dissociated losses but all elements of the same problem.

All aphasics lose some comprehension; and most aphasics, and their friends and families, are more disturbed by their failure to understand what people say to them than by not being able to read, write or speak. For this reason it relatively easy to raise funding for projects that investigate aphasic comprehension. But despite a good deal of focused research over the last twenty years or so the neurology and psychology of auditory comprehension are less well understood than those of vision. Something is known about how the signals we receive through our eyes are transformed by the brain into meaning-ful images; much less about how some of the signals we take in through our ears are translated into what we recognize as meaningful language. It is not, for example, understood how we accomplish 'auditory streaming' – the so-called cocktail-party syndrome, by which we can hear two or more voices at once and differentiate and understand them at the same time. Most aphasics lose this capability. John, who enjoys cocktail parties as much as ever, seems to have retained it. The only voice he cannot hear and understand is his own.

As with all symptoms of aphasia for which there are no universally accepted explanations, hypotheses about anosognosia for disrupted language vary according to the perspective from which the problem is considered. Dr Jonathan Miller refers me to a theory of the nineteenth-century neuropsychologist Hermann von Helmholtz, according to which the brain produces what Dr Miller calls 'a fast-forward carbon copy of its order to act or speak; the outgoing order deposits an invoice, which remains in the brain, of what you *expect* to do or say'. If, for example, a limb is amputated, the brain, in the absence of feedback from the limb, may confuse the invoice with the completed order.

Just as John continues to experience the sensation of talking normally, so some amputees register normal sensation in a limb or organ that has been detached from the body. Usually it is a limb, although there are also cases of phantom appendixes after appendec-tomy, phantom breasts after radical mastectomy, phantom penises after amputation. Signals to and information about the missing body-part may continue to be registered by the brain for months or years.

But as the brain reorganizes itself in response to the amputation something else happens, at least to some patients. The topographical map of the brain's body image is organized differently from the body it represents. The brain map, for example, represents the hand in an area that is closer to the face and shoulder than to the arm; the feet are close to the genitals. V. S. Ramachandran – Director of the Center for Brain and Cognition at the University of California, San Diego, and adjunct Professor at the Salk Institute, La Jolla – describes a patient who, when he shaved or stroked his face, experienced sensation in a missing hand; and another, a woman, whose amputated foot reappeared when she made love. Professor Ramachandran's explanation – which he has confirmed with magneto-encephalography (MEG) scanning – is that in the absence of feedback from missing limbs the areas which normally register input from them go quiet and are colonized by adjacent areas.

I came across Professor Ramachandran's account of his experiments with amputees with phantom limbs at about the time I interviewed Dr Wheeldon. For a time I speculated that a neurological explanation of John's anosognosia might be that something similar had happened in his brain. Was it possible, I wondered, that brain regions or mechanisms responsible for John's surviving language capabilities had overwhelmed nearby or related structures that no longer function?

The analogy with phantom-limb syndrome works to the extent that anosognosia could plausibly be caused by a failure to update mental representations. But there is a crucial difference. Patients with phantom limbs know perfectly well, even when the limbs are causing extreme pain, that the limbs are not there. They never try to use them. Some anosognosics may be, like John, distantly aware of lost function, but they have no automatic reality check. Their consciousness of the problem, such as it is, is second-hand.

Anosognosia is by definition a disturbance of consciousness. Freud said that we are all conscious of only 10 per cent of what is actually going on in our brains, and many thinkers today would agree that normal consciousness is extremely limited. But consciousness today, as one scientist put it to me, 'is of uncertain scientific status'. Although it has been known since the 1820s that taking in sensory stimuli and turning them into responses are two different brain processes, how the two collaborate to produce what we call consciousness is an unresolved philosophical and neurological quandary. Certain brain areas seem to be necessary for conscious awareness. The thalamus, the sub-cortical 'inner room' that straddles both hemispheres, is crucial for awareness of information received by the senses, apart from smell. (Dr Wise, who calls the thalamus 'the centre of the universe', found from John's brain scans that his thalamus, although intact, was cut off by surrounding brain damage.) The left temporal lobe, essential for language, is also an important centre of consciousness.

The neural correlates of consciousness are elusive, and so is an agreed definition of what we mean by the word. Antonio Damasio identifies what he calls *core consciousness*, which is 'about one moment – now – and one place – here' and is 'the rite of passage into' *extended consciousness*, in which 'both the past and the anticipated future are sensed along with the here and now in a sweeping vista as far-ranging as that of an epic novel'. Core consciousness, he maintains, is not affected by brain damage. He cites anosognosia as evidence that extended consciousness can be disrupted selectively and without impairment of core consciousness.

The elements of individual consciousness, whatever and wherever they may be, do not in normal people necessarily reflect the observable realities that can be detected in or by another person. There is no way of proving that your perception of the colour red, let alone of how your voice sounds, is the same as mine. But if our actions were guided by such phenomenological conundrums, we would be existentially paralysed. John, who was and is decisive almost to a fault, is the sort of person who gathers his thoughts, makes up his mind, and acts. He wrote most of his books from first sentence to last with scarcely a change or need for correction. A dithering general, he used to say, would lose the battle to a weaker army with a decisive leader. Now John prepares his thoughts, decides to speak, opens his mouth to do so, and acts on the reasonable assumption that after a lifetime of speaking effectively he is speaking now.

The influence of pre-morbid experience and personality on the way an individual reacts and adapts to loss of function following brain damage cannot be discounted. Synaptic networks are shaped by experience, and it may be that the brain under stress activates connections that release 'realities' wired into the brain since early life, but which do not tally with objective reality. Dr Edwin A. Weinstein, an American specialist in anosognosia, has written that consciousness of disability depends to a considerable extent on pre-morbid personality and on 'the *meaning* of the incapacity in terms of past experience':

Patients with enduring explicit verbal denial were described by relatives and colleagues as having been conscientious, highly work-oriented, orderly, disciplined people. They were considered to have been stubborn and rigid, with a need to be 'right', with a concern for 'principles'. They were regarded as having great will-power and believed that the flesh was the servant of the spirit. They had seen illness and incapacity as a failure and weakness involving a loss of integrity and prestige. They were regarded as not empathic and as reserved rather than emotional. Woodrow Wilson, who denied incapacity after a massive right hemisphere stroke, and who actually sought a third term in office, had such a 'denial personality'. He had believed that good health and success in life depended on following the rules for right living, so illness represented a moral dereliction.

Some of this applies to John. He is indeed conscientious, work-oriented, orderly, disciplined, stubborn (but not rigid), intolerant (but only of his own mistakes), with great will-power. He never believed that illness in others was a 'moral dereliction', but it is true that he denied his own failing health until it finally caught up with him on the day of his stroke.

But Weinstein's profile of a typical anosognosic does not entirely fit. John has always been extremely, sometimes alarmingly, empathic, unreserved and openly emotional. The following passage from the same article seems to me to cast doubt on generalizations about personality:

Patients who had been more emotional and open with their feelings, and who had expressed them in such 'physical' symbols as those relating to the body, looks, food, violence, and sexual activity were more likely to develop paranoid forms of denial with ideas of being beaten, starved, or sexually abused.

As well as being emotional and unusually, for an Englishman, open with his feelings John also was and is unusually (for an Englishman) physical. Beauty, food, sex were and are extremely important to him. He keeps his red-head's temper in check because he despises it and fears, so he used to tell me, that it could erupt into violence. (Hence his perhaps sublimating interest in war.) Paranoia about anything is utterly alien to his sunny and trusting nature.

I have no doubt that John's character, personality, and not least his cavalier attitudes to ill-health and danger were shaped by the months he spent as an adolescent in a wheelchair and his years as a young man risking his life at sea. John in his formative years must have become very adept at denying pain and life-threatening experience. Before his stroke I was sometimes infuriated by his fearless insouciance about the dangers of ill-health and poverty. Since his stroke I have come to admire the same qualities. You could call it denial behaviour, or you could call it courage, optimism, or getting his priorities straight. Whatever you call it I do not accept that his pre-morbid personality is entirely responsible for his anosognosia. But it may explain why he carries it off with such spirit and grace.

Occasionally, self-monitoring does return, sometimes suddenly, out of the blue, as happened to Douglas Ritchie.

Last Friday evening I listened while I talked. It is the first time I have done so since I had the stroke. Or is it the first time I have been consciously aware of my doing so? Before that I was talking but not listening. I was aware of the fact that I was talking but the listening was not conscious. But since last Friday listening has been part of my talking. Not all the while but a good part of it. I have heard my voice begin in a quavering sort of tremble and in a second strengthen to a normal voice. I have heard my voice like an actor's. Hesitations and stammers were there but expression was there also.

I know that until and unless John listens while he talks I will never again have a real conversation with him. Until he monitors his speech he will not speak. He still talks to me in my dreams: we have been having dream conversations for so long that he is quite fluent by now and we have both nearly forgotten what it used to be like when he couldn't speak. During my waking hours I never pass up an opportunity – blowing out the candles on a birthday cake, seeing a new moon – to wish that John would talk, really talk, as he does when I'm asleep.

I would do anything to recall John's speech, except the one thing that might actually work, which is to force his awareness of his voice by confronting him with it over and over on tape and to refuse to allow him ever again to say *da woahs*. I could ask our friends to stop conspiring in the fiction that he makes sense when he talks. If we ridiculed and bullied him, insisted that he either shuts up or uses real words to convey his meaning . . . But I cannot sacrifice his voice. It's not just that I can't bear to hurt him. It's more to do with a weakness in myself. I need his voice. I *do* understand it. It makes me laugh. It tells me things – about the world and myself as well as about John's thoughts – that are beyond words. The Chinese say that before you can conquer a beast you must first make it beautiful. John's voice is beautiful. Perhaps, for all my efforts to learn about the science of aphasia, I am the one who is in denial, and that is why life with him seems, despite everything, to be so joyous.

John's non-language has, in fact, become more comprehensible since, three years after the stroke (at about the time Elizabeth found that his vocalized reading of printed text was following the correct stresses and rhythms) *da woahs* was interspersed with more *ers*, *ums*, *ohs*, *ahs*, *aarghs*, *gahs*, *nos* and *oh my Gods*. His voice is now less fluent. He pauses more often as though searching for a word. His slight stutter has returned: the utterance sometimes splutters out as *d-d-d-DA woahs*. He is more frustrated than he was by his inadequate powers of expression. When he sees that we don't understand, he tries more often to rephrase his comments, enunciating more slowly and emphatically. These are good signs.

17

Hope

Dear John,
I'm so sorry. It must be, among other things, a most
extraordinary thing to have happen – one of the most
extraordinary things that ever happened to a human being.
I don't suppose anyone outside can really begin to imagine
what it's like. Sheila says the wonderful thing is that you
remain absolutely yourself in spite of it. It does sound as
if it is a kind of enchantment, as in a fairy story. And the
point of enchantments in fairy stories – all enchantments,
I think, in all fairy stories – is that eventually they are
lifted, and everything is as it was.

Letter from Michael Frayn, August 1992

From my diary.

28 January 1998. Steven Pinker – in London promoting his latest
book, How the Mind Works – lectured yesterday evening at the
Royal Society of Literature. J and I very curious to see what the great
language guru is like. Cherubic face peeping through clouds of frizzy
grey hair. Talks a mile a minute. Perhaps a little pleased with himself,
but has good reason to be. Packed audience. The London literary
intelligentsia want to know how their minds work. J on the edge of
his seat throughout and afterwards joined the queue of fans wishing
to ask questions. I tried to deflect him, just had a feeling Pinker
might not be keen to meet an old man on a stick seeking the answer
to a wordless question which Pinker wouldn't be able to answer
even if he could understand it. How does the mind of an aphasic
work? And Pinker was in fact clearly embarrassed.

I hadn't fully realized until that encounter (which I minded more than John) that John still has faith that there is someone, somewhere – probably, like Pinker, in a great university – who will explain and perhaps help. At the bottom of Pandora's box full of woes and tribulations there was hope.

30 July. John had his stroke six years ago today. Two weeks later when he was lying speechless and paralysed in Dr X's hellish hospital one of the nicer junior doctors, a woman, said, There is always hope. You must never give up hope. Coming as it did only a few days after Dr X had pronounced J a hopeless case and told me to put him in a home and forget about him, I thought the junior doctor's cliché a bit tasteless. But she was right. J survived – *and* walked – against the expectations of Drs X and Y. And now he is writing. Many words. Some specialists are 'surprised' by such late recovery of writing. (I suspect that what they really mean is that they don't believe me or think I'm exaggerating.) Elizabeth says she is surprised that they are surprised, but she does caution me that he has not actually written a complete sentence without help. I have reminded her of his Christmas note in 1995, 'I feel my writing returning'. But I have to admit that that was nearly three years ago.

14 September. Something stupendous has happened. Yesterday, without help, John wrote two complete and original sentences. I happened to be in the room with Susan, who was about to help him write a thank-you letter to the director of the National Art Collections Fund. We had lunch with him in his office last week. John had a lovely time hearing all the latest gossip about the arts world. Something made me lose patience and say, Look, this is *your* friend, and *your* world, so *you* write the letter. John wrote:

13 September, 1998
Dear David,

I then said, Fine, now what is the expression of gratitude you need? John wrote:

Thanks you for lunch

13 September 1998

Dear David,

Thanks you for lunch in your office on
Thursday. I have certainly been in luck!

Yours ever

John

I said, Now your choice of what follows is limited. Do you want to say where? John wrote:

in your office

When?

on Thursday.

Then he wrote, without prompting:

I have

And I stupidly said, Now you need either a verb or a noun. But he wrote:

certainly

And laughed at me. He finished the letter by himself:

been in luck!
Yours ever,
John

The only guidance I gave him, apart from the questions, was to remind him, as he wrote, of an (obvious) principle of finite state grammar, i.e. that each word you select limits the choice of the words that can legally follow. This seems to me a very different matter from previous letters, which were mostly composed by the friends.

Susan's diary entry, 13 September. *Luck indeed! No, not luck, just sheer glorious genius – & a new command of language. We who were witnesses were in luck. John himself, of course, is stout Cortez facing the Pacific.*

14 September. Telephoned Elizabeth with the news. She is pleased but reminds me that I did in fact guide John.

29 September. John has written more letters, finding his own words as I stand over him, merely reminding him that each word limits his choice of what can follow. Narrowing the choice must reassure him that he is not required to select from a terrifying infinity of possibilities.

To Miranda, after her dance celebrating her fiftieth birthday:

20 September 1998

Dear Miranda,

Thank you for the delicious dance on Friday. I was flattered to be on your party list and to partic... ...

Love

John

partic...

rejou

participate

15 October. Article in today's Guardian about bionic brain implants that can operate a computer by the power of thought. The implants are the size of the tip of a ballpoint and made of glass containing an electrode that picks up electrical impulses from the nervous system. Two disabled volunteers found that they could control the cursor on a computer screen by just thinking about moving parts of their body. The scientists responsible, at Emory University in Atlanta, Georgia, hope the technology will allow people who are completely paralysed to operate artificial limbs. Roy Bakay, who led the team, told New Scientist magazine, 'If you can run a computer, you can talk to the world.'

I've put the article in my Future Possibilities file along with two older ones. According to the Sunday Times (25 April 1993) a team of scientists at a Japanese electronics company were trying to determine whether a computer linked up to brain waves could be used 'to read people's minds'. They have proved the existence of silent speech by measuring the distinctive pattern of brain waves emitted by sub-vocally articulated thought. Using silent speech alone a person can move a cursor around a computer screen. (Won't do for J who has no silent speech?)

A more detailed and promising article in the New York Times (7 March 1995) says that scientists at the New York State Department of Health in Albany have showed that it is possible for a totally paralysed person using brain waves alone to move a computer cursor around a display screen. Dr Jonathan R. Wolpaw, who heads the project at the Health Department's Wadsworth Center for Laboratories and Research, is quoted as saying that although the technology is still in its infancy early results are encouraging.

Rereading this article, which I had filed away without paying enough attention, I notice Dr Wolpaw said that his group gets the best results by positioning the electrodes over the left and right hemispheres. Apparently nobody knows how the subjects control their own brain waves. It's a leap in the dark, but if Elizabeth is right that language is never lost I can't help wondering if aphasics with intact right hemispheres and pre-verbal thinking might also be able to communicate with a computer by using their brain waves.

17 October. J's improved writing has emboldened me to write to Dr Wise taking up his offer to scan J's brain for his research into recovery from aphasia. I slightly exaggerated J's writing skills, to make his case seem more interesting.

24 October. Letter from Dr Wise saying that he'd be delighted to scan J's brain with MRI and PET. Recovery of writing so late is unusual. But the project he's doing now is only about recognition of single words. Can he also do a PET scan on my brain, as a normal control? An MRI won't be necessary for me because they assume my brain is normal. I've agreed to take part.

Sunday, 7 November. Rain. It's rained so much lately that the garden is soggy and the river almost always flooding the towpath so John can't take his favourite walks. Early this morning we heard that John's sister Joan had died. She was ten years older and they had little in common, but there was a lot of affection there. To take John's mind off the loss we did some work on his latest letter to Vicky, a former student who sometimes takes him out for the day. He wrote:

Dear

(couldn't think of her name but made five dashes for five letters),

Thank you for taking me to Dulwich yesterday! The Pieter de Hooch was your wonderful plan! Pieter was completely the follower of Vermeer

(a lot of trouble with Vermeer, but when he got the V I said it was also the first letter of the person to whom he was writing and then he got Vicky quickly).

I loved the young boy and the . . .

He drew a picture frame and in it a small figure in the bottom left corner and in the top right something that could have been a window or a picture or a map or mirror. Then he wrote 'landscape'.

11 November. Tomorrow we fly to Rome where J will be ceremonially received into the Accademia dei Lincei, which is one of the oldest and most exclusive of European scholarly academies – Galileo was a founding member. J has often written about it. It has a bias towards the sciences and invites very few foreigners to be members. He seems more excited by this honour than by any of the many others he has received in his life.

13 November. Rome, Trastevere, guesthouse of the Accademia dei Lincei. The inaugural ceremony today was very long and very chaotic, as such occasions tend to be in Italy. J unusually silent,

almost in a state of shock. He finds it hard to walk on the cobbled streets of Trastevere. The guesthouse is austere, spotlessly clean, bathrooms miles away from bedrooms: the way Italian pensioni used to be when I first travelled in Italy with John.

14 November. No time until today to visit the Villa Farnesina, one of J's favourite places in Rome, and tantalizingly next door to the guesthouse. John could hardly wait. He walked quickly to the centre of the first room to admire the frescoes. I had my back to him when I heard his voice howling. He was howling like a trapped animal and rooted to the spot. He wouldn't move and I couldn't move him until two of the guards and a German tourist carried him outside the building. Then he seemed to recover, but he kept pointing to the ground with his stick and expressing horror. Something about the patterned marble floors of the villa must have disturbed him.

20 November. Since we got back from Rome J hasn't wanted to go out walking on his own. When I walked with him in the park yesterday, he had another panic attack on a path that curves up a slight rise. When I asked Ellie about the episode at the Villa Farnesina she said Parkinson's patients sometimes react that way to patterned floor surfaces but she doesn't know why the curved path would bother him. The doctor says J has no symptoms of Parkinson's. He has no idea why J reacted in the way he did. He will try to make an appointment for J to be examined at Queen Square – he calls it the 'holy of holies' – but we'll probably have to wait at least six months.

9 December. My PET scan took two hours. Richard Wise says it cost £4,000. They cover you with blankets because the room has to be kept chilly for the sake of the machinery. Needle in left arm delivering the positrons, head strapped into the halo of the machine. You listen to lists of common nouns and verbs, all of one syllable, spoken by a brisk woman's voice at varying rates from very slow to the pace of rapid conversation. Richard Wise says don't think about anything, don't worry about understanding the words or try to make sense of them, they are words that anybody of average intelligence

will understand. But after a while I think that I may not actually *be* understanding them – lists of single, unrelated words seem to lose their meaning. I worry that when they discover that I am failing to understand the words Richard Wise will decide that my brain is not after all normal and certainly not fit to understand anything he might explain to me about J's brain. It is very boring (as Richard Wise had warned me) listening to single words. I am tempted to try to discover some hermetic meaning or purpose in them. There seem to be a lot of ships, wrecks, kings, dukes . . . I think about how Billy Wilder got Greta Garbo to act the wonderful scene in the film of Queen Christina where she is standing in the prow of a ship sailing away for ever from Sweden. The more he asked her to think about her tragic situation, the more wooden her expression. Finally he told her to think about absolutely nothing. And that, so the story goes, was how he achieved the famous shot. Which is supposed to prove that some people are able to empty their minds of all thought. But Richard Wise says that scanning has shown that the brain in a resting state is never neutral, i.e. it's impossible not to think. (When they scan for specific brain functions they allow for other kinds of thinking, which is called 'noise'.)

Afterwards I am relieved when Richard's assistant Alex Leff tells me the experiment is designed to locate word recognition rather than actual comprehension, which is different. The words were chosen because the brain is more activated bilaterally by concrete words: abstract words are more concentrated in the language centres. (Why then are some aphasics, including J, better at abstract words?)

10 December. J's MRI. Apparently it's a very noisy experience because afterwards John made a noise – bah, bah, bah – like a hammer. Richard says it's also claustrophobic. Some people panic. John is braver than some. Richard will tell us the results some time next year, after he's done J's PET.

13 January 1999. J's PET. Richard says J is the first aphasic to be tested for location of word recognition by this method. Alex says there have been studies of more sophisticated comprehension tasks:

phonemes, abstract vs. concrete, word type . . . This one is simple, but they think it may have a higher success rate. They want to find out how John, who in the weeks after his stroke couldn't point to common objects when you said or wrote their words, is now able to recognize concrete words.

I sit in the control room, which is crammed with grey boxes containing many gigabytes of computing power; these apparently only take in the first stages of data which will be reprocessed on other computers to produce a virtual image of J's brain and the areas of it that do or don't light up as he listens to the words. Richard may be trying to gain insight into J's inner world, but the technician monitoring the computer screen (which only tells them whether the experiment is working) is at the same time glancing through the Express and eating chilli-flavoured corn chips. Another technician is reading the On Line section of the Guardian. Atmosphere like the back room of a police station in a television thriller. Alex Leff wanders around. I say something about J's memory for words having improved, whatever the outcome of the PET. Leff reminds me sternly that it's not a memory issue: J's semantic, episodic and visuo-spatial memory are all obviously intact.

15 January. Since our return from Rome he has refused to write another of his 'own' letters under my guidance. I haven't nagged him. I suspect that the contrast between the writing that won him membership of the Accademia dei Lincei and the simple sentences that he can manage, but only with help, is simply too stark. John has gone back to conveying his messages through his loyal interpreters, Ann, Anthony and Susan.

30 January. Ann's diary entry. *John did very well. The Russian roulette revolver chamber that seems to be in his brain was in the right position. He wrote a long letter to Charlotte about 2 Metropolitan Museum books she had sent. He wanted to comment in detail on these books, finding writing the words a bit more difficult than kissing his fingers – his reaction to the pictures. But he did well.*

5 February. Charlotte has sent me a copy of the finished letter.

> 30 January 1999
>
> Dear Charlotte,
>
> From Van Eyck to Bruegel and Heroic Armour of the Italian Renaissance are giving me lots of pleasure! Heroic Armor has so many good views of the stupendous helmet by Negroli. Hieronymus Bosch (Style) in the other book is vast, murky and desolate. Hans Memling's Annunciation is one of the most beautiful there is!
>
> With love from,
> John

I don't know exactly how much of it was Ann's and how much John's, but the style reads more like John's.

10 February. Ann's diary entry. *Winter jasmine out. John was on a roll again, only hitting a few empty cylinders – what does go on in his brain? He finished a letter to David by telling D how Fritz Saxl had interviewed him in 1947 for a job at the Warburg but J went to America after Jesus College instead. He indicated the interview by a drawing, which Sheila, who says she knew nothing about it, interpreted.*

13 February. David, very excited about this letter, has returned a copy:

> 10 February 1999
>
> Dear David,
>
> What wonderful memoir. I have never read it before. I heard Saxl

lecture 1947, in London. How interesting to read about the library
before it came to England.
In 1947 Saxl and others interviewed me for a job at the Warburg.
I didn't take it because
to America. With love from,
John.

I guessed about an interview from John's drawing, which showed three men sitting behind a table and one man facing them. But it's the first I've heard about the Warburg having offered him a job, or him having turned it down because he wanted to go to America. David has checked this in the Warburg records. It's true! J has communicated something that none of us knew. That must surely be significant however much guidance he had.

25 March. Christina has alerted me to an article in today's Independent headlined 'Brain machine restores "speech"'. It says that two patients who are totally paralysed and unable to talk have managed to communicate by using their brain waves alone to control a computer. Niels Birbaumer and colleagues at the University of Tübingen in Germany describe in the journal Nature how they enabled two 'locked-in' patients suffering from total paralysis to express their thoughts and feelings to their friends and family. The article quotes Dr Birbaumer as saying, 'We don't know how it works. These centres in the brain for self-control are far away from the language areas.'

26 March. Read the Nature article in the library and wrote to Birbaumer asking if his method might work for 'a very brilliant' aphasic with intact semantics.

8 April. Long telephone conversation with Richard W about the results of J's scans. The MRI shows that it's a 'pretty bad' stroke

affecting the vascular territory of the middle carotid artery – as I already know. But Richard says the result of the PET scan is really interesting. J's left superior temporal gyrus ('Wernicke's') has not been destroyed. On the MRI it looked atrophied, but the PET showed it 'activating 19 to the dozen'. It has been pushed by the stroke to a different location, i.e. there has been movement of the temporal lobe.

11 April (my birthday). Susan's diary entry. *V. brief visit because of traffic, I'm afraid. John is writing an* IMPORTANT *letter – and it strikes me forcibly that his progress is really excellent. But alas, had to leave before he finished.*

11 April. This is my birthday card from John:

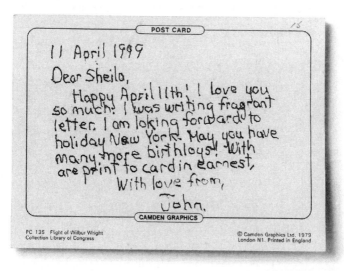

The picture side of the card is a photograph of Wilbur Wright in his aeroplane.

16 April. Amazed to receive a letter in this morning's post from Niels Birbaumer. I hadn't really expected him to reply. He finds J's case 'extremely interesting' and thinks he could 'try to treat this condition with our system'. Will I bring 'my patient' to Germany for

a few days to discuss and take first measurements? For the rest of the day John has spoken to me in a German accent.

17 April. I notice from the Nature article that Niels Birbaumer works at the University of Padua as well as Tübingen. Since J and I are going to be in Venice at the end of the month I've emailed him suggesting that if he is by any chance in Padua then it might be convenient both ways to have our first meeting either there or in Venice, which is only 10 minutes away.

26 April. Email from Birbaumer proposing Venice, Saturday, 1 May, 12 noon at Florians in the Piazza San Marco. How will he recognize us?

1 May. Venice. J looking especially striking. Venice always sets him glowing and the blue summer jacket we bought at Gatwick on the way to Morocco suits him. Even on a sunny Saturday in the Piazza he stood out from the throng and Birbaumer picked him out immediately. Niels Birbaumer 50-ish, medium height, springy build, casual-worldly manner, excellent American English and fluent Italian. Says he doesn't think of himself as belonging to any particular country, certainly not Germany. Works in Germany and Italy because those are the two European countries that provide the best government funding for his kind of research. Describes himself as a psychophysiologist interested in electrical brain activity. He is convinced that most people, including aphasics, can learn how to communicate with a computer by training their brain waves.

We settled over our drinks at Florians and talked for several hours. He has many novel and exciting (at least to me) ideas about language and language recovery. He thinks, for example, that Chomsky's theory of innate language is false. Chomsky is wrong that animals can't learn language. *Of course* they can learn language. That has been proved with dolphins and monkeys. He has worked with dolphins in Hawaii and taught them over 400 words. They could learn an infinite number of words but don't use them because words are not useful in their environment.

Animals and humans learn language by associating words with

sound responses in the environment, like a child babbling. First you find words for what you can see, hear, feel. That's why the language centres are located near the sensory areas of the brain. But in principle any other parts of the brain could learn language. The brain is everywhere the same. (He said this several times. So much for Brodmann's discrete brain areas, which are still a standard reference in textbooks.) The brain is basically a learning organ, it can change. It's not like the colon. It is a dynamic, associative organ that has nothing to do with the rest of the body.

Whatever an MRI tells you, you don't know where anyone's language capacities are located. Semantic memory is all over the brain. (So the 'holistic' position is still alive and kicking.) We all overuse the language area. If no cells are left in J's language cortex he has to find a new area. He has to relearn language through associative learning. We will experiment with muscular activity to find which part of the body communicates with the language centre: the mouth, eye, shoulder, finger. Try the right shoulder. Search for the part of the brain closest to intact language. Try a sensor in the mouth. All sensory modalities must be searched. The object is to create a new associative halo constructed around letters and words. The only question is about the strategy. *There is no question about the possibility.*

J excited, awed. *Da woahs, da woahs.* Nods vigorously when I ask why, if Birbaumer is so certain that language can be regained in this way, it is not routine practice. He says dryly that rehabilitation is not popular because there's no money in it.

He has invited me to a conference about brain-computer interface to take place in June in up-state New York. I will learn more about it there and if I am persuaded that it would be appropriate for J, he will certainly take him for retraining in Tübingen in September. The retraining will be free. All we have to pay for is accommodation. The brain-wave training has an added benefit: it stimulates the whole brain, IQ is improved by 10–20 points. Not, as Birbaumer says, that IQ is John's problem. He is convinced that if his method is going to work for any aphasic it will work for John.

We struggled over the ridiculously expensive bill for our drinks. He won.

5 May. Horrible journey home. Plane very late. Car broke down on the motorway from the airport. We weren't towed home until 6 a.m. Doctor came to take J's blood pressure: 140/80 – the lowest reading since his stroke! For John, travel and its complications are the best medicine.

10 May. Letter to Polly:

10 May 1999

Dear Polly,
    We are flying to Venice on Friday to look after some dogs......
    We are now back home after a delightful holiday! I managed to visit most of the churches in Venice, while Sheila was writing her book. I also re-visited the Accademia with enormous pleasure! In the San Rocco I was transported by the Tintoretto.
            With love from,
                John.

25 May. Richard and Alex came to the house today to explain more about the results of J's scans and to give him some comprehension tests. Having reread the scans Richard has now changed his mind. The MRI shows that J's Wernicke's has after all been destroyed by the stroke. The PET shows that when passively listening to single words he has switched hemispheres: he is activating part of his right temporal lobe which in normal people is only active on the left side.

I asked him about Birbaumer and his idea that the brain is the same everywhere. He has never heard of Birbaumer or his method or theories. He says the cellular architecture of the brain doesn't *look* the same everywhere. Brodmann's different-looking areas are accepted. They look different because the pattern of wiring is different and the cell-shapes are different. That is why recovery involves a shift to the homologous region on the other side. But why not go to the conference and check out his ideas for myself.

10 June. Drove to Cambridge yesterday to visit Elizabeth. It was intended to be a social call, but she couldn't resist trying to get John

to speak some words. They both seemed to be enjoying themselves so much that I asked if she would take him back as a patient. She said, Only if John says please, please I beg you to take me back. John distinctly said please and then something that sounded like I beg and me back.

11 June. No further panic attacks and J is altogether so much back to normal that the doctor agrees with me there's no point in putting him through a visit to Queen Square, where he would certainly have to wait for hours. Also they've told me they won't accept Richard Wise's MRI and I don't want him to have to endure another one.

16 June. Rensselaerville, NY. Up the Hudson by the same train from Penn Station I used to take to Vassar. Memories of life before John. After the Poughkeepsie stop the train heads towards the Catskills, where John and I had a passionate weekend before we were married. I haven't been up here since then. Taxi sent by the Institute met me at Albany station. The towns we passed through on our way to Rensselaerville seemed both strange and familiar, as though my memories were old American films.

The buildings of the Rensselaerville Institute are scattered about in the woods of what was once a huge private estate. The literature on the desk in my room says that the Institute is a forum for innovation, a leading organization in the field of change: 'the long winding driveway lends itself well to speculation of an eccentric nature'. This conference is the first ever international meeting about Brain-Computer Interface Technology. It is sponsored by the National Center for Medical Rehabilitation Research, National Institute of Child Health and Human Development, National Institutes of Health, and is hosted by the Brain-Computer Interface Project at the Wadsworth Center, New York State Department of Health and State University of NY – which is headed by Jonathan R. Wolpaw, who was quoted in the New York Times article in my Future Possibilities file. The programme looks tough. Three days of breakfast at 7 a.m., papers delivered all day with short coffee breaks. Discussions and demonstrations after dinner.

After settling in I joined the others for a reception and dinner in the Weathervane Restaurant. Scientists from Russia, Hungary, UK, Germany, Austria, Canada, Italy, as well as the USA. Age range mid-20s to late-70s. Jonathan Wolpaw tells me that virtually everyone working in the field is present. Five years ago there were 5 labs throughout the world doing BCI. Now there are 20. Neurofeedback has opened a whole new era in rehabilitation. It's all so new they haven't had time to think of all the applications.

17 June. I am the only non-scientist at this conference. But scientists are so much more patient with ignorance of their field than humanists. You wouldn't be treated very well at a conference on Shakespeare if you hadn't read Hamlet. Today I learned that the goals of BCI include mentally driving a wheelchair, solving non-trivial arithmetic and visuo-spatial problems, as well as communicating in words. Wolpaw doesn't seem to think it would work for aphasia: 'We're still at too primitive a stage to address these higher levels.' But Birbaumer is as optimistic as ever. He uses electrical waves called slow-cortical potentials that are not affected by lesions and can be found everywhere in the brain: 'The mechanism is universal. The electrical traces are caused by intra-cortical activity.' Patients cannot verbalize the experience of communicating with the computer via their brain waves because the electrodes are placed far from the language centre. Training is in the pre-frontal area. People with damaged pre-frontal lobes, e.g. schizophrenics, cannot do it. John, whose pre-frontal lobes are in mint condition, will be able to do it.

18 June. A kind scientist called Emanuel Donchin, who seems to be the grand old man of BCI, has been working on ways humans can communicate with computers since the late 1950s. He tells me that the aim is getting information from the mind to the computer. Some people have thought that EEGs can actually communicate thoughts directly: the logic is that EEG can reflect each individual 'thought word'. But that hasn't quite worked and Manny says it can't.

He started working on a wave called P300 to measure effects of workload on pilots, astronauts, nuclear plant workers. In the late 1960s biofeedback and biocybernetics were used by the US Defense Agency. But in the 1970s final, failed attempts to eavesdrop on the brain were followed by backlash. In the 1980s the first brain-computer interface was constructed by a computer scientist who made the mistake of taking signals from the eyes. In the mid-1980s the son of a pilot fell off his bike and was referred to Manny for clinical help as a locked-in patient. The child was not helped, but the paper Manny wrote about his attempts to get him to communicate was published in 1988 and put BCI on the map. 'Very primitive. Was the olden days.'

19 June. 3 a.m. Stayed up late to phone J before he went to sleep. I hang up after three rings then ring again, so he knows it's me. He insists on sending Anie home after she's given him his supper. It worries me to think of him sleeping in the house alone, but that's the way he wants it. So much to tell him! Had to admit that I understand about 10% of the technical papers. But there's an air of intense, pioneering excitement that keeps me on my toes all day. These people from all over the planet are going somewhere. I tell J Birbaumer is still interested in his brain waves. J replies in a German accent.

20 June. Conversation with an enthusiastic neurologist from Atlanta, Georgia, who talks about the evolution of 'cursor cortex', e.g. direct control of computer cursor from human neo-cortex without any bodily movement. 'If locked-in people could use a mouse they could run whole companies on the Internet even though totally paralysed.' When I ask him about applications to aphasia he says that in 3–5 years – given funding – he will implant a speech area. He will implant electrodes for single or groups of phonemes and go into the intact area of the brain for the neural correlates. 'The nerves are like the members of an orchestra. The idea is to grab a few members and retrain them.'

21 June. New York. Staying with my mother, who is cross with me for not bringing John. Says he's the best company and the most interesting man she knows. (But she's got very deaf.) Flew to Boston for the day to see Alfonso Caramazza who gave me lunch at the Harvard Faculty Club. My account of the BCI conference made him angry, especially the neurologist who claimed he would implant

electrodes for phonemes. Caramazza says that's ridiculous. Nothing is known about phonemes except that they are in the temporal/parietal areas. The brain sciences are at a very early stage. Something is known about the brain, something about function. We know that damage to the temporal and frontal lobes causes naming deficits, that the temporal and parietal lobes are crucial for comprehension. But there are too many unknowns. When function becomes a given, fixed, then we can ask intelligent questions about the brain.

He is sceptical about Richard Wise's conclusion from his scans that J has transferred recognition of single words to his right hemisphere. He's 'not a fan of pretty pictures', it's just a modern phrenology. It's a big step from showing a few pretty pictures to saying that transfer has happened. And what scanning doesn't tell you is *how* it's happening. Caramazza deplores 'fancy technologies' that attract all the funding and the best students. Also sceptical about my claims that John can now write, sometimes even sentences. I admitted that we had to guide him a bit, but he still thought I was exaggerating.

But he is encouraging about the book. Says I have one great advantage over even his most dedicated graduate students: I have lived for 7 years with an aphasic. So I am in a position to write about the phenomenology of aphasia. (He wrote down the word phenomenology in case I didn't understand it.) That challenge scares me more than if he'd said I was too dim to understand the aphasiology. The phenomenology of J's aphasia is exactly what I've been trying to get at for all these years. But I still can't really imagine what it is like to be John without words.

25 June. Home! Short day flight but I was so impatient to see J that I thought it would never end. J waiting for my taxi outside the house in his red cashmere cardigan. Anie had prepared and left supper for us. I kept him up half the night telling him about the States, and making plans. He was particularly pleased that Caramazza (a Harvard professor) had been encouraging about the book. I told J not to be such an academic snob. (I didn't, of course, tell him that Caramazza was sceptical about his recovery.) While we were talking J found pencil and paper and wrote the word October. This means he thinks that whatever happens with Elizabeth or in Germany I

must finish my book by then. I've been at it for more than a year and must stop dithering.

13 July. Went to see Brian Butterworth at Queen Square. As an expert in numeracy he is surprised that J can add and subtract in however many columns. Butterworth says J's aphasia sounds unusual 'even in my world': such a restricted vocabulary combined with such good understanding combined with the beginnings of recovered output in writing. Thinks that John's apparently good comprehension could be achieved by computation. He may be using his intelligence to make sense of what he registers as jumbled words. He offered to ask the Queen Square aphasia therapist if she would consider testing and perhaps treating J.

J may prefer to return to Elizabeth. There are so many possibilities, and at least three specialists – Birbaumer, Butterworth and Elizabeth – who believe there is still hope. I sometimes think I have too many irons in the fire. Am I being obsessive? (J always said I was obsessive once I got going.) But what do we have to lose by trying everything? Some of our friends think I'm a bit batty to go on hoping. But others agree with me that John is so bright, so full of life, that with everything else in place language must follow.

30 July. Doctor's visit. J's blood pressure is fine. I told the doctor that today is the seventh anniversary of the stroke. He says J is doing very well, and that the more time that passes after the accident the less chance there is of another stroke.

8 August. Drove down to Hampshire for Sunday lunch in JJ and Amanda's cottage. Pouring with rain. Heavy traffic. Roads lined with drenched hitchhikers holding signs saying ECLIPSE. I've been so absorbed in plans that it took JJ to tell me that there will be a total eclipse on Tuesday. People are heading for Cornwall for a first sight as it enters England. J went for a walk around JJ's garden and came back bleeding from his bad arm which he had gashed – without, apparently, noticing it. As we were leaving I hit a stone and got a flat tyre, which JJ had to change.

9 August. Started the day in a bad mood. Monday blues. The friends are all away on holiday and I'm too busy to help John with his correspondence. When I got back from buying a new spare tyre I was furious to see that J had gone out without waiting for me to tie his laces. Then I found two notes in his handwriting on my desk. One was on a piece of scrap paper:

> Dear Caramagne,
> I will thanks you for agreeing to advice Sheila to carre on.
> With best,
> John Hale

Next to the draft was one of his correspondence cards printed with Professor Sir John Hale. On this he had written:

> Dear Caramazza,
> I will thank you for agreeing to advise Sheila to carry on.
> With best,
> John Hale

Nobody was with him. Nobody prompted or guided him or even suggested he should write to Caramazza, about whom we haven't spoken since I got back from the States. I carry a copy of the card with me everywhere, show it off to friends as though it were a photo of a grandchild. (Note the style: John addresses Caramazza by his surname, one professor to another.) John has reminded me, in his own way, by his own volition – *in his own words* – without instruction, prompting or guidance, that I owe it to him, to other aphasics and to all the people who have helped us to get on with telling the story of how John, seven years after he was silenced by a very bad stroke, began to write again.

11 August. We watched the eclipse move towards London on television, then stood in the garden facing away from the sun because I'd forgotten to buy the glasses you're supposed to wear when looking at an eclipse. As the moon covered the sun everything went dark and we could feel the chill on our backs. Nina's coming round this evening. I'll run out and get some supper for her before the shops close.

Afterword

Let fame, that all hunt after in their lives,
Live registered upon our brazen tombs
And then grace us in the disgrace of death –
When, spite of cormorant-devouring time
The endeavour of this present breath may buy
That honour which shall bate his scythe's keen edge
And make us heirs to all eternity.

Shakespeare, Love's Labour's Lost, *Act I, sc. i*

John died peacefully in his sleep next to me in bed at four in the morning of 12 August. Many weeks later I found among the piles of condolence letters a note from Nina, written before she heard, thanking us for supper and saying how particularly well John had looked that evening. Five weeks short of his seventy-sixth birthday, he had continued to act the part of a man in the prime of life. He played the role so convincingly that he fooled us all: his doctor, his family, his friends, and above all me. I would like to think that he fooled himself, but I'm less sure about that.

We gave thanks for John's life on a relentlessly beautiful morning, with the sun shining on his coffin through the high leaded windows of our local eighteenth-century church by the river. Bamber Gascoigne, my oldest English friend and our mainstay in the last seven years of John's life, gave the address. He spoke of the acclaim John would have received if he had died, as he nearly did, after his stroke in 1992:

But John didn't die in 1992. He lived on to see *The Civilization of Europe in the Renaissance* win prizes and international acclaim. He lived on to be showered with further honours including, only last year, membership of the prestigious Italian Academy of the Lynxes, *dei Lincei*, which boasts among its former members Galileo.

But more important than all that, he survived to build a new life at least as impressive in its own way as his previous one. Surely no one else has spent seven years as a fully active mind, trapped in a cage of silence, without ever lapsing into bitterness and resentment. That was John's final achievement. It should serve as an encouragement to others with the affliction of aphasia.

Most of this book was written before John died. I wrote it in the last years of his life as a kind of love-letter, as a way of satisfying his curiosity about his condition; and because he wanted to see me happy and he believed that anyone who can write at all is happier when writing. It was, however, a long time after his death before I could so much as glance at the manuscript.

I shut the door on our house. It was abhorrent, a brick, book-lined mausoleum from which the spirit had fled. I moved in with Bamber and Christina, and returned only every now and again to collect the bills and the bereavement letters. Wise friends reminded me that I was not the only one who grieved for John; my loss was also theirs. JJ tried to comfort me by saying that we should be grateful that his father had not survived another, more diminishing stroke. How could anyone understand that John had filled every corner of my life and that without him at its heart my world was empty of all meaning?

I decided to sell the house. It was too big, too impractical, too far from central London, above all too empty. Then I moved back and realized that I could not live anywhere else. Gradually, cautiously, I began once again to research the condition that had silenced, and yet not silenced, my eloquent husband. I fell ill. When I recovered I found I was suffering from the mock aphasia that writers call writer's block. The deadline for the book, which had been commissioned in the autumn before John died, came and went. It was a long time before I was able to take the draft manuscript out of its hiding-place, look at it, and finally try to turn it into a publishable book.

If I were to start writing about John's aphasia today, two years three months and twelve days after his death, it would inevitably be a very different book. It would, for one thing, be much angrier.

When John had his stroke in 1992 I was innocent of all thoughts about the larger issues of health-care provision and management of old age, except those that applied immediately to his well-being and recovery. Looking back now I can see all too clearly that John survived his stroke – and lived on to contribute so much to the lives of other people – only because he was extremely fortunate. He was blessed with a robust temperament and constitution, a large circle of loyal friends and family, and a wife still young enough to fight for his life. Without so much resilience and support he would probably have died, as thousands of stroke victims do each year, of neglect.

Nine years ago I saw Dr Z as a white knight in what seemed a battle between two policies of the management of geriatric illness: humanity and common sense versus the brutal and inefficient bureaucracy exemplified by Dr X. But the reality is that Dr X and Dr Z can coexist in the same system because there is in Britain no forum for ideological confrontation, much less ethical debate about public health care. British consultant doctors are all powerful, but only within their own domains. Although euthanasia is illegal in Britain, no patient dependent on the National Health Service has an absolute legal right to treatment of any kind. The 'Beveridgian' model of health care established at the end of the Second World War was never intended to do much more than provide the grateful needy with false teeth and glasses; and the underlying attitude, still accepted by most elderly patients as well as doctors, is that the public is extremely lucky to be granted such privileges as individual doctors deem proper and affordable. The 'Bismarckian' model, which pre-vails in many continental countries, is founded on very different principles. In those countries decent health care is not a gift of the state. It is one of the fundamental planks of a just society. Its provision is financed in various ways, but never directly by the state. Continental countries train too many rather than, as in Britain, too few doctors. More and more British doctors are admitting that they cannot possibly do justice to the numbers of patients they are expected to treat, that patients of all ages are endangered by bureaucratic chaos and their doctors' unrealistically excessive work load. Why don't they speak out? Because the British medical pro-fession is imbued with a culture of getting on with the job and not complaining: fatalistic acceptance seems to weigh heavier than responsibility for the welfare, even the survival, of individual patients. It is easier for doctors who don't like things as they are to leave the profession, as many are now doing, than to criticize its standards.

In a Britain that has no publicly accountable authority with a strong enough mandate to do more than suggest minimum standards of health care, the power of doctors over their submissive patients is dictated not by ethics but by the Treasury. When medical accidents are reported in the press, they are often quantified not in terms of human suffering but of the cost to the Health Service of the extra time the unfortunate patients will spend in hospital as the result of medical error. The European Convention on Human Rights may make it harder for British doctors to refuse the right to life in clear-cut cases without risking litigation. But in an under-funded service that is supposed to be run like an efficient business the Dr Xs may come to outnumber the Dr Zs.

In the years since John's stroke shocked me into investigating the realities of geriatric health care in Britain, I have had, reluctantly, to accept that our experience of Dr X's hospital was far from what the statisticians like to call 'anecdotal'. Rationing of health care may be inevitable in any country, under any system of provision, whether funded by government, employers or private insurance. But it is in Britain that the old are the most likely candidates for exclusion. The income of British people between sixty-five and seventy-five – the age group that was discouraged from saving by the high taxation that funded the welfare state in the post-war decades and that is now rewarded with some of the lowest state pensions in Europe – is 38 per cent below the national average and continues to decline after the age of seventy-five. Students in medical schools are encouraged to despise old fogeys and their geriatric illnesses. The National Health Service classes patients over sixty-five as geriatric – however alert, active or productive they may be – and therefore subject to a policy of separate but equal which, like all apartheids, is more equal for some than others.

One in twenty British 'geriatrics' claims that they have at some time been refused treatment because of their age, but the true percentage is likely to be much higher because this generation, the one that fought the war and learned how to do without in the lean years afterwards, was brought up not to complain. Educated or not, they tend to have faith, as indeed John did, in professional integrity and British standards of decency. If the doctor tells them their case is hopeless or that they will never walk or talk again, they assume that the doctor is telling the truth and doing his/her best. Accustomed to rationing, queuing and turn-taking, many British old people would say that three-score-years and a bit is a fair bite at life.

In 1900, when John's father was beginning to practise medicine in Kent, average life expectancy was forty-seven, and only 4 per cent of the population lived to be over sixty-five. John's father charged the sick what they could afford to pay. Other poor patients were less fortunate. Many died in hospitals as dismal as Dr X's. But it would not have occurred to doctors in 1900 that they had a right, much less an obligation, to suspend their Hippocratic oaths when confronted by patients who had passed their sixty-fifth birthday. A century later, life expectancy in industrialized countries is seventy-four for men and almost eighty for women. Over 12 per cent of the population is over sixty-five, and 4 per cent is over eighty. The forecast for 2020 is a population that is 20 per cent 'geriatric', with the over-eighties curve rising most steeply. And that is discounting the effects of the life-prolonging treatments that will eventually follow advances in microbiology and the decoding of the human genome. Ageism (a crusading neologism coined in America in the 1960s at about the same time that Medicare was introduced) is bound to flourish in a country like Britain where the old are marginalized by poverty, where the nuclear family has been blasted by social change without adequate substitutes, where there are not enough doctors or nurses to go round, and where a dying, ethically confused welfare state places more value on cost-effectiveness and the bottom line than on individual lives. I do not believe that any society that treats its old and helpless citizens the way they are treated in Britain deserves to call itself civilized.

If John was lucky to survive his stroke, so those of us who loved him were lucky to enjoy seven extra years of the humour, kindness, curiosity and sheer love of life that lit up every room he entered. He had made everybody feel better just by being alive and present. And when he was no longer there, nobody ever suggested that his absence might be 'a relief'. On the contrary. People still tell me they miss him. Friends write and telephone on his birthday and the anniversary of his death to say that they remember him as vividly as ever. There have been many beautiful descriptions of John and the impression he made in his last seven years. One that sticks particularly in my mind was written by David Chambers, the former student and friend who had seen John's last book through the press, in an unsigned obituary in *The Times*: 'for those in his company, the infinitely modulated exclamations, chuckles and ironical groans which accompanied his enchanting smile seemed almost to amount to conversation. Gregarious as ever . . . he proved that, even with aphasia, life can be exhilarating.'

Notes

1 John

5/13. *The copy of T. A. Coward's classic*: T. A. Coward, *The Birds of the British Isles and their Eggs*, 4th edn., 1933.

8/32. *His first major book*: *England and the Italian Renaissance*, 1954, 3rd edn., 1996.

22/3. *You see this hand posture in Italian art*: J. A. V. Bates, 'The communicative hand', in J. Benthall and T. Polhemus (eds.), *The Body as a Medium of Expression*, 1975.

4 The Geriatric Ward

59/17. *her two later puzzle books*: V. E. Griffith *et al.*, *A Time to Speak*, 1983, 1991; and *Puzzle Book*, 1992. Both are available from the Stroke Association, CHSA House, Whitecross Street, London EC1Y 8JJ.

5 The Royal Star & Garter

68/1. *Dr Johnson*: quoted in J. Boswell, *Life of Johnson*, 1791.

69/1. *The risk of stroke caused by hypertension could be halved*: S. Pollock (ed.), *More Positive Steps*, Stroke Association, 2000.

69/5. *It is now known that simvastatin*: A. Coghlan, 'Wonder drugs: should doctors now be doling out cholesterol pills like sweets?', *New Scientist*, 24 Nov. 2001

69/11. *In an interview published in the 'New Scientist'*: A. Coghlan, in *New Scientist*, 24 Nov. 2001.

69/25. *During the Second World War*: from the introduction by Kenneth Bloor to G. Wint, *The Third Killer*, 1965.

69/34. *In 2001 a large Australian-based study called PROGRESS*: *Different Strokes Newsletter*, 16, Aug. 2001; J. Hancock, 'The high cost of stroke', *The Times*, 21 Nov. 2001.

70/12. *studies in the United States*: *Newsletter of Integrated Neurological Services*, Spring 2001.

70/20. *The operation, carotid endarterectomy*: S. Pollock, *More Positive Steps*.

70/24. *Now a study at the University of Wisconsin*: *Different Strokes Newsletter*, 17, Nov. 2001.

70/33. *One woman in five*: statistics in this paragraph are from C. Wolfe et al. (eds.), *Stroke Services & Research: An Overview, with Recommendations for Future Research*, 1996.

71/13. *Different Strokes*: 162 High Street, Watford, WD17 2EG. Tel. 01923 240615.

71/28. *Guy Wint, in an attempt*: Wint, *The Third Killer*.

72/32. *According to one survey*: S. Ebrahim and J. Redfern, *Stroke Care – A Matter of Chance: A National Survey of Stroke Services*, Stroke Association, 1999.

72/36. *And the chances of seeing a neurologist*: C. Hancock, 'Case for more consultants', *The Times*, 21 Nov. 2001.

73/5. *The World Health Organization definition of stroke*: C. Wolfe et al., *Stroke Services & Research*.

75/36. *Abciximab*: V. Griffith, 'Drug may help stroke victims', *Financial Times*, 10 April 1999.

76/1. *Another drug, being developed in Australia*: M. Cooper, 'Good Samaritan', *New Scientist*, 1 Sept. 2001.

76/5. *In April 2001 Dr Michael Chopp of the Henry Ford Health Sciences Center*: S. Reinberg, 'Infused bone-marrow stromal cells improve neurologic status after stroke in rats', *Stroke: Journal of the American Heart Association*, April 2001.

76/12. *In August 2001, in the first operation of its kind on a human patient*: H. Cleaver and D. Derbyshire, 'Stem cell therapy repairs a heart', *Daily Telegraph*, 25 Aug. 2001.

76/24. *The most exciting development*: R. Matthews, 'Clot-busting cure for strokes', *Sunday Telegraph*, 6 Oct. 1996.

76/36. *where more than three-quarters of consultants are 'uncertain' about the effects of thrombolytic therapies*: Ebrahim and Redfern, *Stroke Care*.

77/2. *Unfortunately, just under half of British consultants*: ibid.

78/5. *Nevertheless, a survey by the Stroke Association in 1999*: ibid.

78/10. *The cost of stroke to society is enormous: £2.3 billion a year in Britain*: N. Hawkes, 'Survival is a lottery for stroke patients', *The Times*, 21 Nov. 2001.

78/11. *Stroke takes up about 20 per cent of acute hospital beds and 25 per cent of long-term beds*: J. Hancock, 'The high cost of stroke', *The Times*, 21 Nov. 2001.

78/12. *holistic rehabilitation, although initially expensive, results in long-term savings*: B. A. Wilson, 'Cognitive rehabilitation: how it is and how it might be', *Journal of the International Neuropsychological Society*, 3, 1997.

79/1. *Dr Wise believes*: in conversation with the author, 9 Dec. 1998.

79/5. *Another is an American neurologist*: Dr Philip R. Kennedy in conversation with the author, 17 June 1999.

6 Vermeer

85/34. *Dr Arnold Schapiro*: in conversation with the author, 1993.

86/21. *Here are two examples*: from *Actual and Complete SATs: 10 SATs*, 4th edn., 1990.

87/15. *The English Stroke Association*: Stroke Association, CHSA House, Whitecross Street, London EC1Y 8JJ. Tel. 020 7490 7999.

87/25. *Action for Dysphasic Adults (now called Speakability)*: Speakability, 1 Royal Street, London SE1 7LL. Tel. 020 7261 9572.

7 The Varieties of Aphasia

95/13. *The Czech linguist Roman Jakobson*: this observation and the interviews that follow are from H. Gardner, *The Shattered Mind: The Person After Brain Damage*, 1974.

96/24. *transcript from the video*: J. L. Nespoulous, C. Code, J. Virbel and A. R. Lecours, 'Hypotheses on the dissociation between "referential" and "modalizing" verbal behavior in aphasia', *Applied Psycholinguistics*, 19, 1998.

97/15. *Professor David Howard*: in correspondence with the author, June 2001.

97/23. *The great British neurologist*: C. Code, 'On the origins of recurrent utterances in aphasia', *Cortex*, 18, 1982; and C. Code, 'Speech automatism production in aphasia', *Journal of Neurolinguistics*, 8, 1994.

98/14. *Dr Wise says*: in conversation with the author, 13 January 1999.

98/37. *Dr Barbara Lacelle*: N. Kerr and B. Lacelle, 'Therapy for aphasia: insiders' points of view', *Journal of Medical Speech-Language Pathology*, 2000.

99/8. *Guy Wint*: G. Wint, *The Third Killer*, 1965.

99/12. *Some have difficulty with other classes of nouns*: A. R. Damasio and H. Damasio, 'Brain and language', *Scientific American*, Sept. 1992.

99/30. *A recovered Swiss aphasic*: Gardner, *The Shattered Mind*.

99/35. *There are aphasics who can say or read aloud certain words*: S. Chiat and E. V. Jones, 'Processing language breakdown', in M. J. Ball (ed.), *Theoretical Linguistics and Disordered Language*, 1988.

100/4. *Dr Nancy Kerr*: Kerr and Lacelle, 'Therapy for aphasia'.

101/5. *Dr Wise describes this*: in conversation with the author, 12 July 1996.

101/19. *Left-brain dominance for communicating in meaningful sequences*: C. M. Leonard, 'Neural mechanisms of language', in H. Cohen (ed.), *Neuroscience for Rehabilitation*, 1999.

101/21. *including male canaries*: M. Specter, 'Rethinking the brain', *New Yorker*, 23 June 2001.

102/1. *There is some evidence that women*: W. A. Lishman, *The Psychological Consequences of Cerebral Disorder*, 1998.

102/11. *According to Dr Wise*: in conversation with the author, 25 May 1999.

103/1. *An Italian-based team of researchers recently reported*: D. Schön *et al.*, 'Naming of musical notes: a selective deficit', *Brain and Language*, 69, 1999.

103/5. *Brian Butterworth*: in conversation with the author, 13 July 1999.

103/29. *It has been calculated that there are 16,383 varieties of acquired dyslexia*: D. Howard and F. M. Hatfield, *Aphasia Therapy: Historical and Contemporary Issues*, 1987.

8 Silent in Sadness

106/36. *The ingenious propositions . . . somewhat surprisingly, true*: Prof. David Howard in correspondence with the author, June 2001.

107/26. *When he tried to say 'raisin'*: cited, with the quotations following, in H. Gardner, *The Shattered Mind: The Person After Brain Damage*, 1974.

108/36. *another member of the French medical establishment*: anecdote from D. Howard and F. M. Hatfield, Aphasia Therapy: Historical and Contemporary Issue, 1987.

110/4. *Freud*: S. Freud, *On Aphasia*, 1891, English trans. E. Stengel, 1953.

110/15. *Freud's paper on aphasia*: these observations are from E. Stengel's introduction to his translation of *On Aphasia*.

111/9. *To speak . . . to propositionise*: J. H. Jackson, *Selected Writings of John Hughlings Jackson*, ed. J. Taylor, 1958.

111/17. *Freud formulated this principle*: Freud, *On Aphasia*.

111/25. *As recently as 1940 the 'regression hypothesis' was invoked by Roman Jakobson*: in *Child Language, Aphasia, and Phonological Universals*, 1940, trans. A. R. Keiler, 1968.

114/16. *Thought, as Watson put it*: quoted from J. Lyons, *Chomsky*, 1970.
114/36. *The title of the book*: R. A. McCarthy and E. K. Warrington, *Cognitive Neuropsychology: A Clinical Introduction*, 1990.

9 Aphasia Today

119/5. *Dr Jonathan Miller warned me*: in conversation with the author, June 1999.
119/23. *One of these papers*: this and the following paper are summarized in I. Glynn, *An Anatomy of Thought*, 1999.
122/20. *Jakobson, in 1940*: R. Jakobson, *Child Language, Aphasia, and Phonological Universals*, 1940, trans. A. R. Keiler, 1968.
122/22. *Abstract linguistics*: W. T. Gordon, *Marshall McLuhan*, 1977.
122/26. *Ferdinand de Saussure*: in *Course in General Linguistics*, 1916/1959.
123/7. *Wilhelm von Humboldt*: in *Linguistic Variability and Intellectual Development*, 1836, trans. G. C. Buck and F. A. Raven, 1971; quoted from Glynn, *An Anatomy of Thought*.
123/9. *Chomsky postulates*: N. Chomsky, *Language and Mind: Current Thoughts on Ancient Problems*, 1997.
125/16. *'Psycholinguistics is crucial,' says Alfonso Caramazza*: this and the quotations that follow are from a conversation with the author, 21 June 1999.
127/10. *and those who did risked their reputation*: D. Howard, *The Role of Randomised Control Trials in Aphasia*, Speakability Mary Law Lecture, Nov. 2001.
127/12. *what Dr Wise calls 'pronouncing'*: in conversation with the author, 12 July 1996.
129/21. *Their early report on the project*: R. J. S. Wise *et al.*, 'Brain regions involved in articulation', *Lancet*, 353, 27 March 1999.
129/26. *. . . says Dr Wise*: in conversation with the author, 25 May 1999.
130/14. *In his book*: S. Pinker, *Words and Rules: The Ingredients of Language*, 1999.
133/26. *an Italian aphasic whose case was written up in 'Nature'*: R. Cubelli, 'A selective deficit for writing vowels in acquired dysgraphia', *Nature*, 353, 19 Sept. 1991.
134/1. *Dr Warrington described a patient*: Glynn, *An Anatomy of Thought*.
134/20. *Elizabeth Warrington and her colleagues described five such cases*: A. Caramazza and J. R. Shelton, 'Domain-specific knowledge systems in the

brain: the animate-inanimate distinction', *Journal of Cognitive Neuro-science*, 10, 1998.

134/28. *Professors Antonio and Hanna Damasio*: A. R. Damasio and H. Damasio, 'Brain and language', *Scientific American*, Sept. 1992.

135/9. *The original theory of category-specific semantic deficits*: references in R. A. McCarthy and E. K. Warrington, *Cognitive Neuropsychology: A Clinical Introduction*, 1990.

135/19. *Professors Antonio and Hanna Damasio*: 'Brain and language'.

136/10. *Professor Caramazza, considering the problem from a different angle*: Caramazza and Shelton, 'Domain-specific knowledge systems in the brain'.

138/5. . . . *says Dr Wise*: in conversation with the author, 12 July 1996.

138/22. *One of the most ambitious of many ongoing interdisciplinary research programmes*: Center for Research in Language, University of California, San Diego, 9500 Gilman Dr., Dept. 0526, La Jolla, CA 92093-0526. Email: *info@crl.ucsd.edu*

138/35. *what the philosopher Galen Strawson calls*: as quoted in Chomsky, *Language and Mind*.

139/3. *as Chomsky has pointed out*: ibid.

139/11. *Some, like the Damasios*: 'Brain and language'.

139/21. *Dr Wise's advice*: in conversation with the author, 25 May 1998.

10 The Chances of Recovery

140/9. *Most group studies*: in conversation with Dr Richard Wise, 12 July 1996.

140/17. *In a lecture addressed to the British aphasia charity, Speakability*: S. L. Small, *The Future of Aphasia Therapy – Is It Just a Dream?*, Speakability Mary Law Lecture, 2000.

141/21. *Guy Wint recovered everything except one word*: G. Wint, *The Third Killer*, 1965.

141/24. *A Norwegian woman*: I. Glynn, *An Anatomy of Thought*, 1999.

142/5. *C. Scott Moss*: H. Gardner, *The Shattered Mind: The Person After Brain Damage*, 1974.

142/32. *writing has been known to return many years after loss of speech*: B. Rapp *et al.*, 'The autonomy of lexical orthography: evidence from cortical stimulation', *Brain and Language*, 69, 1999.

143/16. . . . *says Dr Wise*: in conversation with the author, 25 May 1999.

143/22. *When I first consulted Dr Wise*: 12 July 1996.

144/33. *The first demonstration that the two hemispheres are not, in fact,* *anatomically symmetrical*: W. A. Lishman, *The Psychological Consequences of Cerebral Disorder*, 1998.

145/11. *The two halves of the brain*: Glynn, *Anatomy of Thought*.

146/14. *When the question of what he wanted to do*: the anecdote is in R. Carter, *Mapping the Mind*, 1998.

146/29. *the French psychologist Jean-Luc Nespoulous and colleagues*: J.-L. Nespoulous, C. Code, J. Virbel and A. R. Lecours, 'Hypotheses on the dissociation between "referential" and "modalizing" verbal behavior in aphasia', *Applied Psycholinguistics*, 19, 1998.

147/11. *When the right hemispheres of recovering aphasics . . . returns to undamaged areas of the left*: A. I. Ansaldo *et al.*, 'The contribution of the right hemisphere to recovery from aphasia: changes in lateralization patterns over time', *Brain and Language*, 69, 1999.

147/19. *Dr Wise, on the basis of scanning experiments*: in conversation with the author, 25 May 1999.

147/37. *Some researchers have suggested*: Lishman, *Psychological Consequences*.

148/24. *Marshall McLuhan*: W. T. Gordon, *Marshall McLuhan: Escape Into Understanding*, 1977.

149/23. *A research project*: N. L. Etcoff *et al.*, 'Lie detection and language comprehension', *Nature*, 405, 11 May 2000.

150/24. *Oliver Sacks describes*: O. Sacks, *Seeing Voices*, 1989.

151/11. *Nancy Kerr taught herself*: N. Kerr and B. Lacelle, 'Therapy for aphasia: insiders' points of view', *Journal of Medical Speech-Language Pathology*, 2000.

151/26. *A British aphasic, Robin Jones*: R. Jones, 'One man's account of recovering from dysphasia', *Speaking Up: The Newsletter of Action for Dysphasic Adults*, 33, 1994.

152/19. *The American aphasic C. Scott Moss*: Gardner, *The Shattered Mind*.

152/23. *'It was so hard to write'*: quoted in Gardner, *The Shattered Mind*.

153/9. *That was written by Nancy Kerr*: Kerr and Lacelle, 'Therapy for aphasia'.

11 The Search for a Cure

154/25. *Dr Wise believes*: in conversation with the author, 9 Dec. 1998.

155/35. *The latest 'Cochrane Review'*: J. Greener, P. Enderby and R. Whurr, 'Pharmacological treatment for aphasia following stroke', *Cochrane Review*, 2001.

156/1. *there are routinely prescribed medications that can actually impede* *recovery . . . tip of the iceberg*: S. L. Small, *The Future of Aphasia Therapy – Is It Just a Dream?*, Speakability Mary Law Lecture, 2000.

156/25. *The outcome of the first major trial*: S. Boseley, 'Parkinson's miracle cure turns into a catastrophe', *Guardian*, 13 March 2001.

157/3. *In the Spring of 2002*: R. Highfield, 'Embryo cell research licences granted', *Daily Telegraph*, 2 March 2002.

157/18. *The dictum that the brain cannot renew itself . . . thousands of new cells each day*: M. Specter, 'Rethinking the brain', *New Yorker*, 23 June 2001.

158/7. *scientists at the University of Pittsburgh Medical Center*: press release from University of Pittsburgh Medical Center, 5 Feb. 1999.

158/18. *In the autumn of 2001 a group of scientists based in Oxford and London*: C. S. L. Lai, S. E. Fisher, J. A. Hurst, F. Vargha-Khadem and A. P. Monaco, 'A forkhead-domain gene is mutated in a severe speech and language disorder', *Nature*, 413, 4 Oct. 2001.

159/35. *Nottebohm has discovered*: Specter, 'Rethinking the brain'.

160/26. *Here is Douglas Ritchie*: D. Ritchie, *Stroke: A Diary of Recovery*, 1965.

161/25. *Robin Jones*: R. Jones, 'One man's account of recovering from dysphasia', *Speaking Up: The Newsletter of Action for Dysphasic Adults*, 33, 1994.

163/7. *from Douglas Ritchie's account*: Ritchie, *Stroke*.

163/11. *Douglas Ritchie explained*: ibid.

163/30. *Nancy Kerr*: N. Kerr and B. Lacelle, 'Therapy for aphasia: insiders' points of view', *Journal of Medical Speech-Language Pathology*, 2000.

163/35. *a Sentence Synthesizer, developed by Marcia C. Linebarger*: M. C. Linebarger *et al.*, 'Competence versus performance in agrammatic production: evidence from an augmentative communication system', *Brain and Language*, 65, 1998.

164/9. *Another new technique, 'Fast ForWard'*: N. F. Dronkers *et al.*, 'Lesion site as a predictor of improvement after "Fast ForWard" treatment in adult aphasic patients', *Brain and Language*, 69, 1999.

12 A Voyage of Exploration

168/11. *Professor Steven Small*: S. L. Small, *The Future of Aphasia Therapy – Is It Just a Dream?* Speakability Mary Law Lecture, 2000.

170/22. *Douglas Ritchie*: D. Ritchie, *Stroke: A Diary of Recovery*, 1965.

171/12. *a telephone survey*: C. Code, 'What does the public know about aphasia?', *Speaking Up: The Newsletter of Speakability*, 54, Nov. 2000.

171/21. *Professor Small runs a rehabilitation clinic*: Small, *The Future of Aphasia Therapy*.

171/32. *Dr Nancy Kerr*: N. Kerr and B. Lacelle, 'Therapy for aphasia: insiders' points of view', *Journal of Medical Speech-Language Pathology*, 2000.

172/2. *While all group trials indicate. . .*: P. Enderby and J. Emerson, *Does Speech and Language Therapy Work?*, 1995.

172/13. *students seeking to study speech and language therapy at the University of Newcastle*: in correspondence with Prof. David Howard, June 2001.

172/23. *according to a review published for the American Speech and Language Hearing Association*: P. D. Jackson and S. T. Hale, *Journal in Communication Sciences and Disorders: A Resource Guide for Authors*, 1990. The reference is in Enderby and Emerson, *Does Speech and Language Therapy Work?*

173/11. *Professor Small has recognized the problem*: Small, *The Future of Aphasia Therapy*.

173/37. *In their book*: D. Howard and F. M. Hatfield, *Aphasia Therapy: Historical and Contemporary Issues*, 1987.

174/15. *the British-based 'Cochrane Library Review' by Jenny Greener and her colleagues*: J. Greener, P. Enderby and R. Whurr, 'Speech and language therapy for aphasia following stroke', *Cochrane Review*, 1999.

174/17. *an American review*: K. D. Cicerone, C. Dahlberg, K. Kalmar *et al.*, 'Evidence-based cognitive rehabilitation: recommendations for clinical practice', *Archives of Physical Medicine and Rehabilitation*, 81:12, Dec. 2000.

174/22. *Professor Small*: Small, *The Future of Aphasia Therapy*.

174/35. *Alfonso Caramazza does not believe*: Chris Code in correspondence with the author, May 2000.

175/12. *David Howard*: in correspondence with the author, June 2001.

175/17. *In his lecture given in 2001 for Speakability*: D. Howard, *The Role of Randomised Control Trials in Aphasia*, Speakability Mary Law Lecture, Nov. 2001.

175/31. *It is very difficult . . . with each other*: A. Basso, E. Capitani and L. A. Vignolo, 'Influence of rehabilitation on language skills in aphasic patients: a controlled study', *Archives of Neurology*, 36, 1979; quoted from Enderby and Emerson, *Does Speech and Language Therapy Work?*

177/1. *Howard and Hatfield explain*: Howard and Hatfield, *Aphasia Therapy*.

182/7. *According to Howard and Hatfield*: ibid.

185/6. *The original proposition by Elizabeth Warrington*: Professor Brian Butterworth in conversation with the author, 13 July 1999.

14 John's Days

208/3. *It started as an article*: S. Hale, 'Diary', *London Review of Books*, 20, 5 March 1998.

210/27. *that Vladimir Nabokov tells us in his autobiography*: V. Nabokov, *Speak, Memory: An Autobiography Revisited*, revised edn., 1967.

220/34 *Professor Butterworth's hypothesis*: in conversation with the author, 13 July 1999.

15 Myths and Metaphors

225/15. *After an earthquake in Turkey*: A. Finkel, 'Mother pulled from the rubble', *The Times*, 23 Aug. 1999.

226/11. *Plato's dialogue between Hermogenes and Cratylus*: Plato, *Cratylus*, in *The Dialogues of Plato*, trans. B. Jowett, 1900.

227/21. *'The Treatise on Man'*: in *The Philosophical Writings of Descartes*, trans J. Cottingham *et. al.*, 3 vols., 1985–91.

227/31. *Noam Chomsky*: N. Chomsky, *Language and Mind: Current Thoughts on Ancient Problems*, 1997.

227/36. *Douglas Ritchie*: D. Ritchie, *Stroke: A Diary of Recovery*, 1965.

228/8. *Nancy Kerr*: N. Kerr and B. Lacelle, 'Therapy for aphasia: insiders' points of view', *Journal of Medical Speech-Language Pathology*, 2000.

228/18. *Marshall McLuhan*: W. T. Gordon, *Marshall McLuhan: Escape Into Understanding*, 1977.

229/25. *Chomsky*: Chomsky, *Language and Mind*.

229/34. *Steven Pinker*: S. Pinker, *The Language Instinct: The New Science of Language and Mind*, 1994.

230/9. *Dr Wise*: in conversation with the author, 13 Jan. 1998.

230/29. *An article about his aphasia*: M. Cleave, 'The silenced sage', *Evening Standard*, 16 June 1994.

232/34. *The structural linguist Ferdinand de Saussure*: in *Course in General Linguistics*, 1916/1959.

232/36. *The anthropological linguist Edward Sapir*: cited in Pinker, *The Language Instinct*.

232/39. *The neurologist Hughlings Jackson wrote*: J. H. Jackson, *Selected Writings of John Hughlings Jackson*, ed. J. Taylor, 1958.

232/14. *Bertrand Russell . . . Wittgenstein*: cited in Pinker, *The Language Instinct*.

233/3. *Antonio Damasio*: A. R. Damasio, *The Feeling of What Happens: Body, Emotion and the Making of Consciousness*, 1999.

233/29. *Dr Wise locates*: in conversation with the author, 9 Dec. 1998.

234/14. *Leibniz . . . Berkeley*: cited by J. Hadamard, *The Psychology of Invention in the Mathematical Field*, 1945.

234/17. *Didert wrote . . .*: quoted by J. Rée, *I See a Voice: Language, Deafness & the Senses – a Philosophical History*, 1999.

235/1. *Francis Galton*: cited by Hadamard, *The Psychology of Invention in the Mathematical Field*.

235/5. *Einstein famously described*: cited ibid.

236/6. *Steven Pinker refutes*: Pinker, *The Language Instinct*.

236/22. *Willem Levelt*: W. J. M. Levelt, *Speaking: From Intention to Articulation*, 1989.

237/23. *Professor Jacques Lordat*: his story is in H. Gardner, *The Shattered Mind: The Person After Brain Damage*, 1974.

237/31. *Dr Wise has no problem*: in conversation with the author, 9 Dec. 1998.

237/33. *Professor Butterworth suggests*: in conversation with the author, 13 July 1999.

237/36 *Douglas Ritchie observed*: Ritchie, *Stroke*.

238/3. *Dr Nancy Kerr forgot*: Kerr and Lacelle, 'Therapy for aphasia'.

16 John's Voice

242/23. *Kopit's play*: A. Kopit, *Wings*, 1978.

243/1. *And yet, there are 'Wernicke's' aphasics*: J. Marshall *et al.*, 'Why does monitoring fail in jargon aphasia? Comprehension, judgement, and therapy evidence', *Brain and Language*, 63, 1998.

243/15. *I asked Dr Wise*: in conversation with the author, 8 April 1999.

243/25. *an article in the London 'Times', about the work of Dr Linda Wheeldon*: A. Ahuja, 'Listening to the censor inside our heads', *The Times*, 19 May 1997.

244/8. *I found her*: in conversation with the author, 18 Jan. 1999.

246/31. *In the milliseconds . . . 'The Hunchback of Notre Dame'*: J. Diamond, *C: Because Cowards Get Cancer Too . . .*, 1998.

247/4. *Vygotsky compared inner speech to 'the other side of the moon'*: quoted from O. Sacks, *Seeing Voices*, 1989.

247/9. *Vygotsky considered*: the observation is from D. Howard and F. M. Hatfield, *Aphasia Therapy: Historical and Contemporary Issues*, 1987.

247/37. *Dr Wheeldon*: in conversation with the author, 18 Jan. 1999.

248/3. *Dr Levelt envisages*: W. J. M. Levelt, *Speaking: From Intention to Articulation*, 1989.

248/23. *And Dr Wise has found physiological evidence*: R. J. S. Wise *et al.*, 'Brain regions involved in articulation', *Lancet*, 353, 27 March 1999.

249/4. *It is not, for example, understood how we accomplish 'auditory streaming'*: Dr Wise, in conversation with the author, 8 Dec. 1998.

249/13. *Dr Jonathan Miller*: in conversation with the author, June 1999.

249/22. *so some amputees register normal sensation*: V. S. Ramachandran and S. Blakeslee, *Phantoms in the Brain: Human Nature and the Architecture of the Mind*, 1998.

250/35. *Dr Wise*: in conversation with the author, 8 April 1999.

251/4. *Antonio Damasio*: A. R. Damasio, *The Feeling of What Happens: Body, Emotion and the Making of Consciousness*, 1999.

251/27. *The influence of pre-morbid experience and personality*: G. P. Prigatano and E. A. Weinstein, 'Edwin A. Weinstein's contribution to neuropsychological rehabilitation', *Neuropsychological Rehabilitation*, 6, 1996.

253/15. *Douglas Ritchie*: D. Ritchie, *Stroke: A Diary of Recovery*, 1965.

17 Hope

259/7. *Article in today's Guardian*: J. Wilson, 'Brain implants "can operate computer by thought power"', *Guardian*, 15 Oct. 1998.

259/19. *According to the Sunday Times*: C. Lloyd, 'Lose your mind in the squid's cool embrace', *Sunday Times*, 25 April 1993.

260/8. *article in the New York Times*: M. W. Browne, 'How brain waves can fly a plane', *New York Times*, 7 March 1995.

266/8. *an article in today's Independent*: S. Connor, 'Brain machine restores "speech"', *Independent*, 25 March 1999.

266/15. *the article quotes Dr Birbaumer*: N. Birbaumer *et al.*, 'A spelling device for the paralysed', *Nature*, 398, 25 March 1999.

Afterword

280/24. *The income of British people . . . decline after the age of seventy-five*: N. Acherson, 'Keep on running . . .', *Observer*, 15 Nov. 1998.

281/17. *A century later, life expectancy . . . with the over-eighties curve rising most steeply*: ibid.

282/10. *obituary in 'The Times'*: 13 Aug. 1999.

Bibliography

Acherson, N., 'Keep on running . . .', *Observer*, 15 November 1998.

Ahuja, A., 'Listening to the censor inside our heads', *The Times*, 19 May 1997.

Ansaldo, A. I., *et al.*, 'The contribution of the right hemisphere to recovery from aphasia: changes in lateralization patterns over time', *Brain and Language*, 69, 1999.

Baddeley, A. D., *The Psychology of Memory*, 1976.

Baldo, J. V., and Dronkers, N. F., 'Verbal and nonverbal short-term memory in patients with conduction aphasia and prefrontal cortex lesions', *Brain and Language*, 69, 1999.

Ball, M. J. (ed.), *Theoretical Linguistics and Disordered Language*, 1988.

Baltes, P. B., and Singer, T., 'Plasticity and the ageing mind: an exemplar of the bio-cultural orchestration of brain and behaviour', *European Review*, 9, February 2001.

Bates, E., and Dick, F., 'Beyond phrenology: brain and language in the next millennium', *Brain and Language*, 71, 2000.

—— and Wulfeck, B., 'Comparative aphasiology: a cross-linguistic approach to language breakdown', *Aphasiology*, 3: 2, 1989.

—— —— 'Cross-linguistic research in aphasia: an overview', *Brain and Language*, 41, 1991.

—— *et al.*, 'Psycholinguistics: a cross-language perspective', *Annual Review of Psycholinguistics*, 52, 2001.

—— *et al.*, 'Comparing free speech in children and adults with left- vs right-hemisphere injury', *Brain and Language*, 69, 1999.

Bauby, J. D., *The Diving Bell and the Butterfly*, 1997.

Benthall, J., and Polhemus, T. (eds.), *The Body as a Medium of Expression*, 1975.

Birbaumer, N., *et al.*, 'A spelling device for the paralysed', *Nature*, 398, 25 March 1999.

Bishop, J. E., 'Stroke patients yield clues to brain's ability to create language', *Wall Street Journal*, 12 October 1993.

Boatman, D., *et al.*, 'Transcortical sensory aphasia: reexamination of the disconnection model', *Brain and Language*, 69, 1999.

Boseley, S., 'Parkinson's miracle cure turns into a catastrophe', *Guardian*, 13 March 2001.

Breitenstein, C., *et al.*, 'Acoustic analyses of emotional prosody following cortical and subcortical brain damage: comparisons with listeners' ratings and perception of emotional prosody', *Brain and Language*, 69, 1999.

Browne, M. W., 'How brain waves can fly a plane', *New York Times*, 7 March 1995.

Bunse, S., *et al.*, 'Changes in semantic ERP-components during aphasia therapy', *Brain and Language*, 69, 1999.

Butterworth, B., *et al.*, 'Language and the origins of number skills: karyotypic differences in Turner's Syndrome', *Brain and Language*, 69, 1999.

Caramazza, A., *Parallels and Divergences in the Acquisition and Dissolution of Language*, 1994.

—— 'The interpretation of semantic category-specific deficits: what do they reveal about the organization of conceptual knowledge in the brain?', *Neurocase*, 4, 1998.

—— and Shelton, J. R., 'Domain-specific knowledge systems to the brain: the animate-inanimate distinction', *Journal of Cognitive Neuroscience*, 10, 1998.

Cardebat, D., *et al.*, 'A functional MRI study of recovery from aphasia in an anomic patient using overt picture naming', *Brain and Language*, 69, 1999.

Carter, R., *Mapping the Mind*, 1998.

Chambers, D. S., Clough, C. H., and Mallett, M. E., *War, Culture and Society in Renaissance Venice: Essays in Honour of John Hale*, 1993.

Chomsky, N., *Syntactic Structures*, 1957.

—— *Topics in the Theory of Generative Grammar*, 1966.

—— *Language and Mind*, 1968.

—— *Language and Mind: Current Thoughts on Ancient Problems*, 1997.

Cicerone, K. D., Dahlberg, C., Kalmar, K., *et al.*, 'Evidence-based cognitive rehabilitation: recommendations for clinical practice', *Archives of Physical Medicine and Rehabilitation*, 81: 12, December 2000.

Clarke, M., *My Experience with Dysphasia: Less Words More Respect*, 1997.

Code, C., 'On the origins of recurrent utterances in aphasia', *Cortex*, 18, 1982.

—— 'Speech automatism production in aphasia', *Journal of Neurolinguistics*, 8, 1994.

—— 'What does the public know about aphasia?', *Speaking Up: The Newsletter of Speakability*, 54, November 2000.

—— (ed.), *The Characteristics of Aphasia*, 1989.

—— et al., 'Mental calculation and number word repetition: a PET study', *Brain and Language*, 69, 1999.

Coghlan, A., 'Wonder drugs: should doctors now be doling out cholesterol pills like sweets?', *New Scientist*, 24 November 2001.

Cohen, H. (ed.), *Neuroscience For Rehabilitation*, 1999.

Connor, S., 'Brain machine restores "speech"', *Independent*, 25 March 1999.

Coward, T. A., *The Birds of the British Isles and their Eggs*, 4th edn., 1933.

Croot, K., 'An acoustic investigation of articulatory impairment in a case of nonfluent progressive aphasia', *Brain and Language*, 69, 1999.

Cubelli, R., 'A selective deficit for writing vowels in acquired dysgraphia', *Nature*, 353, 19 September 1991.

Damasio, A. R., *Descartes' Error: Emotion, Reason and the Human Brain*, 1994.

—— *The Feeling of What Happens: Body, Emotion and the Making of Consciousness*, 1999.

—— and Damasio, H., 'Brain and language', *Scientific American*, September 1992.

Damasio, H., et al., 'A neural basis for lexical retrieval', *Nature*, 380, 11 April 1996.

Dante Alighieri, *Inferno*, trans. Mark Musa, 1971.

Davis, M. H., et al., 'Spot the difference: investigations of conceptual structure for living things and artifacts using speeded word-picture matching', *Brain and Language*, 69, 1999.

Dehaene, S., and Cohen, L., 'Language and elementary arithmetic: dissociations between operations', *Brain and Language*, 69, 1999.

Delazer, M., and Girelli, L., 'Language and numerical skills: an introduction to past and present issues', *Brain and Language*, 69, 1999.

De Lillo, Don, *The Body Artist*, 2001.

Descartes, R., *The Philosophical Writings of Descartes*, trans. J. Cottingham, et al., 3 vols., 1985–91.

Diamond, J., *C: Because Cowards Get Cancer Too . . .*, 1998.

Dick, F., et al., 'Interpretation of complex syntax in aphasic adults and children with focal lesions or specific language impairment', *Brain and Language*, 69, 1999.

'Dr Foster' (an independent company that provides information about healthcare provision in the UK), 'The *Times* hospital consultant guide: part 3: Neurology', *The Times*, 21 November 2001.

Dronkers, N. F., et al., 'Lesion site as a predictor of improvement after "Fast ForWard" treatment in adult aphasic patients', *Brain and Language*, 69, 1999.

Durward, M., *et al.*, Speaking Without Words, 2000.

Ebrahim, S., and Redfern, J., *Stroke Care – a Matter of Chance: A National Survey of Stroke Services*, Stroke Association, 1999.

Edelman, G., and Greenwood, R., *Jumbly Words, and Rights Where Wrongs Should Be: The Experience of Aphasia From the Inside*, 1992.

Enderby, P., and Emerson, J., *Does Speech and Language Therapy Work?*, 1995.

Ferroni, L., *et al.*, 'Evidence of the interaction between the modules of the lexical-semantic system: the rehabilitation of the grapheme-phoneme conversion mechanism', *Brain and Language*, 69, 1999.

Finkel, A., 'Mother pulled from the rubble', *The Times*, 23 Aug. 1999.

Freud, S., *On Aphasia*, 1891, English trans. E. Stengel, 1953.

Friedmann, N., ' "That" and "what" in agrammatic aphasia', *Brain and Language*, 69, 1999.

Gardner, H., *The Shattered Mind: The Person After Brain Damage*, 1974.

Girelli, L., and Delazer, M., 'Differential effects of verbal paraphasias on calculation', *Brain and Language*, 69, 1999.

Glynn, I., *An Anatomy of Thought*, 1999.

Goldrick, M., *et al.*, 'Lexical and postlexical processes in spoken word production', *Brain and Language*, 69, 1999.

Goodglass, H., *Understanding Aphasia*, 1993.

Gordon, W. T., *Marshall McLuhan: Escape Into Understanding*, 1977.

Greener, J., and Grant, A., 'A survey of speech and language therapists in Scotland who manage people aphasic after stroke', *Health Bulletin*, January 1998.

—— Enderby, P., and Whurr, R., 'Speech and language therapy for aphasia following stroke', *Cochrane Review*, 1999.

—— —— —— 'Pharmacological treatment for aphasia following stroke', *Cochrane Review*, 2001.

Greenfield, S., *The Human Brain: A Guided Tour*, 1997.

Gregory, R. L. (ed.), *The Oxford Companion to the Mind*, 1987.

Griffith, V. E., *A Stroke in the Family*, 1970.

—— *et al., A Time to Speak*, Stroke Association, 1983, 1991.

—— *et al., Puzzle Book*, Stroke Association, 1992.

Gupta, K., *Human Brain Coloring Workbook*, 1997.

Hadamard, J., *The Psychology of Invention in the Mathematical Field*, 1945.

Hale, J. R. *England and the Italian Renaissance*, 1954, 3rd edn., 1996.

—— *The Civilization of Europe in the Renaissance*, 1993.

—— (ed. and trans.), *The Literary Works of Machiavelli*, 1961.

Highfield, R., 'Embryo cell research licences granted', *Daily Telegraph*, 2 March 2002.

Howard, D., *The Role of Randomised Control Trials in Aphasia*, Speak-ability Mary Law Lecture, November 2001.

—— and Hatfield, F. M., *Aphasia Therapy: Historical and Contemporary Issues*, 1987.

Jackson, J. H., *Selected Writings of John Hughlings Jackson*, ed. J. Taylor, 1958.

Jakobson, R., *Child Language, Aphasia, and Phonological Universals*, 1940, trans. A. R. Keiler, 1968.

Jones, R., 'One man's account of recovering from dysphasia', *Speaking Up: The Newsletter of Action For Dysphasic Adults*, 33, 1994.

Katz, R., *et al.*, 'Aphasia management in five health care systems', *Brain and Language*, 69, 1999.

Kelson, M., *et al.*, *Speaking Out About Stroke Services: The Views of People Affected by Stroke. A Survey to Inform the Implementation of the National Service Framework for Older People*, Stroke Association, June 2001.

Kerr, N., and Lacelle, B., 'Therapy for aphasia: insiders' points of view', *Journal of Medical Speech-Language Pathology*, 2000.

Koenig, P., *et al.*, 'Neural basis for motion and cognition verbs', *Brain and Language*, 69, 1999.

Kopit, A., *Wings*, 1978.

Kotulak, R., 'Stroke rehab goal: rewiring the brain', *Chicago Tribune*, 26 July 1998.

Lai, C. S. L., Fisher, S. E., Hurst, J. A., Vargha-Khadem, F., and Monaco, A. P., 'A forkhead-domain gene is mutated in a severe speech and language disorder', *Nature*, 413, 4 October 2001.

Laiacona, M., and Capitani, E., 'A case of prevailing deficit of nonliving categories: is associative information more impaired than perceptual information?', *Brain and Language*, 69, 1999.

Leff, A. P., *et al.*, 'Synaptic reorganization in the contralateral hemisphere following left posterior temporal lobe infarction' (forthcoming).

Lesser, R., and Milroy, L., *Linguistics and Aphasia: Psycholinguistics and Pragmatic Aspects of Intervention*, 1993.

Levelt, W. J. M., *Speaking: From Intention to Articulation*, 1989.

Linebarger, M. C., *et al.*, 'Competence versus performance in agrammatic production: evidence from an augmentative communication system', *Brain and Language*, 65, 1998.

Lishman, W. A., *The Psychological Consequences of Cerebral Disorder*, 1998.

Lloyd, C., 'Lose your mind in the squid's cool embrace', *Sunday Times*, 5 April 1993.

Love, T., et al., 'Perfusion MRI as a measure of cognitive/linguistic deficits', Brain and Language, 69, 1999.

Luria, A. R., The Man with a Shattered World, 1972.

Lyons, J., Chomsky, 1970.

McCarthy, R. A., and Warrington, E. K., Cognitive Neuropsychology: A Clinical Introduction, 1990.

McCrum, R., My Year Off: Rediscovering Life After a Stroke, 1998.

Marshall, J., 'Current themes in aphasia therapy', Speaking Up: The Newsletter of Action For Dysphasic Adults, Winter 1994.

—— 'Calling a salad a federation: an investigation of semantic jargon', Journal of Neurolinguistics, 9, 1996.

—— et al., 'Why does monitoring fail in jargon aphasia? Comprehension, judgement, and therapy evidence', Brain and Language, 68, 1998.

Martin, R. C., et al., 'Access to count/mass information without access to phonology in an anomic patient', Brain and Language, 69, 1999.

Matthews, R. 'Clot-busting cure for strokes', Sunday Telegraph, 6 October 1996.

Merleau-Ponty, Maurice, The Structure of Behaviour, trans. A. L. Fisher, 1965.

Nabokov, V., Speak, Memory: An Autobiography Revisited, revised edn, 1967.

Nai, W., et al., 'Syntactic and semantic processes in the intact brain: an event-related study with fMRI', Brain and Language, 69, 1999.

Nespoulous, J.-L., Code, C., Virbel, J., and Lecours, A. R., 'Hypotheses on the dissociation between "referential" and "modalizing" verbal behavior in aphasia', Applied Psycholinguistics, 19, 1998.

Nickels, L., and Howard, D., 'When the words won't come: relating impairments and models of spoken word production', in L. Wheeldon (ed.), Language Production, 1998.

Ohnesorge, C., and Van Lancker, D., 'Cerebral lateralization of common and proper nouns: evidence from normal processing', Brain and Language, 69, 1999.

Parr, S., et al., Talking About Aphasia, 1997.

Pinker, S., The Language Instinct: The New Science of Language and Mind, 1994.

—— Words and Rules: The Ingredients of Language, 1999.

—— 'Talk of genetics and vice versa', Nature, 413, 4 October 2001.

Plato, Cratylus, in The Dialogues of Plato, trans. B. Jowett, 1900.

Pollock, S. (ed.), More Positive Steps, Stroke Association, 2000.

Pomeroy, V. M., and Tallis, R. C., 'The Stroke Association's Therapy

Research Unit (SATRU): an overview of the first eighteen months', *Stroke Matters*, June 1998.

Prigatano, G. P., and Weinstein, E. A., 'Edwin A. Weinstein's contribution to neuropsychological rehabilitation', *Neuropsychological Rehabilitation*, 6, 1996.

Radford, T., 'The human cells that will revolutionise medicine' and 'How the human machine gave up another of its secrets', *Guardian*, 6 November 1998.

Raichle, M. E., 'Visualizing the Mind', *Scientific American*, April 1994.

Ramachandran, V. S., and Blakeslee, S., *Phantoms in the Brain: Human Nature and the Architecture of the Mind*, 1998.

Rapp, B., *et al.*, 'The autonomy of lexical orthography: evidence from cortical stimulation', *Brain and Language*, 69, 1999.

Raskin, A. H., 'The words I lost', *New York Times*, 19 September 1992.

Rée, J., *I See a Voice: Language, Deafness & the Senses – a Philosophical History*, 1999.

Reinberg, S., 'Infused bone-marrow stromal cells improve neurologic status after stroke in rats', *Stroke: Journal of the American Heart Association*, April 2001.

Ritchie, D., *Stroke: A Diary of Recovery*, 1965.

Robson, J., *et al.*, 'Written communication in undifferentiated jargon aphasia: a therapy study', *International Journal of Language and Communication Disorders*, 33, 1998.

Rogers, A., 'How to grow circuits from brain cells', *New Scientist*, 12 June 1999.

Ryle, G., *The Concept of Mind*, 1940.

Sacks, O., *Seeing Voices*, 1989.

Saussure, F. de, *Course in General Linguistics*, 1916/1959.

Schön, D., *et al.*, 'Naming of musical notes: a selective deficit', *Brain and Language*, 69, 1999.

Schutz, Alfred, *The Phenomenology of the Social World*, 1972.

Sharma, A., 'An introduction to the British Association of Stroke Physicians', *Stroke Matters*, 2 June 1999.

Small, S. L., 'Pharmacotherapy of aphasia: a critical review', *Stroke*, 25, June 1994.

—— *The Future of Aphasia Therapy – Is It Just a Dream?*, Speakability Mary Law Lecture, 2000.

Specter, M., 'Rethinking the brain', *New Yorker*, 23 June 2001.

Sutherland, S. (chairman), *With Respect to Old Age*, report by the Royal Commission, 1999.

Swinney, D., *et al.*, 'Temporal parameters in language comprehension in aphasia', *Brain and Language*, 69, 1999.

Tavistock, H., and Levin, A., *A Chance to Live*, 1991.

Thioux, M., *et al.*, 'Functional neuroanatomy of the semantic system: the case for numerals', *Brain and Language*, 69, 1999.

Tyrrell, P., 'Thrombolysis in Germany', *Stroke Matters*, 1 March 2000.

Wade, N., 'Brain stem cell is discovered, twice', *New York Times*, 15 June 1999.

Weinstein, E. A., 'Behavioral aspects of jargonaphasia', in J. Brown (ed.), *Jargonaphasia*, 1981.

Wheeldon, L. R., and Levelt, W. J. M., 'Monitoring the time course of phonological encoding', *Journal of Memory and Language*, 34, 1995.

Wilson, B. A., 'Cognitive rehabilitation: how it is and how it might be', *Journal of the International Neuropsychological Society*, 3, 1997.

—— 'Research and evaluation in rehabilitation', in B. A. Wilson and D. L. McLellan, *Rehabilitation Studies Handbook*, 1997.

Wilson, J., 'Brain implants "can operate computer by thought power"', *Guardian*, 15 October 1998.

Wint, G., *The Third Killer*, 1965.

Wise, R. J. S., *et al.*, 'Brain regions involved in articulation', *Lancet*, 353, 27 March 1999.

Wolfe, C., *et al.* (eds.), *Stroke Services & Research: An Overview, with Recommendations for Future Research*, 1996.